MIDWEST
State Park
Adventures

Discover the beauty of America's heartland, one state park at a time.

Presented by members of the
Midwest Travel Writers Network

Veronica Bareman
Sara Broers
Matthew & Thena Franssen
Dannelle Gay
Brandy Gleason
Theresa L. Goodrich
Lindsay Hindman
Dustin & Kelly Ratcliff
Tim & Lisa Trudell
Alicia Underlee Nelson
Jamie Ward
Roxie Yonkey

Also Available:
Midwest Road Trip Adventures, 2nd Edition

MIDWEST State Park *Adventures*

Discover the beauty of America's heartland, one state park at a time.

MIDWEST TRAVEL WRITERS NETWORK

X THE **LOCAL TOURIST**

Copyright © 2023 by The Local Tourist
Published in the United States by The Local Tourist
thelocaltourist.com

All rights reserved. No part of this book may be reproduced in any form, or by any means, electronic or mechanical, including photocopying, recording, or any information browsing, storage, or retrieval system, without permission in writing from the publisher, except for the use of brief quotations in a book review or as allowed by copyright law.

ISBN 978-1-958187-10-4

Every effort has been made to ensure the accuracy of the information presented in this book. If you are inspired to visit any of these destinations, please confirm all details and amenities before making plans.

Cover design by Theresa L. Goodrich
Cover photos by: Theresa L. Goodrich, Brandy Gleason, and Veronica Bareman

CONTENTS

Introduction 1

How to Use This Book 3

Illinois 5

    Illinois State Parks Facts & Important Information 7

    Illinois State Parks Map 8

  Region: Northeastern 9

    Kankakee River State Park 9

    Adeline Jay Geo-Karis Illinois Beach State Park 10

    Moraine Hills State Park 11

  Region: East Central 12

    Weldon Springs State Park 12

    Lincoln Trail Homestead State Park 13

    Wolf Creek State Park 14

  Region: South 14

    Giant City State Park 14

    Cave-in-Rock State Park 16

    Fort Massac State Park 17

  Region: West Central 17

    Pere Marquette State Park 17

    Horseshoe Lake State Park 19

    Nauvoo State Park 20

  Region: Northwestern 21

    Starved Rock State Park 21

    Mississippi Palisades State Park 23

    White Pines Forest State Park 24

Illinois State Parks Amenities	26
Indiana	29
Indiana State Park Facts & Important Information	30
Indiana State Parks Map	32
Region: Northern Indiana	33
Pokagon State Park	33
Indiana Dunes State Park	34
Tippecanoe River State Park	35
Region: Southern Indiana	35
Clifty Falls State Park	35
Charlestown State Park	37
O'Bannon State Park	37
Region: Eastern Indiana	38
Ouabache State Park	38
Summit Lake State Park	39
Whitewater Memorial State Park	40
Region: Western Indiana	41
Turkey Run State Park	41
Shades State Park	42
Prophetstown State Park	43
Region: Central Indiana	44
Brown County State Park	44
McCormick's Creek State Park	46
Spring Mill State Park	46
Indiana State Parks Amenities	48
Iowa	51
Iowa State Park Facts & Important Information	52

Iowa Road Trips Map	53
Region: East	54
Maquoketa Caves State Park	54
Pikes Peak State Park	55
Cedar Rock State Park	56
Region: North	56
Clear Lake State Park	56
Fort Defiance State Park	58
Gull Point State Park	58
Region: Central	59
Ledges State Park	59
Dolliver Memorial State Park	60
Walnut Woods State Park	61
Region: South	62
Lacey Keosauqua State Park	62
Lake Darling State Park	63
Lake Macbride State Park	64
Region: West	64
Viking Lake State Park	64
Prairie Rose State Park	65
Waubonsie State Park	66
Iowa State Parks Amenities	68
Kansas	73
Kansas State Park Facts & Important Information	74
Kansas State Parks Map	76
Region: North	76
Milford State Park	76

- Tuttle Creek State Park 78
- Glen Elder State Park 78
- Region: East 79
  - Hillsdale State Park 79
  - Eisenhower State Park 80
  - Flint Hills Trail State Park 81
- Region: South 82
  - Cross Timbers State Park 82
  - Crawford State Park 83
  - Elk City State Park 84
- Region: West 85
  - Historic Lake Scott State Park 85
  - Cedar Bluff State Park 86
  - Little Jerusalem Badlands State Park 87
- Region: Central 88
  - Wilson State Park 88
  - Kanopolis State Park 89
  - El Dorado State Park 90
- Kansas State Parks Amenities 92
- Michigan 95
  - Michigan State Park Facts & Important Information 96
    - Michigan State Parks Map 98
  - Upper Peninsula Region 99
    - Fort Wilkins Historic State Park 99
    - Porcupine Mountains Wilderness State Park 100
    - Tahquamenon Falls State Park 101
  - Northwest Region 102

    Petoskey State Park 102

    Wilderness State Park 103

Silver Lake State Park 104

Northeast Region 104

    Mackinac Island and Fort Mackinac Historic Park 104

    Tawas Point State Park 106

    Hartwick Pines State Park 107

Southwest Region 107

    Holland State Park 107

    Fort Custer Recreation Area 109

    Saugatuck Dunes State Park 109

Southeast Region 110

    Sanilac Petroglyphs Historic State Park 110

    Maybury State Park 112

    Belle Isle Park 112

Michigan State Parks Amenities 114

Minnesota 121

    Minnesota State Park Facts & Important Information 123

    Minnesota State Parks Map 124

    Region: Northwest 125

        Itasca State Park 125

        Lake Bronson State Park 126

        Maplewood State Park 127

    Region: Northeast 127

        Gooseberry Falls State Park 127

        Grand Portage State Park 129

        Lake Vermillion State Park 130

v

Region: Southeast 130
    Forestville/Mystery Cave State Park 130
    Frontenac State Park 132
    Nerstrand Big Woods State Park 132
Region: Southwest 133
    Blue Mounds State Park 133
    Upper Sioux Agency State Park 135
    Minneopa State Park 135
Region: Central 136
    Banning State Park 136
    Charles A Lindbergh State Park 137
    Interstate State Park 138
Minnesota State Parks Amenities 140
Missouri 145
    Missouri State Park Facts & Important Information 147
    Missouri State Parks Map 148
Region: Northeast 149
    Long Branch State Park 149
    Mark Twain State Park 150
    Thousand Hills State Park 151
Region: Central 151
    Finger Lakes State Park 151
    Arrow Rock State Historic Site 152
    Katy Trail State Park 153
Region: St. Louis (East) 155
    Meramec State Park 155
    Route 66 State Park 156

  Castlewood State Park 156

 Region: Lakes (Southwest) 157

  Bennett Spring State Park 157

  Ha Ha Tonka State Park 158

  Roaring River State Park 159

 Region: Southeast 160

  Echo Bluff State Park 160

  Johnson's Shut-Ins State Park 160

  Elephant Rocks State Park 161

 Missouri State Parks Amenities 163

Nebraska 167

 Nebraska State Park Facts & Important Information 168

 Nebraska State Parks Map 169

 Region: Northeast 169

  Niobrara State Park 169

  Ponca State Park 171

 Region: North Central 172

  Smith Falls State Park 172

 Region: Southeast 174

  Platte River State Park 174

  Eugene Mahoney State Park 175

  Indian Cave State Park 177

 Region: West 179

  Chadron State Park 179

  Fort Robinson State Park 180

 Nebraska State Parks Amenities 183

North Dakota 185

North Dakota State Park Facts & Important Information 186

North Dakota State Parks Map 189

Region: North 189

Lake Metigoshe State Park 189

Icelandic State Park 191

Grahams Island State Park 192

Region: East 192

Fort Ransom State Park 192

Turtle River State Park 194

Region: South 195

Fort Abraham Lincoln State Park 195

Beaver Lake State Park 196

Region: West 197

Sully Creek State Park 197

Little Missouri State Park 199

Lewis and Clark State Park 199

Region: Central 200

Fort Stevenson State Park 200

Lake Sakakawea State Park 202

Cross Ranch State Park 203

North Dakota State Parks Amenities 205

Ohio 207

Ohio State Park Facts & Important Information 209

Ohio State Parks Map 210

Region: Northeast 211

Geneva State Park 211

Mosquito Lake State Park 212

- Punderson State Park 213
- Region: Southeast 214
  - Hocking Hills State Park 214
  - Salt Fork State Park 215
  - Burr Oak State Park 216
- Region: Southwest 217
  - Hueston Woods State Park 217
  - Caesar Creek State Park 218
  - Shawnee State Park 219
- Region: Northwest 220
  - Maumee Bay State Park 220
  - Indian Lake State Park 221
  - South Bass Island State Park 222
- Region: Central 222
  - Mohican State Park 222
  - Deer Creek State Park 224
  - Alum Creek State Park 225
- Ohio State Parks Amenities 227

South Dakota 231
- South Dakota State Park Facts & Important Information 233
- South Dakota State Parks Map 234
- Region: West 234
  - Custer State Park 234
  - Bear Butte State Park 236
  - Spearfish Canyon Nature Area 236
- Region: Central 237
  - Oahe Downstream Recreation Area 237

ix

    Indian Creek Recreation Area 238

    Farm Island State Recreation Area 239

    Randall Creek State Recreation Area 240

Region: Northeast 240

    Fort Sisseton Historical State Park 240

    Sica Hollow State Park 242

    Hartford Beach State Park 242

    Sandy Shore State Recreation Area 244

Region: Southeast 244

    Lewis & Clark, Pierson Ranch, & Chief White Crane State Recreation Areas 244

    Palisades State Park 246

    Good Earth State Park 246

    Adams Homestead and Nature Preserve 247

South Dakota State Parks Amenities 249

Wisconsin 253

    Wisconsin State Park Facts & Important Information 254

    Wisconsin State Parks Map 256

Region: Southeast 257

    Kohler-Andrae State Park 257

    High Cliff State Park 258

    Big Foot Beach State Park 259

Region: East 260

    Peninsula State Park 260

    Copper Culture State Park 261

    Rock Island State Park 261

Region: South Central 262

  Devil's Lake State Park 262

  Mirror Lake State Park 263

  Rocky Arbor State Park 263

 Region: Southwest 264

  Wyalusing State Park 264

  Blue Mound State Park 266

  Belmont Mound State Park 266

 Region: Northwest 267

  Amnicon Falls State Park 267

  Pattison State Park 268

  Big Bay State Park 269

Wisconsin State Parks Amenities 271

State Contact Information 274

Index 277

INTRODUCTION

Welcome to the fabulous world of Midwestern state parks, presented by authors who live in the states we've covered.

Our status as residents is an important distinction. We're locals, which means we each have a viewpoint that simply can't be captured by someone who doesn't live here. We've visited these parks, and even though none of our states is small, consider these resources an extension of our backyards.

I live in Illinois, and have been a resident since 2001. This state is my playground. Now, I feel like I've added eleven more.

When we started this project, we all knew about the geological diversity of our states, of the breadth of landscapes available for anyone to explore. I'm not sure we realized the extent of the entire region's diversity. I know I didn't, and as a life-long Midwesterner, I've seen quite a lot.

I grew up in Indiana. Weekend trips to Turkey Run and McCormick's Creek State Parks filled my summers. My current residence is thirty minutes from one state park, and I've got five within an hour. It's a Mother Nature jackpot.

That's the Midwest for you.

There are more than 500 official state parks in these twelve states. We've featured 171. After much deliberation, we decided to feature one state from each of five regions per state. Then we'd include two more parks per region, for a total of fifteen per state. The exceptions are Nebraska and North Dakota, which have eight and thirteen state parks, respectively.

We would have loved to tell you about each and every park, but we figured you wouldn't want to carry around a book that's 1000+ pages, and that's what it would take.

However, we wanted to make sure you could learn more about the parks we didn't include. Each state includes a table listing every state park plus a select list of amenities. There's an appendix with contact information for the states' park management organizations.

Putting this information together was...challenging. Each state runs things differently from the next, and the park systems are ever changing. It's been a truly collaborative process, and I am prouder than I could possibly express with the work these authors have put in to ensure you get the most accurate and up-to-date information.

That being said, this is a book, and things change. In fact, one state changed its regions the week before we were scheduled to publish. That author had to select different parks and essentially rewrite her chapter. But, she did it. And she did it well.

(This is a not-so-subtle reminder to confirm everything before you visit any of these parks. There are also reminders in each chapter. We'd hate for you to get to a park to find out something you hoped to see wasn't available.)

There are enough parks in this book to provide years of exciting experiences. I hope—we all hope—that this guide helps you enjoy these great outdoors and plan your next Midwest State Park Adventures.

Theresa L. Goodrich
Publisher, The Local Tourist

How to Use This Book

While our authors have made a concerted effort to confirm the information we've provided in *Midwest State Park Adventures*, make sure you also confirm while you're planning your visits. Like roads, state parks are often under some form of construction or development. Depending on the work being done, sections may be closed. The website for each state's parks management organization can be found in the Amenities section near the back of each chapter.

Each state features a note about accessibility. While we would have preferred to include detailed information about ADA compliance, space limitations and frequent changes mean we need to defer to the individual state park management organizations.

There are maps at the beginning of each state. These are meant as guidelines to show you the approximate location of the parks. Knowing whether a state park is in the north, south, east, west, or center of the state can help you decide if it's one you can add to your itinerary.

While we've aimed for consistency, the difference in our states means the information provided is unique based on the location. For example, we've included a table with every state park at the end of each chapter. Some states include lodging facilities in their parks; others do not. For those that do not, we've removed that option from the table. There are also notes specific to each states' amenities.

Although each of the contributing authors has their own writing style, the states are similar in that they're part inspiration and part itinerary. This is the kind of book you should feel free to mark up and bookmark.

We hope you'll be inspired to explore these public lands in the heartland of America.

ILLINOIS

by Theresa L. Goodrich

When you think of Illinois, two images probably come to mind: corn fields and Chicago. While the Prairie State does have abundant farmland and is also home to the third largest city in the country, its landscape is much more diverse than those two features imply.

There are prairies—it is the Prairie State, after all—and there are also steep bluffs, winding rivers, and sandstone cliffs. There are hardwood forests and world-renowned wetlands. Glaciers carved this landscape, leaving evidence of their passage with limitless horizons and unique geological formations.

Illinois state parks showcase all of it.

I've visited every state park in my home state, and I can verify each one is unique. From the shores of Lake Michigan to the banks of the Ohio River, from the Indiana border to the Mississippi, Illinois state parks provide some of the most beautiful and diverse landscapes in the Midwest. Camp along the Mississippi River and hike the hills of Shawnee National Forest. See bald eagles and bison. Duck under waterfalls and kayak whitewater rapids. Discover the surprising cornucopia of flora and fauna in the remnants of the prairies that used to cover the plains.

But it's not just the scenery that makes these parks so special. They're steeped in history, whether preserving the stories of the original inhabitants or introducing you to the settlers and pioneers who forged their way west. More than learning about history, you can experience it: Explore caves where scoundrels used to hide. Walk in the steps of the Potawatomi, Sauk, and Fox. Then imagine what the world was like when Lewis and Clark searched for a way to the Pacific Ocean. You can trace travel routes and visit the safe havens that made up the Underground Railroad. Learn about the struggles of the early settlers and the people who built the Land of Lincoln.

With forty-five state parks in Illinois, there's always something new to discover and explore. I'm excited to introduce you to several of my favorites, and to invite you to experience these natural and cultural juggernauts for yourself.

Illinois State Parks Facts & Important Information

- Illinois has 45 state parks and over 130 total parks, forests, fish and wildlife areas, and recreation areas.
- Entrance to Illinois state parks is free.
- Fort Massac was the first state park, designated in 1908.
- At 8,000 acres, Pere Marquette is the largest state park in Illinois.
- Many Illinois state parks and recreation areas prohibit alcohol. This can be a seasonal restriction, in specific locations of the park, or in the entire park and year-round.
- Pets are allowed, but must be leashed.
- You can reserve campsites at 32 sites in Illinois. Most campsites offer electricity and showers.
- Rock climbing is allowed at four Illinois state parks: Ferne Clyffe, Giant City, Mississippi Palisades, and Pere Marquette.

A note about accessibility

The Illinois Department of Natural Resources has a stated goal of expanding opportunities for people of all abilities to participate in outdoor activities. On their website, each park includes a section listing its accessibility features, including access to hunting, showers, fishing, and trails.

You can find out more at dnr.illinois.gov/parks/accessibility.html

Illinois State Parks Map

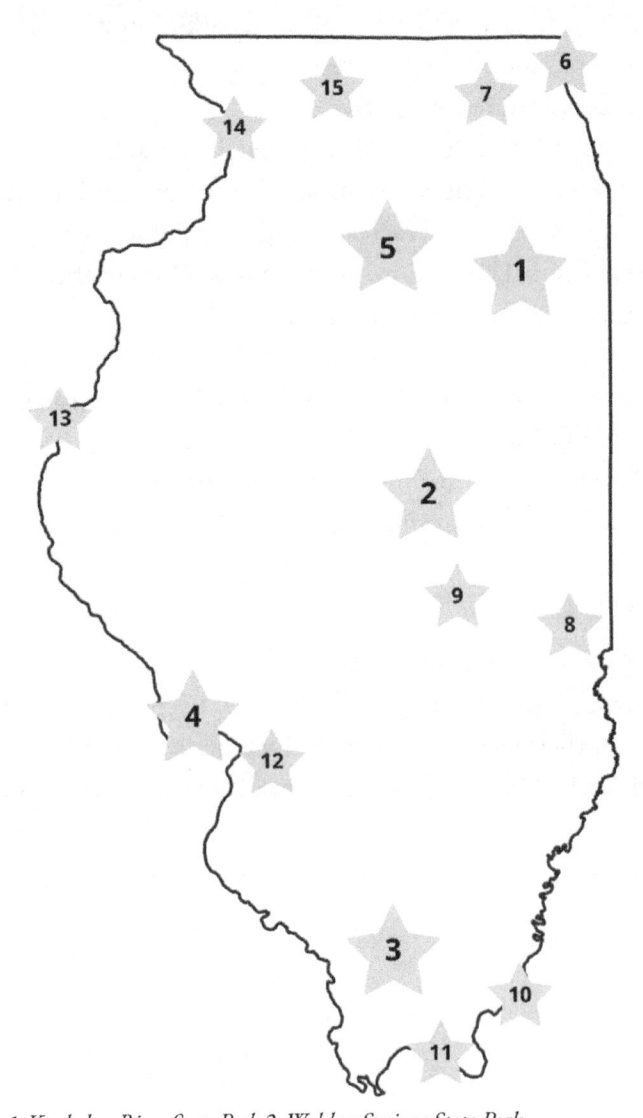

1. Kankakee River State Park 2. Weldon Springs State Park
3. Giant City State Park 4. Pere Marquette State Park 5. Starved Rock State Park
6. Adeline Jay Geo-Karis Illinois Beach State Park 7. Moraine Hills State Park 8. Lincoln Trail State Park 9. Wolf Creek State Park 10. Cave-in-Rock State Park 11. Fort Massac State Park
12. Horseshoe Lake State Park 13. Nauvoo State Park 14. Mississippi Palisades State Park
15. White Pines Forest State Park

Region: Northeastern

Kankakee River State Park

More than a million people visit Kankakee River State Park each year, drawn by its abundant fishing, rich history, and miles of trails. About an hour from Chicago, the park's proximity makes it a popular day trip from the city. The shallow gravel-bottomed river is on the federal Clean Streams Register and is filled with crappie, catfish, bluegill, walleye, and multiple types of bass, making it an angler's dream.

The location has been popular for centuries. Once known as the River of the Miami, it attracted members of that Native American tribe as well as the Illini, Kickapoo, and Mascouten, and later the Potawatomi, Ottawa, and Chippewa. They were followed by fur trappers, traders, and farmers.

Throughout the park are vestiges of its history. It was the site of the last Great Council of the Potawatomi in 1830. Only three years later, the Treaty of Camp Tippecanoe ended the Black Hawk War and the tribe ceded their land along the Kankakee and Illinois Rivers. A boulder along the Rock -reek nature trail marks the burial site of Potawatomi Chief Shaw-waw-nas-see. Another marker commemorates the log cabin village of Rockville, which had been founded in 1840.

In 1938, Chicagoan Ethel Sturges Dummer donated 35.6 acres for the establishment of a state park. Today, Kankakee River State Park straddles the eponymous river for eleven miles and encompasses nearly 4,000 acres.

Visitors to Kankakee River State Park can enjoy several outdoor activities, including hiking, biking, and horseback riding. More than a dozen miles of trails include a variety of terrains, from a bicycle path along the river to a more rugged hike through limestone canyons to a waterfall. The Riverwalk Trail is wheelchair accessible, with a shelter, picnic tables, and grills. There's also an equestrian trail, open April 1 through October 31. After hunting season, if there's enough snow on the ground, the park's open for snowmobiling.

Swimming is one activity that's not allowed; while the Kankakee River is lovely and clean, its current is unpredictable. However, canoeists are welcome. You can either bring your own craft or rent from a nearby concessionaire. There's a boat ramp at Warner Bridge Day Use Area and a launch at the Area 9 parking lot. Only craft with motors of 10 horsepower or less are allowed.

Bow hunting is allowed, and there's an archery range in the park. Firearm hunting is permitted for duck, pheasant, turkey, dove, rabbit, squirrel, fox, coyote and raccoon.

Like many Illinois state parks, alcohol is prohibited, including in the campgrounds.

Kankakee River State Park's campgrounds are open seasonally, and you'll need to reserve your spot at camp.exploremoreil.com. Potawatomi Campground has 110 Class A sites, which means electricity and showers are available. There are ADA-accessible campsites. Chippewa Campground, the park's Class BE (electricity only, no showers) campground, was undergoing construction at time of publication, but it is set to reopen in 2023. There's also an equestrian campground. Like the equestrian trail, it's open from April 1 through October 31.

Adeline Jay Geo-Karis Illinois Beach State Park

Illinois has 63 miles of Lake Michigan shoreline, and Adeline Jay Geo-Karis Illinois Beach State Park protects ten percent of them. This stretch of dunes and swales is the only remaining beach ridge shoreline in the state. But the unique park's features go beyond the beach; it's also home to lowland wetlands and black oak savannahs. There are even colonies of prickly pear cactus.

The state first acquired pieces of what is now Illinois Beach State Park in 1948, but its beginnings date back sixty years before that. In 1888, renowned landscape architect Jens Jensen and Waukegan nurseryman Robert Douglas floated the idea of a regional park. Legislative efforts didn't start until the 1920s. By 1964, the first Illinois Nature Preserve was established.

There are 6.5 miles of trails where you can see more than 650 species of plants. You can also swim, fish, and picnic.

For an overnight visit, camp in the Class A campground, which is open from April 1 through December 30. The Illinois Beach Resort and Conference Center is open year-round, and is the only resort within an Illinois state park. There's also a 1,500-slip marina on the north side of the park.

Note: there are two park units, both with entrances from Sheridan Road. The park offices and resort are in the South Unit.

Moraine Hills State Park

Moraine Hills and McHenry Dam State Parks are a two-for-one deal. McHenry Dam came first, founded in 1939 with just fifteen acres along the Fox River. Moraine Hills State Park, with 2500 acres, opened in 1976 after Illinois acquired Lake Defiance.

McHenry County is littered with moraines, or large piles of boulders, stones, and debris left behind by glaciers. A big piece of ice broke off and melted, forming Lake Defiance. This 48-acre body of water is one of the few glacial lakes in Illinois still in its near-natural condition.

Fishing both the Fox River and Lake Defiance is popular. While the McHenry Dam area provides boating access to the river, fishing on the lake is only allowed from designated piers along the boardwalk. Hunting, including archery, shotgun, and waterfowl, is also popular. While the park is closed during specific weekends in November for shotgun hunting, all trails are open during archery season.

Over eleven miles of trails wind through the park; most of them are wheelchair accessible. Three of the trails are surfaced with crushed limestone, while the fourth is paved. To learn about the park's geology and its history, take one of the guided hikes. The Visitor Center, open based on availability of volunteer docents, has exhibits dedicated to "The First Americans," the geological formations found in the park, and native plants and animals.

Region: East Central

Weldon Springs State Park

Weldon Springs State Park is 550 acres of year-round outdoor fun with a dose of history. In addition to standard summer activities like boating, fishing, picnicking, and camping, winter visitors can go sledding, tobogganing, ice-fishing, and cross-country skiing.

The park gets its name from both Judge Lawrence Weldon, who purchased the property before the Civil War, and natural springs that trace their origin to an ancient river. The Teays River was so huge it stretched fifteen miles wide in DeWitt County, where the park is located. Glaciers buried the river, but groundwater continued to flow over the impervious layer of bedrock.

Judge Weldon leased his property to the Weldon Springs Company at the turn of the twentieth century. It soon hosted an annual assembly called a Chautauqua. For ten days each summer from 1901 to 1921, locals would hear public speakers and entertainers. Reverend Billy Sunday spoke regularly, and notable speakers included Hellen Keller and Carrie Nation. In 1936, Lincoln Weldon, the Judge's son, donated fifty acres to the City of Clinton for the creation of Weldon Springs State Park. Twelve years later, it became an Illinois state park.

To the right of the main entrance is a look into nineteenth century life. The Union School Interpretive Center, a one-room schoolhouse built in 1865 and later moved to its current spot, serves as the park's visitor center. Children of all ages are encouraged to touch the taxidermist-mounted creatures on display. There are also insect cards as well as exhibits detailing the evolution of the park. What had once been open prairie became a railroad holding, then a venue for the Chautauqua Assemblies, and finally a state park.

Next door inside the Texas Township Community Building, moved to the park in 1995, visitors can see collections of bird nests, animal tracks, grasses, and other items that represent the flora and fauna of the region.

Of course, you can experience that for yourself by hiking over ten miles of trails. There are eight large picnic areas plus smaller spots throughout the park. Each picnic site includes cooking grills or fire rings, access to water, and toilet facilities. The larger picnic areas even have electrical service. You can reserve a shelter at six of those spots.

The campground offers 75 Class A sites and there's a playground. There are three accessible campsites as well as areas for tent campers. Backpackers can hike to a few primitive spots along Salt Creek. Those sites are known to flood in the spring, so call ahead.

Whether you're visiting for the day or camping, don't miss Veterans Point. Originally planned to be a patio with a flagpole, a rock with a plaque, and engraved bricks, donations so greatly exceeded the original plans they were able to dedicate a much more elaborate memorial. Time your visit to coincide with Memorial Day, Flag Day, July 4, Patriots Day, POW/MIA Recognition Day, Veterans Day, and Pearl Harbor Remembrance Day to see fifty "Flags of Freedom."

Lincoln Trail Homestead State Park

At only 162 acres, Lincoln Trail Homestead State Park is tiny, but it's definitely worth a visit. The reason is in the name: it's the site of Abraham Lincoln's first Illinois homestead.

Thomas and Sarah Lincoln built their first home in the Prairie State along the Sangamon River in 1830. While they only lived there a year and the cabin is long gone, a marker, erected by the D.A.R. in 1904, marks the approximate location.

The Whitley family later settled the land and built a dam to power a sawmill. Both a bit of the mill and the Whitley cemetery are preserved, making this park a dual memorial for both the country's 16th president and nineteenth century pioneers.

Lincoln Trail Homestead State Park is now a peaceful preserve that's ideal for birdwatchers. According to the Illinois DNR, 299 out of 300 bird species found in Illinois have been spotted in the area. Ten percent of those are threatened or endangered.

Fishing and canoeing are allowed in the Sangamon River, and there are three nature trails. There are also two picnic shelters; both are handicap accessible.

This park is not to be confused with Lincoln Trail State Park, Lincoln Trail Homestead State Park is a separate entity.

Wolf Creek State Park

Wolf Creek is about as close to another state park as one can get: it shares a body of water, facing Eagle Creek State Park across Lake Shelbyville.

The lake, like many in Illinois, was formed by a dam. Construction began in 1963, and what had previously been the site of several mines, a power plant, and gas and oil pipelines became a natural retreat.

The sprawling lake is characterized by several coves. Because the lake was formed by flooding, there are lots of submerged ridges and tributary springs, making this a prime fishing spot. With 304 Class A and 78 Class C camping spots, Wolf Creek State Park is one of the largest campgrounds in the state. There's also an equestrian campground and 140 more sites are available in the Lick Creek area of the park.

Wolf Creek is also a great swimming hole, with a developed beach that's open from the end of May to the beginning of September. There's a high-water beach when the lake floods. There are also several hiking trails, a snowmobile trail, and an equestrian trail.

Region: South

Giant City State Park

Named for massive sandstone formations, Giant City's unique geology makes it one of the best state parks in the Midwest. Ferns, moss, wildflowers, and other flora carpet the landscape like a verdant blanket. The park sits a stone's throw from Carbondale and is a short drive to the Mississippi River.

Humans have taken advantage of this lush environment for 10,000 years. As you hike through the woods, which are also part of Shawnee National Forest, you'll encounter shelter bluffs with black ceilings, a remnant from ancient campfires. Evidence of occupation is displayed as soon as you enter the park: near the entrance is a stone wall built between 600 and 800 A.D.

Now comprised of over 4,000 acres, including the 110-acre Fern Rocks Nature Preserve, the park began at about a quarter of that size. Illinois created Giant City State Park in 1927 with 1100 acres. Nine years later, the Civilian Conservation Corps completed the lodge and twelve overnight cabins. The lodge has been expanded and remodeled over the years, but they've taken care to preserve the historic character, and there are several original furnishings and decorations. Be sure to check out the two-story lobby and the photos and clippings that line the walls. For stunning panoramic views of the park, climb to the observation deck of the 1970 water tower.

Inside the lodge, the Bald Knob serves breakfast, lunch, and dinner, and there's a cocktail bar where you can relax after a long day on the trails.

Hiking is the highlight of Giant City, especially if you want to see the many features that attract a million and a half visitors each year. At only a mile, the Nature Trail is a great introduction to the park. It's a moderate loop with sheer bluffs, the same bluffs that inspired early settlers to say the area resembled "giant city" streets. If you want to see the balanced rock on the cover of this book, hike this trail.

Post Oak Trail was specifically designed for visitors with mobility constraints. While it's wide enough for wheelchairs, there are some uneven surfaces. Wildflowers are present throughout the temperate months of March through September.

Serious outdoor adventurers will want to hike Red Cedar Trail. It's twelve miles; as the Illinois DNR states, it "provides an invigorating challenge to the truly dedicated backpacker." There's a campsite at the halfway point so you can rest and recoup.

You can pick up interpretive trail brochures at the Visitors Center, which also has information on the geology and history of the park, as well as nearby tourist destinations.

Giant City is popular for camping and there are 86 Class A campsites. It's a good idea to reserve a site as soon as you know you plan to visit, especially if it's on a weekend. There are also 14 Class C tent-only sites that are first-come, first-served. Equestrian campers have their own campground.

If you want adventure and a world that will take your breath away, plan a trip to Giant City.

Cave-in-Rock State Park

On the shores of the Ohio River is a geologic wonder that's been the source of intrigue for centuries. Carved out of a limestone bluff, Cave-in-Rock is exactly what it sounds like. At 55 feet wide, the limestone cave's size made it the perfect hideout for pirates, bandits, and other ne'er-do-wells. Early travelers floating past would have been subject to attacks by scallywags like Samuel Mason and his gang. It's rumored that Jesse James hid out in its cavernous depths. If you've seen *How The West Was Won*, you might recognize it. The cave was featured in the 1962 film.

Since 1929, this place of lore has been a state park. Originally 64.5 acres, it's now over 200. Visitors can climb the steps down to the infamous cave and explore its depths. The walls are lined with graffiti dating back hundreds of years. On the surface, campers have their choice of 34 Class A campsites with electricity and 25 Class B/S sites. Accessible sites are available.

For more comfort, the Lodge offers duplex cabins, each with eight suites. The family-style restaurant serves lunch and dinner on the weekends, or you can bring your own lunch and have a picnic. There are also several hiking trails. A visit to Cave-in-Rock State Park makes a great jumping off point for a tour of the Ohio River Scenic Byway in Illinois.

Fort Massac State Park

Welcome to Fort Massac State Park, the first state park in Illinois. Established in 1908, the Daughters of the American Revolution prompted the founding of the park to protect what had been a prominent military site.

According to legend, Hernando DeSoto built the first European fortification on the site around 1540. Later, the French and British fought over the location until George Rogers Clark and his Long Knives secured it for the Americans during the Revolutionary War.

Today, the park features a replica of the fort from 1802 and a statue of Clark overlooking the Ohio River. The replica looks the same as the structure explorers Meriwether Lewis and William Clark (George's younger brother) would have seen in 1803 before continuing west, placing the park on the Lewis and Clark National Historic Trail.

You can learn more about the fort's history in the Visitor Center, and you can also learn about the people who were there first. Fort Massac has one of the best Native American artifact collections in Illinois.

The park offers boating, fishing, disc golf, hunting, picnicking, and hiking, as well as living history weekends, where reenactors bring the past to life. Every October, the Fort Massac Encampment attracts around 200,000 people. Down the road, you can visit a superhero. Fort Massac is in the town of Metropolis, and their Superman statue is one of the most popular regional attractions.

There are 50 Class A vehicular campsites as well as separate spots for tent campers.

Region: West Central

Pere Marquette State Park

Pere Marquette State Park, situated along the Illinois and Mississippi Rivers meet, is the state's largest and a crowning jewel in the state park system. Named for explorer Pere Jacques Marquette, who traveled with

Louis Joliet, it's a bonanza of beautiful forests, impressive cliffs, and scenic river views.

Native American communities once roamed the hills, ravines, and prairies of the area, hunting wildlife, foraging for food, and eventually establishing homes. Archaeologists have identified six distinct cultures in this region. Signs of their presence, such as pottery shards, spear points, and agricultural tools, have been discovered throughout the park. Additionally, burial mounds can be found in various locations, including one at McAdams Peak.

Make your first stop the Visitor Center, which is appropriately impressive. As soon as you enter, you'll find an impressive 3D map of the park, along with numerous displays and exhibits showcasing the Illinois River, local wildlife, historical stories, and geology.

You can grab trail maps inside the center. During regular office hours, park staff are present to explain the trail system and offer advice on the best routes. You'll also find several informative park videos worth watching in the Audio/Visual room of the Visitor Center. For those interested in exploring the park's scenic areas, you can schedule free guided hikes for any group size. To organize one, simply call the visitor center and set up a date and time.

Since its establishment in 1931, Pere Marquette State Park has grown to over 8,000 acres of beautiful forests. The hiking trails are some of the best features of the park, with options for all skill levels.

Birdwatching is another highlight of Pere Marquette State Park. In fact, the park is known for being a winter home for bald eagles. If you visit between December and February, you can take part in Eagle Watching Days, where you can learn more about these incredible birds and their migration patterns.

With its location at the confluence of two major rivers, you better believe boating and fishing are major attractions at Pere Marquette. Anglers can catch a variety of fish species, including catfish, bass, and bluegill.

Camping at Pere Marquette State Park is always a pleasant experience. The campground has 80 Class A campsites with electricity and a few Class B/S sites. There are accessible sites available and modern shower facilities.

For a more upscale stay, the historic Pere Marquette Lodge, built in the 1930s by the CCC, has both guest rooms and stone cabins. The impressive structure, built with limestone and large timber beams, boasts a 50-foot vaulted ceiling, handcrafted chandeliers, and a massive 700-ton stone fireplace in the extraordinary Great Room. The recently renovated hotel also offers a life-size, handcrafted chess set, a terrace with views of the picturesque Illinois River, an indoor pool, a popular restaurant, and a local winery. You can remember your stay with a purchase at the gift shop.

Pere Marquette State Park is a special place that's simultaneously close to St. Louis while being a world away.

Horseshoe Lake State Park

At 2,400 acres, Horseshoe Lake is the second largest natural lake in Illinois. (The largest is Lake Michigan.) The park is a stone's throw from the Mississippi River, although you could say it *is* the Mississippi, or it used to be. The lake's an oxbow, a remnant of Big Muddy.

Horseshoe Lake State Park is a few miles from Cahokia Mounds State Historic Site, which is a UNESCO World Heritage Site, and across the river from Gateway Arch National Park in St. Louis. That prime location makes this a great home base for exploring the region. Cahokia dates back to 700 AD, but archaeologists have found evidence of human activity at Horse Lake dating back to 8000 BC.

Today's visitors enjoy four miles of hiking trails; fishing, including from an accessible pier, for bass, crappie, bluegill, carp, buffalo, and channel catfish; and picnicking. Public hunting blinds are available for waterfowl hunters. There's also a small campground, with 26 tent or trailer campsites. There's no electricity, but there are water hydrants. The campground is open from May 1 to September 30.

Nauvoo State Park

Nauvoo State Park provides a unique blend of natural beauty and historical significance. Spanning 148 acres, this park packs a lot into its small footprint.

Previously a Fox village of 400 to 500 lodges, Mormons settled along the Mississippi River in 1839 while escaping from religious persecution. Joseph Smith, the founder of the Church of Jesus Christ of Latter-day Saints, changed the town's name to Nauvoo. One of the most famous missionaries was Brigham Young, who led the Mormons west to Utah after Smith was murdered.

Today, visitors can delve into the fascinating history of the Mormon pioneers by touring the neighboring Historic Nauvoo District. To go beyond their story, explore the on-site Nauvoo State Park Museum. The site of the town's first vineyard, there's a wine cellar and press room. Exhibits also include Native American artifacts.

Enveloped within the park's boundaries is 13-acre manmade Lake Horton. It's stocked with largemouth bass, channel catfish, and bluegill. There's a primitive boat launch and only electric trolling motors are permitted.

The park's main trail is an easy 1.5 miles that winds around the lake. There's also a 3/8-mile accessible trail that begins in the campground, which has 105 campsites. Winter visitors can go sledding and cross-country skiing. Both the modern restrooms and museums are closed in the winter.

The annual Nauvoo Grape Festival takes place each Labor Day weekend and celebrates the town's history as well as its historic industries of wine and cheese.

Region: Northwestern
Starved Rock State Park

Starved Rock State Park, a stunning natural oasis located along the Illinois River in La Salle County, offers visitors an unparalleled opportunity to explore the complex history and unexpected beauty of the region. Designated as Illinois' second state park in 1911, inside Starved Rock are 18 awe-inspiring canyons carved out of St. Peter Sandstone by glacial meltwater. These dramatic geological formations provide a unique and memorable experience for all who visit.

Sprawling over 2,630 acres, the park has over 13 miles of well-maintained hiking trails, which meander through the verdant landscape, leading to eight seasonal waterfalls, sandstone overhangs, and spectacular panoramic views. The topography means the trails are uneven and many of them contain stairs. Illinois, Ottawa, and Kaskaskia canyon trails cross creek beds, so be prepared to get muddy. This topography means that there aren't any ADA compliable trails. It's always a good idea to start at the visitor center to inquire about trail conditions.

The diverse flora found within the park, including white and red oak, maple, hickory, white pine, eastern red, and northern white cedar, creates a thriving ecosystem that supports a wide array of wildlife. Fauna include bald eagles, who fish the Illinois River throughout the year, but are especially busy in January.

Throughout the year, Starved Rock State Park offers numerous recreational activities such as hiking, camping, fishing, boating, and hunting. In addition, special events, guided tours, and educational programs are frequently scheduled, ensuring that visitors of all ages and interests can find something to enjoy. The Starved Rock Visitor Center, open year-round, serves as a hub of information and resources for visitors looking to learn more about the park and its history.

Starved Rock State Park is one of the most popular camping spots in Illinois. Reservations are required and all 133 sites fill quickly. You can make them up to six months in advance, and it's a good idea to do so.

I'd like to point out one particular rule for campers: a maximum of one family (two parents and minor children) or four adults is allowed per campsite. As the Illinois DNR says on their site, that is "non-negotiable."

For those seeking a more luxurious experience, Starved Rock Lodge, built in the 1930s by the CCC and listed on the National Register of Historic Places, provides comfortable accommodations, a restaurant, and a rustic atmosphere that perfectly complements the natural surroundings. With a variety of guest rooms, cabins, and conference facilities, the lodge caters to a wide range of needs, from romantic getaways to corporate retreats.

The history of Starved Rock State Park is as fascinating as its natural wonders. Evidence suggests that the area has been inhabited by humans as early as 8000 BC, with various Native American cultures flourishing over the millennia. The Illinois Confederation, which included the Kaskaskia subtribe, occupied the region from the 16th to early 19th centuries. French explorers Louis Joliet and Father Jacques Marquette passed through the area in 1673, with Marquette later founding Illinois' first mission in the Kaskaskia village.

Fort St. Louis was constructed atop Starved Rock in 1682-83 due to its strategic position above the Illinois River. However, facing pressure from Iroquois war parties during the French and Indian wars, the fort was abandoned in the early 1700s. Despite briefly serving as a hub for traders and trappers, by 1720, all traces of the fort had vanished.

The name "Starved Rock" originates from a Native American legend surrounding the death of Chief Pontiac of the Ottawa tribe, who was killed by a Peoria brave (a sub-tribe of the Illinois Confederation). As a result, a series of battles ensued to avenge Pontiac's death. According to the legend, during one of these skirmishes, a group of Illinois sought refuge atop a 125-foot sandstone butte. The Ottawa and Potawatomi tribes surrounded the butte, holding their ground until the Illinois succumbed to starvation. That butte became known as Starved Rock.

Today, Starved Rock State Park stands as a testament to the rich history and breathtaking natural beauty of Illinois. With its picturesque bluffs, diverse ecosystem, and wide range of recreational opportunities, the park remains a favorite destination for locals and tourists alike. Whether you're an avid hiker, a history buff, or simply looking to escape the daily grind, Starved Rock State Park offers a truly unforgettable experience.

Mississippi Palisades State Park

Situated near the confluence of the Mississippi and Apple rivers in northwestern Illinois, the 2,500-acre Mississippi Palisades State Park is steeped in Native American history. The term "palisades" refers to a series of high, steep cliffs typically found along a river, and Mississippi Palisades, located 3 miles north of Savanna, certainly lives up to its name. You'll find caves and potentially dangerous sinkholes—limestone formations that descend straight down. Erosion has created fascinating rock formations, such as Indian Head, which resembles an eagle's profile, and Twin Sisters, a pair of human-like figures atop the bluffs. In 1973, the U.S. Interior Department recognized the remarkable nature of this area by designating a portion of it as a National Natural Landmark.

The park's 15-mile rugged trail system serves as a gateway to its diverse array of plant and animal life. The northern part of the park features five trails that are generally wider and less challenging than the five southern trails, which are narrow and situated extremely close to the bluff. The southern trails can be hazardous when wet.

Mississippi Palisades is popular among campers, offering 241 Class A and B campsites in both shaded and open areas. Electrical hookups are available at 110 sites, and three buildings with showers and flush toilets operate from May 1 through October 31.

Anglers are consistently drawn to Mississippi Palisades due to the diverse fish population in the Mississippi River and its backwaters. Catfish and carp are the most commonly caught species, but bluegill, crappie, and bass can also be found.

White Pines Forest State Park

Situated in the heart of the Rock River Valley, the 385-acre White Pines Forest State Park serves as the southern boundary of the historic Chicago-Iowa Trail. The park offers a perfect getaway for families, with activities such as hiking, fishing, camping, and picnicking.

The landscape is adorned with majestic trees, moss-covered cliffs, and trailing vines near the meandering banks of Spring and Pine creeks. During the blooming season, the park is filled with vibrant patches of trout lily, bloodroot, blue-eyed grass, spring beauty, and hepatica.

A unique feature of the park is the concrete fords that span the creeks, enabling visitors to drive through the flowing streams. An accessible path leads to the stream bank for wildlife watching and fishing.

White Pines is popular for camping and picnicking, offering shaded picnic areas along Pine Creek and over 100 campsites for visitors to enjoy.

The White Pines Lodge, originally built by the Civilian Conservation Corps in the 1930s, has been updated with modern amenities. It comprises 13 one-room cabins, 2 cabins with 4 rooms, and 1 cabin with 2 rooms, totaling 23 guest rooms. The White Pines Lodge Restaurant is known for its homemade delicacies, banquet facilities, and a dinner theater.

White Pines Forest State Park provides seasonal archery and firearm deer hunting. Additionally, when the ground is covered in snow, cross-country skiing trails become available for visitors to enjoy.

Theresa L. Goodrich is an Emmy-winning author and the force behind thelocaltourist.com, a site dedicated to telling in-depth stories of magnificent, quirky, and unique places. A passionate member of the Midwest Travel Network, Theresa is slightly obsessed with writing, road trips, camping, and history. She's turned these interests into multiple books, including the Two Lane Gems *series,* Living Landmarks of Chicago, Planning Your Perfect Road Trip, *and the* Alex Paige Mystery *series. She's driven, often literally, to inspire you to get off the interstates and explore the parks, towns, and communities that make this country, and especially the Midwest region, a constant and welcome surprise.*

Learn more about Theresa at thelocaltourist.com and follow her on social media @thelocaltourist.

Illinois State Parks Amenities

Please confirm availability of amenities with the state park system. For more information on Illinois State Parks, visit their website at dnr.illinois.gov/parks.html

A few notes about the amenities:
- RV – Partial Hookups include access to electricity and water, but not sewer.
- Tent: Tent only sites available.
- Primitive: Remote camping. This often means camping without any amenities or man-made structures. However, primitive campgrounds in Illinois often have access to grills, toilets, and sometimes even showers. They're noted as primitive because they're remote and you're required to walk in.
- Restrooms: Indicates the highest functional type of restroom available. Most Illinois campgrounds have Vault toilets. Shower houses are only available for campers.
- Shower buildings often close by November 1.
- Paddling: Boat access; this could be kayaking, canoeing, and/or powered boats.
- Swimming: Selected if swimming is available, either at a beach or a pool.

Notes about specific state parks:
- Adeline Jay Geo-Karis Illinois Beach State Park has an on-site hotel.
- Horseshoe Lake State Park is marked as Tent, but trailers can camp as well. There aren't any hookups.
- Matthiessen State Park's camping is equestrian-only.

Illinois

State Park Name	Hiking # of miles	Camping RV - Partial Hookups	Tent	Primitive	Lodging Cabin	Lodge
Adeline Jay Geo-Karis Illinois Beach State Park	6.8	✓	☐	☐	☐	✓
Apple River Canyon State Park	4.5	☐	✓	☐	☐	☐
Argyle Lake State Park	5	✓	✓	✓	☐	☐
Beall Woods State Park	6.25	☐	✓	☐	☐	☐
Beaver Dam State Park	8	✓	✓	☐	✓	☐
Buffalo Rock State Park	2.6	☐	☐	✓	☐	☐
Castle Rock State Park	6	☐	☐	✓	☐	☐
Cave-in-Rock State Park	2	✓	✓	☐	☐	✓
Chain O' Lakes State Park	8.5	✓	☐	☐	✓	☐
Delabar State Park	2	✓	✓	☐	☐	☐
Dixon Springs State Park	2.7	✓	✓	☐	☐	☐
Eagle Creek State Park	6.5	✓	☐	✓	☐	☐
Ferne Clyff State Park	26.75	✓	✓	✓	☐	☐
Fort Defiance State Park	N/A	☐	☐	☐	☐	☐
Fort Massac State Park	7	✓	✓	☐	☐	☐
Fox Ridge State Park	8	✓	☐	☐	✓	☐
Gebhard Woods State Park	61	☐	☐	✓	☐	☐
Giant City State Park	17	✓	✓	✓	✓	✓
Horseshoe Lake State Park	4	☐	✓	☐	☐	☐
Illini State Park	3.7	✓	✓	☐	✓	☐
James Pate Philip State Park	4.1	☐	☐	☐	☐	☐
Jubilee College State Park	40	✓	✓	☐	☐	☐
Kankakee River State Park	13.5	✓	✓	☐	☐	☐
Lake Murphysboro State Park	3	✓	✓	☐	☐	☐
Lincoln Trail Homestead State Park	1	☐	☐	☐	☐	☐
Lincoln Trail State Park	2.5	✓	✓	☐	☐	☐
Lowden State Park	4	✓	✓	✓	✓	☐
Matthiessen State Park	5	☐	☐	☐	☐	☐
Mississippi Palisades State Park	15	✓	☐	☐	☐	☐
Moraine Hills State Park & McHenry Dam State Park	11.4	☐	☐	☐	☐	☐
Morrison-Rockwood State Park	3.5	✓	☐	☐	☐	☐
Nauvoo State Park	2	✓	✓	☐	☐	☐
Pere Marquette State Park	12	✓	✓	☐	✓	✓
Prophetstown State Park	1/3	✓	☐	☐	☐	☐
Red Hills State Park	8	✓	☐	☐	✓	☐
Rock Cut State Park	40	✓	☐	☐	✓	☐
Rock Island Trail State Park	26	☐	☐	✓	☐	☐
Sangchris Lake State Park	15	✓	✓	✓	✓	☐
Siloam Springs State Park	15+	✓	✓	✓	✓	☐
Starved Rock State Park	13	✓	☐	☐	☐	✓
Walnut Point State Park	2.25	✓	✓	☐	☐	☐
Weldon Springs State Park	10+	✓	✓	✓	☐	☐
White Pines Forest State Park	6	✓	✓	☐	✓	✓
William G. Stratton State Park	N/A	☐	☐	☐	☐	☐
Wolf Creek State Park	7	✓	✓	☐	✓	☐

Midwest State Park Adventures

State Park Name	Restrooms	Visitor/ Nature Center	Swimming	Paddling	Store	Picnic	Fishing
Adeline Jay Geo-Karis Illinois Beach State Park	Flush	☐	☑	☑	☑	☑	☑
Apple River Canyon State Park	Vault	☐	☐	☐	☐	☑	☑
Argyle Lake State Park	Flush	☑	☐	☑	☑	☑	☑
Beall Woods State Park	Flush	☑	☐	☐	☐	☑	☑
Beaver Dam State Park	Showers	☐	☐	☑	☑	☑	☑
Buffalo Rock State Park	Flush	☐	☐	☐	☐	☑	☐
Castle Rock State Park	Vault	☐	☐	☑	☐	☑	☑
Cave-in-Rock State Park	Showers	☐	☐	☐	☑	☑	☑
Chain O' Lakes State Park	Showers	☐	☐	☑	☑	☑	☑
Delabar State Park	Vault	☐	☐	☐	☐	☑	☑
Dixon Springs State Park	Flush	☐	☑	☐	☐	☑	☑
Eagle Creek State Park	Showers	☐	☐	☑	☑	☑	☑
Ferne Clyff State Park	Showers	☐	☐	☐	☐	☑	☑
Fort Defiance State Park	Vault	☐	☐	☐	☐	☑	☑
Fort Massac State Park	Showers	☑	☐	☐	☐	☑	☑
Fox Ridge State Park	Showers	☐	☐	☑	☐	☑	☑
Gebhard Woods State Park	Vault	☐	☐	☑	☐	☑	☑
Giant City State Park	Showers	☑	☐	☐	☑	☑	☑
Horseshoe Lake State Park	Vault	☐	☐	☑	☐	☑	☑
Illini State Park	Showers	☐	☐	☑	☐	☑	☑
James Pate Philip State Park	Flush	☑	☐	☐	☐	☑	☐
Jubilee College State Park	Showers	☐	☐	☐	☐	☑	☑
Kankakee River State Park	Showers	☑	☐	☑	☐	☑	☑
Lake Murphysboro State Park	Showers	☐	☐	☐	☐	☐	☐
Lincoln Trail Homestead State Park	Vault	☐	☐	☑	☐	☑	☑
Lincoln Trail State Park	Showers	☐	☐	☑	☑	☑	☑
Lowden State Park	Showers	☐	☐	☑	☐	☑	☑
Matthiessen State Park	Showers	☐	☐	☐	☐	☑	☐
Mississippi Palisades State Park	Showers	☐	☐	☑	☐	☑	☑
Moraine Hills State Park & McHenry Dam State Park	Flush	☑	☐	☑	☑	☑	☑
Morrison-Rockwood State Park	Showers	☐	☐	☑	☐	☑	☑
Nauvoo State Park	Showers	☑	☐	☑	☐	☑	☑
Pere Marquette State Park	Showers	☑	☐	☐	☐	☑	☐
Prophetstown State Park	Showers	☐	☐	☐	☐	☑	☑
Red Hills State Park	Showers	☐	☐	☑	☐	☑	☑
Rock Cut State Park	Showers	☐	☑	☑	☑	☑	☑
Rock Island Trail State Park	Flush	☑	☐	☐	☐	☐	☐
Sangchris Lake State Park	Showers	☐	☐	☑	☐	☑	☑
Siloam Springs State Park	Showers	☐	☐	☑	☐	☑	☑
Starved Rock State Park	Showers	☑	☐	☑	☐	☑	☑
Walnut Point State Park	Showers	☐	☐	☑	☐	☑	☑
Weldon Springs State Park	Showers	☑	☐	☐	☐	☑	☑
White Pines Forest State Park	Showers	☐	☐	☐	☑	☑	☐
William G. Stratton State Park	N/A	☐	☐	☑	☐	☑	☑
Wolf Creek State Park	Showers	☐	☑	☑	☐	☑	☑

INDIANA

By Jamie Ward

Indiana is home to twenty-four state parks and two state forest recreation areas. Within the state parks are over 700 miles of trails, seven inns and hotels, and over 7,000 campsites. Each park has a story and unique attractions notable to its location.

Colonel Richard Lieber is the father of Indiana state parks. After visiting Yosemite National Park, he was inspired to create the Indiana state parks system. Lieber opened the first state park, McCormick's Creek

State Park, and Turkey Run State Park during the state's centennial celebration in 1916 without public funds. As the Director of the Indiana Department of Conservation, he organized the development of ten state parks and five state memorials.

Indiana State Park Facts & Important Information

- The Indiana state parks system manages: twenty-four state parks and seven satellite locations, seven inns, eight reservoirs, two state forest recreation areas, two off-roading riding areas, seventeen marinas, fifteen beaches, 150 cabins, and over 7,000 campsites.
- As of 2023, cars, trucks, and campers have a standard entrance fee for in-state ($7.00) and out-of-state ($9.00) plates. For pedestrians, bicycles, buses, and passenger vans, the entrance fee is $2.00 per person. These rates may vary per park and apply when a gate attendant is on duty.
- Reserve campgrounds and inns through the Indiana DNR website.
- Camping amenities have a reduced rate between November and April due to reduced amenities. Full amenities are available between May and October.
- Most Indiana State campgrounds sites have a standard check-in time of 2:00 pm local time and check-out time of 5:00 pm local time. Cabin and Inn times may vary.
- Pet owners must always keep their dogs and cats on a leash with a maximum length of six feet.
- Using metal detectors and removing fossils from Indiana state parks is prohibited unless you have obtained special permission.
- Always be courteous and conscious of the carry-in and carry-out trash policies in the day-use areas of the parks. If you bring trash in with you, please take it out with you.

- Guests can find electric charging stations at most State Park Inns.

Jamie's tip: Annual State Park Permits are a great way to save money. This one-time fee permits one vehicle entry to the Indiana state parks and Recreational areas from January through December of that year. In-state annual entrance permits (AEPs) are $50.00. Out-of-state annual entrance permits are $70.00. Discounts are available to seniors, Veterans, and disabled individuals.

A note about accessibility

The Hoosier state has been advancing on ADA-Handicap Accessibility in its state parks. Many of the parks have ADA-accessible trails and facilities. Some parks have options to rent an all-terrain power wheelchair or scooter for free. Call the state park ahead about how and where to rent.

Midwest State Park Adventures

Indiana State Parks Map

1. Pokagon State Park 2. Clifty Falls State Park 3. Ouabache State Park 4. Turkey Run State Park 5. Brown County State Park 6. Indiana Dunes State Park 7. Tippecanoe River State Park 8. Charlestown State Park 9. O'Bannon State Park 10. Summit Lake State Park 11. Whitewater Memorial State Park 12. Shades State Park 13. Prophetstown State Park 14. McCormick's Creek State Park 15. Spring Mill State Park

Region: Northern Indiana

Pokagon State Park

I affectionately refer to Pokagon State Park as the "best State Park for all seasons." There is something to do here for every season of the year. Pokagon is most famous for its winter toboggan run but offers many other recreational activities yearly. Boating, swimming, fishing, sand volleyball, and ice fishing are popular around Lake James and Snow Lake, which surrounds the park. Trine State Recreation Area is adjacent to Pokagon and offers kayak, paddleboat, and trolling motor power rowboat rentals. Hiking, horseback riding, cross-country skiing, biking, basketball, and sledding are other recreational activities in the park.

Pokagon is tucked in the corner of northeast Indiana, just north of Fort Wayne and a short drive from the Michigan and Ohio borders. The name "Pokagon" was chosen to honor father and son Leopold and Simon Pokagon, the last two most prominent leaders of the Potawatomi tribe. The state park inn was named Potawatomi Inn to remember the Native American heritage and those who made their home in this region of Indiana.

The Potawatomi Inn is a northern wilderness, fishing theme lodge with over 120 guest rooms and twelve cabins. The hotel has two restaurants, and guests can access the indoor pool, hot tub, sauna, and game room. Some of my fondest memories of visiting Potawatomi have been sitting in their large family room areas, playing board games around the fireplaces on winter nights with my daughters.

A quarter-mile dual-track refrigerated toboggan run is Pokagon's most prominent attraction. It's open every weekend from the end of November through the end of February, with extended hours on winter break. Four riders can ride per toboggan run; it's a blast! A Warming Station with concessions and bathrooms keeps guests toasty while taking breaks or waiting.

Jamie's Pokagon State Park Tips:
- Consider staying overnight at the Potawatomi Inn when visiting in the winter. Staying for a weekend ensures extra time to enjoy all the available winter activities. The toboggan runs get busy and is only available on a first-come, first-served basis.
- Take advantage of the Indiana State Park's Winter Inn specials with a cozy weeknight stay. The BOGO Winter specials are perfect for quiet getaways with views of frozen Lake James, intimate restaurant dinners, warm nights in front of the inn fireplaces, and relaxing in the sauna and hot tub.
- Cross-country skis and snowshoes are available for rent at the Warming Station.

Indiana Dunes State Park

Swim in Lake Michigan, hike the dunes, and camp at Indiana Dunes State Park, surrounded by its own National Park (Indiana Dunes National Park). The Indiana Dunes State Park is worthy of praise and is famous for its majestic dunes. It is a State Park that you should add to your bucket list. While the beach and lakeshore are popular visitor attractions, I prefer to draw attention to the park's other significant characteristics and features.

Beyond the lakeshore are over 1,500 acres of wooded wetlands, marsh, and various habitats and landscapes. The views of the marsh and the 3 Dune Hiking Challenge trails are superior to the lakeshore views facing the city. They showcase plant life, wildlife, and "tree graveyards" (forests buried by sand and re-exposed by wind erosion) and are excellent for birding. The 3 Dune Hiking Challenge is indeed a challenge! Although it is only a one-and-a-half-mile trail, it's the most strenuous trail in the park, with a 552 vertical feet climb. The payoff is phenomenal views from the top of all three dunes.

Tippecanoe River State Park

The river, trails, and camping are the most prominent attractions at Tippecanoe. My fondest memories of the Tippecanoe River State Park include tube floating down the Tippecanoe River, tent camping in the campground, and meeting Smoky, The Bear. Those looking to fish or float along the Tippecanoe will appreciate the primitive River Tent Campground with a boat launch. The Horsemen's Camp also has primitive camping. This State Park is a nature and water explorer's paradise.

For a less primitive camping experience, the campground provides electrical sites, modern amenities, and Rent-A-Camp cabins. Other unique Tippecanoe attractions are the ninety-foot fire tower, the historic Tepicon Recreation Hall (listed on the National Register of Historic Places), the marsh, and the Nature Center.

Region: Southern Indiana
Clifty Falls State Park

Southern Indiana is known for its scenic views of the Ohio River, limestone formations, and waterfalls.

Clifty Falls State Park is the perfect location to glimpse it all! Enter the park at the North Gate and start your visit at Little and Big Clifty Falls. An ADA-accessible paved loop path is adjacent to the parking lot. The way leads to some of the best Little and Big Clifty Falls views, so don't forget a camera. From here, an optional Trail 7 leads to an overlook of the falls and ravines for more rugged hiking.

The park has four significant waterfalls: Little Clifty, Big Clifty, Tunnel, and Hoffman Falls. Tunnel Falls is the tallest waterfall, cascading at eighty-three feet. The trails at Clifty Falls are considered moderate to very rugged; they are definitely for those seeking a hiking adventure. The ADA-accessible paved loop path and Trail 10 are best for easy hikes and those with limitations. If you have any physical restraints, please keep this in mind.

Brought's Folly, a manufactured 1852 historic railroad tunnel, sets Clifty Falls apart from other state parks. It was initially built to form a railway from Madison to Indianapolis; the project wasn't finished due to a lack of funds. The famous tunnel is open seasonally to visitors from May 1st to October 31st. It is not unusual to spot a few bats; it is closed during the winter for bat hibernation.

If you are a modern camper, you'll be happy to find modern camp amenities in the campground, such as showers, flush toilets, and laundry facilities. In the summer, the picnic shelters, playgrounds, and playfield areas are busy with families picnicking and enjoying the park. An outdoor Olympic-sized swimming pool, wading pool, and waterslides are also open to visitors.

If you prefer sleeping in a hotel or inn, Clifty Falls is one of the state parks with an inn. The Clifty Inn overlooks historic downtown Madison and the Ohio River. Unfortunately, you must ignore the smokestack at the neighboring power plant to appreciate this view. However, the inn was here first. In 1922, it began as an old stone farmhouse converted to guest rooms until the hotel was built in 1924. Over the decades, additions and renovations were added to make it the seventy-plus-room hotel it is today. The affordable rates, indoor swimming pool, free Wi-Fi, and private suites are some guest favorites.

The attached Clifty Inn Restaurant is one of my favorite State Park restaurants. They have some of the best fried chicken and buffets in southwest Indiana. Whether you stay overnight at the inn, camp or just visit for the day, make room for breakfast, lunch, or dinner at the restaurant while you're there.

Jamie's Clifty Falls State Park Tips:
- Wear waterproof hiking boots or shoes for hiking. The trails are sometimes wet or flooded, especially after rainfall.

- The best views of the waterfalls can be found in the Winter and Spring when the falls cascade the most. The creek and canyon offer impressive year-round scenic views.
- Bring a flashlight to navigate the tunnel if you plan to visit Brought's Folly.

Charlestown State Park

Charlestown State Park is the third largest state park known for its RV camping, waterfalls, and abandoned 1920s Rose Island Amusement Park. This park is located on an undeveloped portion of an old Indiana Army Ammunition plant. It is home to the historic Portersville Bridge, which connects the Charlestown State Park to Rose Island, where a 1920s amusement park and hotel once stood. If state parks could win prizes, Charlestown would win the "most unique and interesting" trophy.

The Porterville Bridge was originally built in 1912 for the White River; the steel bridge was restored and relocated to Charlestown State Park in 2011. It now crosses the Fourteenmile Creek into the interpretive Trail 7 on Rose Island. Although it's not technically an "island," it is a peninsula that can only be reached by bridge or ferry. After the Great Depression, the amusement park slowed, and in 1937 a flood ruined it past repair.

Trail 7 features historical markers with audio excerpts and a few remnants that remain on the island. I've found old bricks and fossils where a hotel once sat. The remains of a fountain, pool, columns for the original Rose Island welcome sign, and a restored main walkway are a bit eerie. Rumors say the island is haunted. There is something a bit spooky about the quietness of the hikes through the island, darkened by forest and remnants of past days.

O'Bannon State Park

O'Bannon State Park is peacefully located along the Ohio River and within the Harrison-Crawford State Forest in the southernmost part of the state. The name honors the late Indiana Governor Frank O'Bannon and his family for contributing to the area's natural resources. Hiking, hunting, fishing, mountain biking, and horseback riding are favored and approved sports at O'Bannon.

A modern campground with more than 230 electric sites is available for tent and RV camping. A Horseman Campgroup with over thirty electric sites and fifty non-electrical modern sites is available, surrounded by eighty miles of horse trails. Experienced backpackers can access The National Recreation Trail, Indiana's longest and most scenic backpacking trail, through O'Bannon's rugged twenty-five-and-a-half-mile Adventure Hiking Trail (AHT). The AHT takes two to three days to complete and has five overnight shelters for backpackers.

Other unique park activities include a Nature Center, fire tower, two nature preserves, cave tours, and an outdoor Family Aquatics Center. The Hickory Hollow Nature Center consists of live animals, an outdoor wetlands pond, and an 1830s farmstead with an authentic 1850s hay press and barn. Guided tours of the Big and Little Wyandotte Caves are available seasonally.

Region: Eastern Indiana

Ouabache State Park

The Ouabache State Park (pronounced "O-bah-chee") was initially the Wells County State Forest and Game Preserve when it was acquired in the 1930s. It's a challenge to spell, but I've heard it called the "Wabash State Park." Ouabache had been known as the "Greatest Wildlife Laboratory in the United States." The park was given this title for game raising, which phased out in the 1960s. In the 1980s, recreation and camping took over and became the main highlights of Ouabache State Park.

Bison existed in Indiana until the early 1800s, and the Ouabache exhibit is a conservation effort to serve these once-endangered mammals. Today, a twenty-acre American Bison (also called buffalo) exhibit exists in the park, across the street from the Fire Tower. Trail 1 loops around the bison exhibit, a double-layered fence acts as a barrier between the bison and visitors. Climb the restored, one-hundred-foot-tall 1930s Fire Tower to glimpse the bison and park from above. The tower was built during the Great Depression by Civilian Conservation Corps workers to spot wildfires. A CCC Worker Statue was built along Trail 5 to honor those workers.

Sports and recreation are the central focus at Ouabache. Options for recreation include a three-mile asphalt bike trail, a bocce court, a baseball diamond, a volleyball pit, tennis and basketball courts, a playfield, a beach, and fishing and water sports on the twenty-five-acre Kunkel Lake. The beach is free to access. And boats, kayaks, paddleboats, and canoes are available to rent at the beach service areas. I enjoy the lake recreation and picnicking at Ouabache, and it's worth the breathtaking view to stay until the sunset over Kunkel Lake.

Tent and RV campers will enjoy the electric camping sites. You won't find an inn, cabins, or full hookups at the Ouabache campground, but you can claim you slept next to bison while camping in Indiana! The campground has modern showers, flush toilets, and a waterfill and dump station. For groups, the youth tent sites are reservable. A rustic lodge is also available on Kunkel Lake and has kitchen and bathroom facilities.

Jamie Ouabache State Park Tips:
- Ouabache is excellent for families and sunset picnics. Pack a lunch or dinner and enjoy a picnic by the lake.
- Bring binoculars for the Fire Tower to better look at the bison. Sometimes the bison hide in locations not viewable from the trail, and binoculars are handy.

Summit Lake State Park

Summit Lake State Park is perfect for campers, anglers, swimmers, and photographers. This State Park is amid Indiana cornfields and small towns on over 2,600 acres, and is a gorgeous backdrop for picnics and hikes. I've spent many evenings watching the sunset over the lake for one of the most scenic sunset spots in east central Indiana. Camping sites are all electric, with water hook-ups and lakeside views along the 800-acre Summit Lake.

The beach is busy and popular in the summer (open Memorial Day through Labor Day), especially for families. The park's fishing and water recreation options are plentiful, with rental opportunities for boating, kayaking, canoeing, and three boat ramps. A picnic area with a volleyball pit and hiking trail is located at the beach. A beach house with restrooms and a concession stand are available, with nearby handicapped parking. (Please note that non-handicap visitors must park further and walk to the beach).

Wildlife photographers love Summit Lake for its abundance of wildlife, especially birds. I've seen more wildlife here than in any other state park, including bald eagles, deer, foxes, osprey, and snakes. There are more than one-hundred species of birds, including the bald eagle.

Whitewater Memorial State Park

By now, you've probably noticed that the east central Indiana area state parks have several things in common: lakes, fishing, wildlife, and water recreation are abundant. The Whitewater Memorial State Park is a complex of all these as well. It consists of Whitewater Lake, Brookville Lake Reservoir, Silver Creek, Hornbeam Nature Preserve, Barton's Bay Marina, and Kent's Harbor Marina. Water sports such as fishing, boating, swimming, canoeing, and kayaking are popular. The beach house and the beach on Whitewater Lake are open from Memorial Day to Labor Day.

Whitewater Memorial State Park was purchased to memorialize those who served in World War II. It's the only memorial park within Indiana's State Park system; they host an annual event to recognize and honor veterans and have a two-mile Veteran Vista Loop trail with an open vista area to view the lake.

Nine miles of bridle trails, a horse stable, and a horsemen's camp are great opportunities for riders to camp and horseback. Water, dump stations, and electricity are available at all the campgrounds. Whitewater Memorial Campground has modern bathrooms and showers. Though the Family Cabins are the most popular lodging option, these modern cabins sleep up to six and come furnished with bedrooms, a kitchen, a bathroom, and a living room.

Region: Western Indiana

Turkey Run State Park

Indiana's second State Park, Turkey Run State Park, is known as a natural geologic wonder. This state isn't so "flat and boring" after all, and Turkey Run's scenic views, deep canyons, ravines, and hemlocks prove that. Colonel Richard Lieber, Indiana's State Park founder, was particularly fond of Turkey Run, and his ashes are buried atop a hemlock grove at the end of Trail 11. The Lieber Memorial honors his memory and resides beside the Log Church (built in 1871). The Lieber Cabin, built in the 1840s, is one of the oldest in the state and is located on Trail 11.

Eleven hiking trails navigate hikers through fourteen miles of mainly moderate to rugged trails. Some require adventurous climbs along ridges, up ladders, down streambeds, and through rocky terrain. Rainy and wet conditions can cause trails to be hazardous and slippery. Use caution if you are hiking with children or have physical limitations. If you have two to three hours, take the 5 Mile Challenge that traverses Falls Canyon-Rocky Hollow Nature Preserve, which explores three canyons, climbs a ladder, and crosses a suspension bridge. The suspension bridge provides a charming look at Sugar Creek and is a beautiful photo opportunity.

The canyons and formations are mesmerizing - carvings in sandstone bedrock have been formed from erosion and glacial meltwaters. Coal was mined here in the late 1800s and early 1900s, and coal seams are still distinguishable on trails today. The saddle barn and shelter houses have been around since the 1930s and were built by the Civilian Conservation Corps. The nature center is open yearly and has live animals and a planetarium.

Turkey Run Inn and Narrows Restaurant sell themselves - after the trails, you'll want rest and nourishment. That is where the park's inn and restaurant come in handy. Turkey Run Inn offers guest rooms and cabins with an indoor heated pool and sundeck, outdoor pool, game room, playground, and lobby lounge with seating and a fireplace. Narrows is known for its Hoosier-famous tenderloin sandwich.

Jamie's Turkey Run State Park Tips:
- Wear waterproof hiking boots or shoes for hiking. The trails are sometimes wet or flooded, especially after rainfall.
- Trail 11 is a short, half-mile trail for an easy hike.
- Take a bathroom break and refill your water bottles before taking the 5 Mile Challenge; there isn't access to bathrooms or water sources along the challenge.

Shades State Park

Shades State Park is a neighbor to Turkey Run State Park. Hikers seeking peace and solidarity will appreciate this park's challenging hiking trails and beautiful naturescapes. Nature lovers will adore the ravines, sandstone cliffs, rock steps, streambeds, and dense forest.

Shades has the perfect starter for a backpacking weekend: a two-and-a-half-mile Back-Pack Trail that ends at a backcountry camp. The camp is one of the best areas in the park to view the stars. Shades has one of the darkest skies in Indiana and regularly hosts Astrology and stargazing events.

Sugar Creek runs through Shades and is popular for canoeing. A canoe camp is available for serious canoers. No reservations are required for either the backpack or canoe camp. Non-electric, primitive tent and RV camping are open in the campground with modern amenities such as flush toilets and showers.

Stories of folklore and rumors surround the meaning behind the name of Shades State Park. However, upon visiting the park and witnessing the heavily wooded areas and shadows of ravines, it's easy to see how Shades got its name. I noticed an immediate temperature drop just hiking through the canyons and streambeds, a cool welcome during the hot summer months.

Prophetstown State Park

Are you looking for a family-friendly state park? Currently Prophetstown State Park is one of the best state parks for family recreation. Prophetstown is between the Tippecanoe and Wabash Rivers, and its name honors a Native American village that settled here. The village was established by Tecumseh and his brother Tenskwatawa (The Prophet) in 1808.

The park provides visitors with hands-on, interpretive experiences through its visitor center, The Farm at Prophetstown, the Native American village, and recreation. The Farm at Prophetstown is a 1920s living history museum with real animals, farming, blacksmithing, gardening, canning, and more. Take a self-guided tour of the farm, visit the farmhouse to purchase products and items sourced directly from the land, and chat with experts working daily in the blacksmith shop, barn, garden, or farmhouse. The farm is free to visit with park admission and is open daily.

A visit to the Aquatics Center is a must during the summer months. It's one of the cleanest pools I've visited at a State Park and Indiana's only outdoor State Park waterpark. The waterpark features a 4,238-foot leisure pool, a thirty-foot tube slide, a body flume, a 523-foot lazy river float area, an adventure channel, a zero-entry pool with play features, and an aquatic activity area with basketball. A bathhouse with showers, changing rooms, and lockers are on-site, as well as a concessions stand and Aquatics Center parking. Camping, hiking, biking trails, and swimming are other popular outdoor activities at Prophetstown.

Region: Central Indiana
Brown County State Park

I adore the Central Indiana state parks, which makes narrowing them nearly impossible. They each have magnificent features and highlights that make them some of "the best" in the state. Brown County State Park is the largest State Park in Indiana, with over 16,000 acres of hills and ravines. It's nicknamed the "Little Smokies" for its likeness to the Great Smoky Mountains. The Fall season is packed with visitors from all over the country, coming to get a glance at the glorious rolling hills of autumn foliage.

Within the thousands of acres, Brown County State Park's winding roads navigate visitors through twenty miles of scenic overlooks. And more, from trails (hiking, mountain biking, and bridle), to a fire tower, lookout towers, campgrounds, creeks, and amphitheater, to a nature preserve and two lakes. The Seven Vista Challenge is a fun way to see all seven scenic vistas in Brown County. Visit all seven sights in the park, snap a photo of yourself in the Vista picture frames, and post your photos on social media using #BC7VistaChallenge.

Suppose you don't fear heights; brave the ninety-foot fire tower for amazing views of Brown County. You'll get a good glimpse of the four campgrounds offering electrical and non-electric sites, a water and dump station, and modern restrooms and showers. The Horseman Campground has primitive and electric sites. The Saddle Barn, located near the inn, offers seasonal trail, pony, and hayrides available during operation days.

The rustic, woodsy-themed Abe Martin Lodge is my favorite State Park overnight option. The lodge has over eighty rooms (many recently renovated), thirty cabins, and fifty rustic cabins. Guest lounging areas are available throughout the lodge, with cozy reading nooks and places to set up a board game or puzzle. Additional amenities include a gift shop, restaurant, indoor aquatics center, and game room. A large outdoor deck expands across the back of the lodge and is the best location for star gazing or relaxing in rockers by a firepit. All guests of the lodge and cabins have free access to the Abe Martin indoor Aquatic Center. The Aquatic Center features a zero-entry swimming pool, water slide, lazy river, water volleyball and basketball, hot tub, and a whirlpool with a waterfall.

Bird and reptile lovers will enjoy the Nature Center. A bird observation room with seating and a large viewing window offers a glimpse at some of Brown County's various birds, including robins, white-breasted nuthatches, blue jays, cardinals, juncos, and crows. Live turtles, snakes, and a beehive display are for those interested in the native reptiles and species of Indiana.

Jamie's Brown County State Park Tips:
- The Family Cabins are more affordable overnight lodging for larger families and groups. These cabins sleep up to eight people, and include access to the Aquatics Center and other hotel amenities.
- The Seven Vista Challenge is available for those with limited mobility. Simply drive to each of the seven vistas rather than hiking or biking.
- You can find a rare and state-endangered Yellowwood tree on Trail 5.
- There are two gate entrances for Brown County State Park. RV's and vehicles with trailers must use West Gate Entrance due to height restrictions at the North Gate Entrance.

McCormick's Creek State Park

McCormick's Creek State Park was declared Indiana's first State Park, and it's been wowing visitors since 1916. The limestone formations, waterfalls, caves, cliffs, and canyons are glorious. McCormick's Creek is on the Indiana Limestone Trail and supplied limestone to create the Indianapolis Statehouse.

The park is named after John McCormick, who settled there in 1816. Remnants of McCormick's old 1800's farm, "Historic Peden Farm Site," remain on the property and can be accessed from Trail 9. The farm remained in the family, last owned by grandson Thomas Alexander Peden. McCormick's real gem is the Wolf Cave, located along Trail 5. The park naturalist offers guided hikes and tours of the cave.

The Canyon Inn was opened the same year as the park, with over seventy rooms. After a hike, I enjoy relaxing on a rocker in front of the fireplace lobby lounging area. Other inn perks include a gift shop, restaurant, outdoor swimming pool, and game room. In the 1970s, the park added a campground, Nature Center, and swimming pool. Modern family cabins and electric and primitive camping spots are also available in the campground.

Spring Mill State Park

What do astronauts, caves, and pioneering have in common? They are all a part of Spring Mill State Park's history and interpretive facilities. Selected caves at Spring Mill are open for guided group and boat tours highlighting cave formations and animals. Cave tours are seasonal and a unique opportunity to see an endangered blind cavefish. Cave River Valley is an off-site location managed by Spring Mill, known for its caves. Guided hikes and cave tours are available with the Spring Mill State Park naturalist.

A restored 1814 Pioneer Village features an operating 1817, three-story limestone gristmill and twenty historic buildings. The village is open from May through mid-October and is lively with interpreters portraying the 1860s through pioneer entrepreneurship and crafts.

Indiana

The Virgil I. Grissom Memorial has his space suit and Gemini III space capsule on display - it's a surprisingly impressive exhibit to find in a State Park! From pioneers to astronauts, the park also pays homage to Virgil "Gus" Grissom. Grissom is the second American to visit space and was from Mitchell, Indiana, where Spring Mill State Park resides.

The word "cool" keeps coming to mind when discussing Spring Mill - there are so many unique and intriguing things to do here. You can also visit the historic Hamer Pioneer Cemetery (where early pioneers are buried), rent a mountain bike, see the Wilson Monument on Trail 4, or fish, kayak, and canoe on Spring Mill Lake. To add to the excitement, the Spring Mill Inn and Millstone Dining Room is undergoing a significant renovation, which is scheduled to be completed in early 2024. They're adding seventy new guest rooms, a heated indoor/outdoor pool, a gift shop, and a game room.

Jamie Ward is the writer and owner of the travel and lifestyle blog Cornfields & High Heels and wrote 100 Things To Do In Indiana Before You Die. *Her love for travel takes her from the West Coast to the East Coast, North to the South, through tiny towns with cornfields and bustling cities with skyscrapers. She is a member of the Midwest Travel Network and frequently writes about her Indiana and Midwest adventures. Jamie resides in central Indiana with her family and enjoys road trips, good coffee, waterfalls, and thrifting.*

Learn more about Jamie at fieldsandheels.com and follow her on social media @fieldsandheels

Indiana State Parks Amenities

Please confirm availability of amenities with the state park system. For more information on Indiana State Parks, visit their website at www.in.gov/dnr/state-parks/parks-lakes/

A few notes about the amenities:
- RV – Full Hookups include access to electricity, water, and sewer at the campsite.
- RV – Partial Hookups include access to electricity and water, but not sewer.
- Tent: Tent only sites available.
- Primitive: Camping in remote areas. Vault bathrooms and water resources are available at most Indiana primitive camping sites.
- Restrooms: Indicates the highest functional type of restroom available.
- Paddling: Boat access; this could be kayaking, canoeing, and/or powered boats.
- Swimming: Selected if swimming is available, either at a beach or a pool.
- Some Indiana state parks have Aquatic Centers.

Notes about specific state parks:
- Redbird State Recreation Area is an off-road vehicle recreation park. However, hiking is allowed on the trails and a Visitor Center is planned.
- Brown County, Clifty Falls, Fort Harrison, McCormick's Creek, Pokagon, Spring Mill, and Turkey Run State Parks have on-site inns and restaurants.
- Fort Harrison State Park has three historic Officer's Homes available to rent that can sleep larger groups or families.

Indiana

State Park Name	Hiking # of miles	RV - Full Hookups	RV - Partial Hookups	Tent	Primitive	Cabin	Lodge	Hotel/Resort
Brown County State Park	20.85	☐	✓	✓	☐	✓	✓	☐
Chain O'Lakes State Park	24.2	☐	☐	✓	☐	✓	☐	☐
Charlestown State Park	15.4	✓	☐	✓	☐	☐	☐	☐
Clifty Falls State Park	14.37	☐	✓	✓	☐	☐	☐	✓
Deam Lakes Recreational Area	9	☐	✓	✓	☐	✓	☐	☐
Falls of the Ohio State Park	0.75	☐	☐	☐	☐	☐	☐	☐
Fort Harrison State Park	14.4	☐	☐	☐	☐	☐	☐	✓
Harmonie State Park	7.75	☐	✓	✓	☐	✓	☐	☐
Indiana Dunes State Park	16.35	☐	✓	✓	☐	☐	☐	☐
Interlake State Recreation Area	2.36	☐	☐	☐	☐	☐	☐	☐
Lincoln State Park	12.5	☐	✓	✓	✓	✓	☐	☐
McCormicks Creek State Park	10.7	☐	✓	✓	✓	✓	☐	✓
Mounds State Park	6	☐	✓	✓	☐	☐	☐	☐
O'Bannon Woods State Park	13	☐	✓	✓	☐	☐	☐	☐
Ouabache State Park	13	☐	✓	✓	✓	☐	☐	☐
Pokagon State Park	13.7	☐	✓	✓	☐	☐	☐	✓
Potato Creek State Park	10.85	☐	✓	✓	☐	✓	☐	☐
Prophetstown State Park	18.85	✓	✓	✓	☐	☐	☐	☐
Redbird State Recreation Area		☐	☐	☐	☐	☐	☐	☐
Shades State Park	10	☐	☐	✓	✓	☐	☐	☐
Shakamak State Park	13.33	✓	✓	✓	☐	✓	☐	☐
Spring Mill State Park	8.875	✓	✓	✓	☐	☐	☐	✓
Summit Lake State Park	4.9	☐	✓	✓	☐	☐	☐	☐
Tippecanoe River State Park	22.6	☐	✓	✓	☐	✓	☐	☐
Turkey Run State Park	14	☐	✓	✓	☐	✓	☐	✓
Versailles State Park	6.5	☐	✓	✓	☐	☐	☐	☐
Whitewater Memorial State Park	9.4	☐	✓	✓	✓	✓	☐	☐

Midwest State Park Adventures

State Park Name	Restrooms	Visitor/Nature Center	Swimming	Paddling	Store	Picnic	Fishing
Brown County State Park	Showers	✓	✓	✓	✓	✓	✓
Chain O'Lakes State Park	Showers	✓	✓	✓	✓	✓	✓
Charlestown State Park	Showers	☐	☐	✓	☐	✓	✓
Clifty Falls State Park	Showers	✓	✓	☐	☐	✓	☐
Deam Lakes Recreational Area	Showers	☐	✓	✓	☐	✓	✓
Falls of the Ohio State Park	Flush	✓	☐	✓	☐	✓	✓
Fort Harrison State Park	Flush	✓	☐	☐	☐	✓	☐
Harmonie State Park	Showers	✓	☐	☐	✓	✓	✓
Indiana Dunes State Park	Showers	✓	✓	☐	✓	✓	✓
Interlake State Recreation Area	Vault	☐	☐	✓	☐	✓	☐
Lincoln State Park	Showers	✓	✓	✓	✓	✓	✓
McCormicks Creek State Park	Showers	✓	✓	☐	✓	✓	✓
Mounds State Park	Showers	✓	✓	☐	✓	✓	✓
O'Bannon Woods State Park	Showers	✓	✓	✓	☐	✓	✓
Ouabache State Park	Showers	☐	✓	✓	☐	✓	✓
Pokagon State Park	Showers	✓	✓	✓	✓	✓	✓
Potato Creek State Park	Showers	☐	✓	✓	✓	✓	✓
Prophetstown State Park	Showers	☐	✓	☐	☐	✓	☐
Redbird State Recreation Area	Vault	☐	☐	✓	☐	✓	✓
Shades State Park	Showers	☐	☐	✓	✓	✓	✓
Shakamak State Park	Showers	✓	✓	✓	✓	✓	✓
Spring Mill State Park	Showers	✓	✓	✓	☐	✓	✓
Summit Lake State Park	Showers	☐	✓	✓	✓	✓	✓
Tippecanoe River State Park	Showers	☐	☐	✓	✓	✓	✓
Turkey Run State Park	Showers	✓	✓	✓	✓	✓	✓
Versailles State Park	Showers	✓	✓	✓	✓	✓	✓
Whitewater Memorial State Park	Showers	☐	✓	✓	✓	✓	✓

IOWA

By Sara Broers

Iowa is home to 56 state parks that offer something for everyone on each visit. Many are set in unique geographic locations, giving you that "wow" factor. Family gatherings, camping, hiking, kayaking, biking, and picnicking are some of the most popular activities in Iowa state parks.

Backbone State Park is Iowa's first state park. It was in 1920 that Iowa's State Park system began. Today, over 16 million people visit these treasures in Iowa. Most Iowa state parks are free to visit, making them easy for everyone to use. Iowa offers four distinct seasons, and each state park offers visitor activities all year. Cross-country skiing and ice fishing are two popular winter activities. January is known for prime bald eagle viewing season along Iowa's rivers and lakes.

I have lived in Iowa all my life, and I have visited most of Iowa's state parks. Over the years, the experiences have continued to evolve. Today you can camp in a yurt, stay in a cabin, or choose to "rough it." Iowa state parks offer sunrise and sunset experiences you can only find in Iowa. The Northeastern section of Iowa is known as the Driftless Region. This area of Iowa was left untouched by the glaciers that covered the area thousands of years ago. Today steep, rugged cliffs soar above, and narrow valleys prevail for your enjoyment. The southeast and southwest state parks offer rolling hills and prairies that appear to be unscathed.

Iowa state parks are known for nature experiences, but Cedar Rock State Park offers something different- architecture. A Frank Lloyd Wright-designed home sits on the property, offering incredible nature and architectural views. Fun and unique are two words that speak to Iowa state parks. Anglers will appreciate the opportunities that several state parks offer. From Clear Lake to West Okoboji Lake in Northwest Iowa, the state parks are nearby, offering outdoor recreation, including fishing, camping, swimming, and boating. You can decide how adventurous you want to be when you visit Iowa state parks.

Iowa State Park Facts & Important Information

- Iowa has 56 state parks
- In 1920, Iowa's first state park came to be
- Iowa's largest state park boasts 2,180 acres
- You can sleep in yurts in one of Iowa's state parks
- An 1848 gristmill in one of Iowa's state parks is on the National Register of Historic Places

A note about accessibility

The ADA Accessibility varies from park to park in the Iowa state park system. A few state parks offer paved walkways around lakes, but most do not. If you require an ADA accessibility venue, I would call the state park to confirm what the park offers. There is not any consistency within the Iowa state park System, in regards to ADA Accessibility.

Iowa Road Trips Map

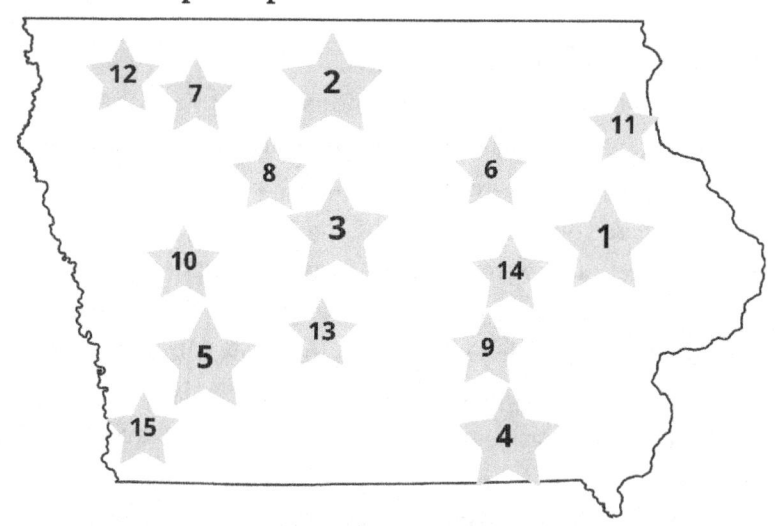

1. Maquoketa Caves State Park 2. Clear Lake State Park 3. Ledges State Park 4. Lacey Keosauqua State Park 5. Viking Lake State Park 6. Cedar Rock State Park 7. Fort Defiance State Park 8. Dolliver Memorial State Park 9. Lake Darling State Park 10. Prairie Rose State Park 11. Pikes Peak State Park 12. Gull Point State Park 13. Walnut Woods State Park 14. Lake Macbride State Park 15. Waubonsie State Park

Quick note: Backbone State Park is Iowa's oldest state park and at time of publication has a lot of construction projects underway.

Region: East

Maquoketa Caves State Park

One of Iowa's unique outdoor attractions can be found at Maquoketa Caves State Park. A highlight of your visit to Maquoketa Caves State Park is a stroll through the 1,100-foot "Dancehall Cave." You can't miss this magnificent cave as you climb down the stairs to enter the caving area at the state park. There are approximately 16 caves throughout this stunning Iowa state park, making it a prime space for caving in the Midwest.

In the mid-1850s, people began caving in the area, and it was in 1921 that the Maquoketa Women's Club purchased land to establish Morehead Caves State Park, which became Maquoketa Caves State Park in 1928.

Most of the park's infrastructure was completed from 1932 to 1939 by the Civilian Conservation Corps (CCC) and the Works Progress Administration (WPA). Both programs resulted from the federal government's efforts to create work for Americans during the Great Depression. Today, we all enjoy and appreciate the work that went into Maquoketa Caves State Park during this challenging time in America. Three CCC overlook shelters, entrance portals, the custodian's residence, cave improvements, trail improvements, two stone latrines, and many other projects were completed for visitors. Over time, the amenity list has grown for all of us to enjoy.

With a six-mile trail system, outdoor adventure enthusiasts will fall in love as soon as their heel hits the ground. The caves and scenic overlooks are all links through the trail system, providing views of the rich landscape that will be engrained with you. If you are into caving, this state park is for you. With several caves to explore, dress accordingly. I can personally attest to the fact that you should wear clothing you do not want to keep. When you are done caving, you will be muddy and will want to toss your clothing into a dumpster. Several caves require you to crawl on your belly, which is dark. Sport a flashlight on the top of your head and you can see all the nooks and crannies hidden within the caves. If tight spaces are not your thing, it's best to avoid sticking your head into one of these low-lying caves.

"Dancehall Cave" is the largest and best cave all around for everyone in your party. It's wide-open and offers an incredible view of the area. There is also an interpretive center within the park. You can learn about the geology of the area, park history, and see how the park has changed over time. This center is open on weekends during the summer, and a video tour of the park is open for viewing.

Maquoketa Caves State Park has always been and continues to be an incredible place for family picnics. Shelter houses are available on a first-come, first-served basis, so plan accordingly. Several picnic tables are scattered throughout the park, making it easy to set up your family picnic area. The campground is a short drive from the caving area. Camp-site reservations must be made through the state park website, which includes primitive hike-in-sites.

The beauty of Maquoketa Caves State Park is stunning all year round. It's one of Iowa's most beautiful state parks, and is free to visit.

Pikes Peak State Park

Pikes Peak State Park is the most recognizable Iowa state park that sits along the Mississippi River. It is located along the famed Great River Road National Scenic Byway. 11 miles of hiking trails include hikes to Bridal Veil Falls, Point Ann Overlook, and views that overlook the Mississippi River throughout your hiking experience. If you look closely, you will find fossils along the trails as you walk the paths that many Native Americans have.

Camping and picnicking have been a highlight for many visiting Pikes Peak State Park. A large, paved overlook area is ADA-accessible and offers visitors a magnificent view of the Mississippi River throughout the year. The campground offers youth group camping campsites, and electric and non-electric campsites.

Winter brings snowshoeing, cross-country skiing, as well as incredible sunrises. Fall offers vibrant colors that are true to the area, making it a prime time of year to explore the Great River Road in Eastern Iowa. No matter what time of year you visit, the magic of Pikes Peak State Park will win you over.

Cedar Rock State Park

Cedar Rock State Park is home to the historic estate of Agnes and Lowell Walter, featuring property designed by Frank Lloyd Wright. The Walter House is a focal point of the park, which does sit near Cedar Rock. The visitor center and The Walter Residence are open seasonally to the public. Free tours are available by reservation through the state park website.

The estate includes the only original Wright-designed boat pavilion still in existence. Cedar Rock is the only Iowa property with one of his coveted signature tiles. I enjoy strolling through the prairie during summer when the flowers are in full bloom. The short walk to the Walter home is beautiful and if you listen as you stroll, you will hear several birds that inhabit the area.

This state park is truly one of a kind, as it's rare to find a state park with a Frank Lloyd Wright-designed property on site. Allow yourself time to take a guided tour of the home and immerse yourself in the beauty of Cedar Rock State Park. Note: There are no shelter houses or designated picnic areas at Cedar Rock State Park.

Region: North

Clear Lake State Park

Clear Lake State Park is in Northcentral Iowa, home to one of Iowa's most popular lakes, Clear Lake. It is located along I-35 and is part-way between Minneapolis and Des Moines. The 3,000-acre lake is a draw for boating, fishing, and sailing. Fishers enjoy fishing for bluegill, largemouth bass, yellow bass, and walleye.

Are you looking to participate in a fishing competition? Look no further than The Clear Lake Walleye Classic. This fishing contest draws in hundreds of fishers annually in May. The lake is what many people come to Clear Lake State Park for, but there is also a lot to see and do in the area. The state park is not spread out, which makes it easy to use. The lake is the main focal point, shining 365 days of a year.

Picnicking is popular in this state park. Several acres of picnic grounds feature tables and grills popular for day use. The historic lodge near the beach offers a rustic fireplace, restroom, kitchen, and venue for all gatherings. Is a family reunion in your future? Clear Lake State Park is a great meeting place for your next reunion. Reservations for the historic lodge can be made through the state park website. A beautiful butterfly garden featuring Iowa prairie grasses sits near the historic lodge. During summer, the prairie is in full bloom. You can never go wrong with a summer visit to Clear Lake State Park. There is a large parking area; if the lot seems full, many visitors find a grassy area to park their vehicles.

The campground boasts more than 150 campsites, featuring full hookups, electric, and non-electric campsites. Modern restrooms are available throughout the campground. There is a campsite for everyone at Clear Lake State Park. The 900-foot beach area is a short walk from the campground, making the beach a family favorite. The day-use lodge is ADA-accessible, as is the fishing pier. Kayaking, canoeing, boating, water-skiing, tubing, and all types of watersports are popular on Clear Lake. You can board your boat near Clear Lake State Park and play in the water all day.

If you don't own a boat, no worries. You can rent a boat in several places in Clear Lake, Iowa. The casual and frequent boater will have a great time on the lake. The Clear Lake Area Chamber of Commerce is a good resource for wanting to know what you need to know about your visit any time of year.

Clear Lake, Iowa, is home to one of the Midwest's best 4th of July festivals. And it's no secret that Clear Lake State Park is a great place to spend any holiday. One quarter of the campsites are available on a first-come, first-served basis. Reserve your campsite through the state park reservation system. You can easily ride your bicycle from Clear Lake State

Park to explore Downtown Clear Lake, Iowa. Once the sun goes down, campfires with s'mores are popular when camping in one of Iowa's premiere state parks. Make your reservations as soon as you consider visiting, and make it happen.

Fort Defiance State Park

Fort Defiance State Park near Estherville, Iowa, in Northwest Iowa. With more than 191 acres of asporous woodlands, you will fall in love with this quiet area in Iowa. The rolling farmlands are nearby, and summertime is incredibly lush and green.

A highlight for many who visit Defiance State Park is an army-style lodge ideal for your next family gathering. You can reserve the lodge through the Iowa state park reservation system. A picnic shelter is available on a first-come, first-served basis.

If you are a birding enthusiast, you will love this state park. Bring your binoculars and be ready to view and listen to the many species of birds that frequent the area. Several trails are for hikers, but equestrian use is also allowed on three different trails. As I hiked through this state park, I was stunned at how quiet things were.

This state park brings on a new feel the Saturday before Halloween. The Estherville Chamber of Commerce hosts a popular Fright Hike. Visitors hike ½ mile through the haunted woods at Fort Defiance State Park. There is a fee to participate in the Fright Hike, but admission to the state park all year long is free.

Gull Point State Park

Gull Point State Park is in the heart of the Iowa Great Lakes Region. The lakes area in Northwest Iowa offers abundant water adventures for everyone. A 1.5-mile self-guided interpretive hiking trail is a great way to learn about the history of the area.

Gull Point Lodge, built during the 1930s by the Civilian Conservation Corps, is the largest in the state. The lodge has a kitchen, fireplaces, an attached patio, and a restroom. Many wedding receptions, family reunions, and events occur at the lodge. Beach, Gull Point, and Trailhead

Shelters are available through the state park reservation system for your picnicking enjoyment. Camping is popular, boasting nearly 100 electrical and non-electric sites.

Boating is the most popular activity in the area. Anglers of all ages will appreciate the opportunity to snag white bass, yellow bass, perch, blue gills, and walleye. Fishers, hikers, bikers, water skiers, sailors, and anyone with a love of the water will have the time of their life at Gull Point State Park. With numerous lakes in the area, the fish will surely be biting somewhere.

Note: Magical sunsets are everywhere in Iowa's Great Lake Region.

Region: Central

Ledges State Park

Ledges State Park was designated as one of Iowa's first state parks in 1924. Many of the buildings within the state park were constructed during the 1930s by the Civilian Conservation Corps (CCC).

This state park is a short drive from Des Moines, making it a popular getaway from the city. An arch stone bridge, a shelter in Oak Woods, and a shelter in Lower Ledges are from the CCC project. The sandstone of the cliffs remains from the prehistoric sea that covered the Midwest nearly 300 million years ago. The cliffs come from the last ice age, 13,000 years ago, when meltwater carved down through the rock. This ice age left a lot of beauty for all of us to admire in Ledges State Park.

When you take Canyon Drive, a winding one-way road along Pea's Creek, you will see the canyon's stunning views and the Des Moines River Valley. Popular overlook locations for hikers are Inspiration Point, Crow's Nest, and Table Rock. A four-mile trail system greets visitors to Iowa's Ledges State Park.

The historic and unique features of this Iowa state park will entertain outdoor enthusiasts. Pea's Creek Canyon offers magnificent views that hikers have talked about for years on end. A fully handicapped accessible interpretive trail to Lost Lake is available for users at the park's southern end. A fun thing to do in Ledges State Park is stream walking along canyon road in Pea's Creek. There's no better way to cool off on a hot summer day in Iowa than hiking through the water in Ledges State Park. Pack sunscreen, water shoes, and summer clothing for a fun hiking experience. The canyon drive closes over the winter and after heavy rain during the summer months. When was the last time you went creek stomping?

Slightly fewer than 100 campsites are available for campers. Seventy-five percent of campsites are reservable, and the remaining are first-come, first-served. You can reserve your campsite through the state park reservation system. Group camping is available, as well as hike-in campsites.

My family and I have camped here numerous times over the years. Keeping a clean campsite is necessary, as racoons frequent the campground. I know this from firsthand experience. If you are camping during the weekend during the midst of summer, you may have the opportunity to enjoy a show at the amphitheater. Ledges State Park is open to hikers, snowshoers, and cross-country skiers in winter.

Winter can be one of your most memorable visits to Ledges State Park. Dress warmly and enjoy the views. A variety of attractions are in the Boone area. The Birthplace of Mamie Doud Eisenhower, Boone History Center, and the Boone Scenic Valley Railroad and Museum are popular with Ledges State Park visitors.

Dolliver Memorial State Park

Dolliver Memorial State Park is home to natural bluffs and geological formations unique to the area, located in the Des Moines River Valley. This state park encompasses five-hundred ninety-seven acres. Two historic day lodges were built during the 1930s as part of a CCC project.

With six miles of trails featuring unique sandstone formations, prairie lands, creeks, and woodlands, hikers of all ages will enjoy Dolliver Memorial State Park. Camping cabins, campsites, and a shelter are all available for rent. A group campsite is also available and is reservable through the state park website.

A popular hiking trail is Bone Yard Hollow. This area is said to have been named by early settlers who found numerous bison bones in the canyon.

History comes to life in Dolliver Memorial State Park as you explore and enjoy the lush green that this state park offers during summer. As you explore, watch for the ancient Native American mounds overlooking the Des Moines River Valley. Pack a picnic lunch, lay out a blanket, and enjoy the views.

Note: Fort Dodge, Iowa, is nearby and is home to Iowa's tallest mural.

Walnut Woods State Park

Walnut Woods State Park is located near Iowa's capital, Des Moines. Visitors can hike the two miles of trails that meander through wooded bottomland along the Raccoon River. You will want to pack your binoculars, as you never know what type of bird will be in the area. Birding is popular all year, but particularly exciting in the spring and fall. Migrating warblers, flycatchers, and a variety of songbirds, hawks, and owls can be viewed in the park.

There are several picnic sites visible from the main road through the park. Grab a picnic table and enjoy your lunch under a shaded tree. Toss a fishing line in the river, hike, camp, or relax on a summer day. Walnut Woods State Park will not disappoint.

A magnificent stone and timber-day-use lodge is available year-round to rent for family reunions, weddings, graduations, and other events. With four seasons, you can visit monthly and experience something different. Winter brings out the cross-country skiers, and fall brings out leaf chasers. Walnut Woods State Park is near I-35 and the intersection of State Highway 5 bypass, making it accessible for all travelers.

Region: South

Lacey Keosauqua State Park

Southeast Iowa is home to Iowa's second state park, Lacey Keosauqua State Park. This state park was dedicated in 1921, originally known as Big Bend State Park. This park spans 1,653 acres while offering an array of outdoor activities.

With 13 miles of winding trails among the valleys and cliffs, tree species and wildlife are abundant while shadowing the Des Moines River. One 3-mile segment of hiking trails follows a bluff of the Des Moines River. The trail touches on the history of the area, from the river crossing of the Mormon's western trek in the mid-1800s to the structures built by the young men of the CCC during the Great Depression.

A series of 19 ancient Native American mounds overlooking the river in the northwest section of the park still stands. These burial mounds were built by the ancient Woodland Culture between 750 and 2,500 years ago.

History comes to life as you hike through Iowa's second state park. Many of the park's structures were built in the 1930s as part of the Civilian Conservation Corps (CCC) and are available for visitors. Lacey-Keosauqua State Park is the first site in Iowa to erect a statue commemorating the invaluable contributions of the CCC to Iowa state parks.

A highlight of Lacey-Keosauqua State Park is a 22-acre lake, and 2 miles down the road is a larger 575-acre Lake Sugema. The fishing pier at Lake Sugema offers convenient access to the water. Anglers appreciate all this area has to offer, making it a fishing paradise. Only electric motors are allowed on Lacey Lake.

Cabins and campsites are available for visitors. Lacey-Keosauqua's Lodge is available for weddings, family reunions, company picnics, meetings, and other gatherings. The Beach House Lodge is available to rent during the warmer months of the year.

Several picnic areas and shelter houses are up for grabs. Pack your picnic lunch, throw in a fishing pole, and enjoy nature in Iowa's quietest county. Nearly 65 campsites await campers, featuring full hookups, electric, electric with water, and non-electric sites. A youth group site and shelter are also available within the campground. 25% of the campsites are available on a first-come, first-served basis. Advanced cabin and campsite reservations can be made through the state park campground reservation system. Firewood sales are available on Memorial Day weekend through the middle of October.

This state park campground is one of my all-time favorites, as it's one place I can camp under the stars surrounded by dark skies. The Villages of Van Buren County are nearby, offering an experience in each village. You will not find fast-food restaurants in Van Buren County or find many stop lights.

Take a step back in time as you camp, explore, and embrace the culture that Lacey-Keosauqua State Park has to offer.

Lake Darling State Park

If you are looking for the ultimate park for a family picnic in Southeast Iowa, look at Lake Darling State Park. A 1.5-mile paved fishing trail is accessible for all, making it one of the few lake trails in the Iowa state park System to do so.

Several hiking trails meander through the wetland habitats around Lake Darling, featuring the native prairie and an 1800s cemetery. Crushed rock and grass make these trails ideal for hikers, mountain bikers, cross-country skiers, and snowmobilers.

The lake is open for water enthusiasts, including paddle boats, stand-up paddleboards, kayaks, and motors of all sizes at a "no wake" speed. There are two boat ramps along the lake, with boat trailer parking nearby. You can rent your boats at the Boat Rental Concession during the warmer months of the year.

Modern cabins are ADA-accessible, and Lake Darling's large campground is sure to have a campsite for you and your family. A newly renovated lodge is available for family reunions, weddings, and large gatherings. A covered patio overlooks the lake, making this a popular rental. A nice feature of Lake Darling State Park is the large number of fishing jetties that line the 302-acre lake.

Lake Macbride State Park

Lake Macbride State Park in Southeast Iowa is named after the "father" of Iowa Conservation, Thomas Macbride. This is Iowa's largest state park; at 2,180 acres, it boasts many outdoor activities. Lake Macbride State Park is a short drive for Cedar Rapids and Iowa City residents, making it an easy escape from the city.

It's important to note that Lake Macbride is split into two units. The northern unit is located at the end of Country Road F-16, 4 miles west of Solon, and features a modern campground. The southern unit is located off County Road F-28 by Fifth Street in Solon and features a non-modern campground.

The north unit's park office offers boat ramps and picnic areas. The beach area in the park's northern unit is the perfect place to be on a hot summer day. Boat rental and concessions are also in the north unit. Multi-use trails run through the state park, offering prairie and lake views throughout your time on the trail. A day-use lodge, and four open shelters are available for rent. From family reunions to corporate gatherings, Lake Macbride offers an opportunity to connect with nature.

Region: West

Viking Lake State Park

Viking Lake State Park offers an array of outdoor recreational opportunities, including boating, fishing, and hiking. If you enjoy lake life, this state park will win you over. This popular Southwest Iowa state park boasts a renovated and restocked 140-acre lake. Bluegill, red-ear sunfish, largemouth bass, channel catfish, crappie, and walleye can be caught in Viking Lake. Viking Lake State Park is a great option if you are looking for an experience overlooking the lake. All sizes of motors are allowed on the lake, with a 5-mph restriction. Four boat ramps are available for anglers wanting to fish from their boats. Shoreline fishing is popular; all you need is an Iowa Fishing License and a fishing pole.

Viking Lake State Park is an hour from Omaha, making it an easy escape from the city to the lake. A swimming beach is used by many on a hot summer day, along with the kayaks, canoes, and smaller boats that are available for rent. I have fond memories of chasing fireflies at Viking Lake State Park when our boys were growing up. Anytime nature comes knocking at your door, reach out and grab it. Viking Lake State Park will speak to you if you allow it to. Make family memories and enjoy nature.

More than 100 campsites welcome campers of all types. Full hookups, electric, non-electric, reservable, and non-reservable campsites are available. This is one of a few Iowa state parks that offer lakeside camping. 25% of the campsites are available on a first-come, first-served basis. 75% are reservable online, through the state park camping reservation site. Shelter reservations can also be reserved through the reservation system.

Two hiking trails are popular, featuring the beauty of the state park. The 6-mile White-Tailed Trail goes around the lake, making it a favorite for all types of hikers. Signage is abundant, as you make your way around the lake. A shorter hike is the Bur Oak Nature Trail, a mile hike featuring the prairie. Beavers, turkeys, ducks, and white-tail deer frequent the state park. As you can imagine, summer brings out the magic in the Iowa prairies. A beach concessionaire is open all summer long, offering bait, kayak, canoe, and pontoon rentals. For a different experience, visit in the fall. The campground is quiet, and the fall foliage is abundant.

Prairie Rose State Park

Prairie Rose State Park offers outdoor recreation in numerous shapes and forms. The rolling hills and shade trees make this an ideal park for camping. Camping cabins and a variety of campsites are reservable through the state park reservation system. Grab a campsite along the shore of the lake to have a front-row seat to an Iowa sunset. If you have a beginning angler in your family, this state park is excellent for shoreline fishing. With two fish cleaning stations and two boat ramps, boating is popular at Prairie Rose State Park. Any size boat can be on the lake, but must be run at "no wake" speeds. Kayaks and canoes are a fun way to stay cool on a hot summer day at Prairie Rose State Park.

Seven miles of hiking trails meander through the park. Hiking, biking, snowmobiling, and cross-country skiing are all popular trail activities. The casual hiker will appreciate the interpretive trail that starts in the northwest area of the park and winds near the shoreline. In addition to hiking, the beach, sand volleyball courts, and horseshoe pits are popular recreation activities. Need a reason to visit in summer? June and July are prime months for viewing Iowa's flower, the wild rose.

Waubonsie State Park

Waubonsie State Park sits in the heart of the Loess Hills in southwest Iowa. The park has historical significance, as it is a Lewis & Clark Historical Trail site. Mountain bikers, equestrians, and anyone with a desire to dive into nature, Waubonsie State Park is calling your name. Nearly 2,000 acres make up the sweeping views of the Missouri River Valley. The trail to the main overlook is accessible to people of all ages and abilities. Eight cabins, equestrian campsites, electric & non-electric campsites, and primitive equestrian campsites are offered in Waubonsie State Park.

An extensive trail system invites adventure for hikers, snowmobilers, mountain bikers, and equestrian enthusiasts. The Sunset Ridge Nature Trail is in the heart of the park and offers views over the Missouri River Valley. The Ridge, Bridge, and Valley Trails offer unique views under a canopy of trees in the valleys: pack water, sunscreen, and a picnic lunch. Make a note of the season, and dress in layers. During the spring and fall, the temperatures in Iowa fluctuate throughout the day. Once you enter Waubonsie State Park, you will have a hard time leaving. The area's beauty will lure you in and offer you a quiet place to connect with nature.

Iowa

Sara Broers is a travel enthusiast and resides in North Iowa. She is the CEO of Travel With Sara, Co-Owner of the Midwest Travel Network, and an author. She is the co-author of Midwest Road Trip Adventures, Midwest State Park Adventures, and the author of 100 Things To Do In Iowa Before You Die. Sara is a proud farmer's daughter and lives on the family farm. She and her husband have two grown sons and three grandchildren.

Iowa State Parks Amenities

Please confirm availability of amenities with the state park system. For more information on Iowa state parks, visit their website at www.iowadnr.gov/places-to-go/state-parks/iowa-state-parks

A few notes about the amenities:
- RV – Full Hookups include access to electricity, water, and sewer at the campsite.
- RV – Partial Hookups include access to electricity and water, but not sewer.
- Tent: Tent only sites available.
- Primitive: Camping in remote areas without amenities like bathrooms, picnic tables, trash cans, or any other man-made structures.
- Restrooms: Indicates the highest functional type of restroom available.
- Paddling: Boat access; this could be kayaking, canoeing, and/or powered boats.
- Swimming: Selected if swimming is available, either at a beach or a pool.

Iowa

State Park Name	Hiking # of miles	RV - Full Hookups	RV - Partial Hookups	Tent	Primitive	Cabin	Yurt	Lodge
Ambrose A. Call State Park	2	☐	☑	☐	☐	☐	☐	☐
Backbone State Park	21	☑	☑	☑	☐	☑	☐	☐
Banner Lakes At Summerset State Park	6.5	☐	☐	☐	☐	☐	☐	☐
Beeds Lake State Park	2	☐	☑	☑	☐	☐	☐	☐
Bellevue State Park	3	☐	☐	☑	☐	☐	☐	☐
Big Creek State Park	27	☐	☑	☐	☐	☐	☐	☐
Black Hawk State Park	1.6	☑	☑	☑	☑	☑	☐	☐
Cedar Rock State Park	1	☐	☐	☐	☐	☐	☐	☐
Clear Lake State Park	0	☑	☑	☑	☐	☐	☐	☐
Dolliver Memorial State Park	5	☐	☑	☑	☐	☑	☐	☐
Elinor Bedell State Park	0	☑	☐	☐	☐	☐	☐	☐
Elk Rock State Park	13	☑	☑	☐	☐	☐	☐	☐
Fort Defiance State Park	2	☐	☑	☐	☐	☐	☐	☐
Geode State Park	2	☑	☑	☑	☐	☐	☐	☐
George Wyth State Park	3	☑	☑	☑	☑	☐	☐	☐
Green Valley State Park	10	☑	☑	☑	☐	☐	☐	☐
Gull Point State Park	1.3	☐	☑	☐	☐	☐	☐	☐
Honey Creek State Park	5	☐	☑	☑	☐	☑	☐	☐
Lacey Keosauqua State Park	13	☐	☑	☐	☐	☑	☐	☑
Lake Ahquabi State Park	6	☐	☑	☐	☐	☐	☐	☐
Lake Anita State Park	5	☑	☑	☐	☐	☐	☐	☐
Lake Darling State Park	4	☑	☑	☐	☐	☑	☐	☑
Lake Keomah State Park	3	☐	☑	☑	☐	☐	☐	☐
Lake Macbride State Park	7	☑	☑	☐	☐	☐	☐	☐
Lake Manawa State Park	3	☐	☑	☐	☐	☐	☐	☐
Lake of Three Fires State Park	10	☐	☑	☐	☐	☑	☐	☐
Lake Wapello State Park	7	☑	☑	☐	☐	☑	☐	☐
Ledges State Park	4	☑	☑	☐	☑	☐	☐	☐
Lewis and Clark State Park	3	☑	☑	☐	☐	☐	☐	☐
Maquoketa Caves State Park	6	☐	☑	☐	☑	☐	☐	☐
McIntosh Woods State Park	1.5	☐	☑	☐	☐	☐	☑	☐
Mini-Wakan State Park	0	☐	☐	☐	☐	☐	☐	☐
Nine Eagles State Park	10	☐	☑	☐	☑	☑	☐	☐
Okamanpedan State Park	0	☐	☐	☐	☐	☐	☐	☐
Palisades-Kepler State Park	5	☑	☑	☐	☐	☑	☐	☐
Pikes Peak State Park	4.5	☑	☑	☐	☐	☐	☐	☐
Pikes Point State Park	0	☐	☐	☐	☐	☐	☐	☐
Pilot Knob State Park	5	☑	☑	☐	☐	☐	☐	☐
Pine Lake State Park	2.5	☑	☑	☐	☐	☑	☐	☐
Prairie Rose State Park	7	☑	☑	☑	☐	☑	☐	☐
Preparation Canyon State Park	2	☐	☐	☐	☑	☐	☐	☐
Red Haw State Park	4	☑	☑	☑	☐	☐	☐	☐
Rice Lake State Park	0	☐	☐	☐	☐	☐	☐	☐
Rock Creek State Park	8	☑	☑	☐	☐	☑	☑	☐
Springbrook State Park	12	☐	☑	☐	☐	☑	☐	☐
Stone State Park	15	☐	☑	☑	☐	☑	☐	☐
Trappers Bay State Park	0	☐	☐	☐	☐	☐	☐	☐
Twin Lakes State Park	7	☐	☐	☐	☐	☐	☐	☐
Union Grove State Park	3	☑	☑	☐	☐	☑	☐	☐
Viking Lake State Park	5.5	☑	☑	☐	☐	☐	☐	☐
Walnut Woods State Park	2	☑	☑	☐	☐	☐	☐	☐
Wapsipinicon State Park	3	☐	☑	☑	☑	☑	☐	☐

Midwest State Park Adventures

State Park Name	Restrooms	Visitor/Nature Center	Swimming	Paddling	Store	Picnic	Fishing
Ambrose A. Call State Park	Vault	☐	☐	☐	☐	✓	☐
Backbone State Park	Flush	✓	✓	✓	✓	✓	✓
Banner Lakes At Summerset State Park	Vault	✓	☐	✓	☐	☐	✓
Beeds Lake State Park	Flush	☐	✓	✓	☐	✓	✓
Bellevue State Park	Flush	✓	☐	☐	☐	✓	☐
Big Creek State Park	Flush	☐	✓	✓	✓	✓	✓
Black Hawk State Park	Flush	☐	✓	✓	☐	✓	✓
Cedar Rock State Park	Flush	✓	☐	☐	☐	☐	☐
Clear Lake State Park	Flush	☐	✓	✓	☐	✓	✓
Dolliver Memorial State Park	Flush	☐	☐	☐	☐	☐	☐
Elinor Bedell State Park	Flush	☐	☐	☐	☐	✓	✓
Elk Rock State Park	Flush	☐	☐	☐	☐	☐	☐
Fort Defiance State Park	Vault	☐	☐	☐	☐	✓	☐
Geode State Park	Flush	☐	✓	✓	☐	✓	✓
George Wyth State Park	Flush	☐	✓	✓	☐	☐	☐
Green Valley State Park	Flush	☐	✓	✓	☐	✓	✓
Gull Point State Park	Flush	☐	✓	☐	☐	☐	☐
Honey Creek State Park	Flush	☐	✓	✓	☐	✓	✓
Lacey Keosauqua State Park	Flush	☐	✓	✓	☐	✓	✓
Lake Ahquabi State Park	Flush	☐	✓	✓	✓	✓	✓
Lake Anita State Park	Flush	☐	✓	✓	✓	✓	✓
Lake Darling State Park	Flush	☐	✓	✓	☐	✓	✓
Lake Keomah State Park	Flush	☐	✓	✓	☐	✓	✓
Lake Macbride State Park	Flush	☐	✓	✓	✓	✓	✓
Lake Manawa State Park	Flush	☐	✓	✓	✓	✓	✓
Lake of Three Fires State Park	Flush	☐	✓	✓	☐	✓	✓
Lake Wapello State Park	Flush	☐	✓	✓	☐	✓	✓
Ledges State Park	Flush	☐	☐	☐	☐	✓	☐
Lewis and Clark State Park	Flush	✓	✓	✓	☐	✓	✓
Maquoketa Caves State Park	Flush	✓	☐	☐	☐	✓	☐
McIntosh Woods State Park	Flush	☐	✓	✓	☐	✓	✓
Mini-Wakan State Park	N/A	☐	☐	✓	☐	☐	✓
Nine Eagles State Park	Flush	☐	✓	✓	☐	✓	✓
Okamanpedan State Park	N/A	☐	☐	✓	☐	✓	☐
Palisades-Kepler State Park	Flush	☐	☐	✓	☐	✓	✓
Pikes Peak State Park	Flush	☐	☐	☐	✓	✓	☐
Pikes Point State Park	N/A	☐	✓	☐	☐	✓	☐
Pilot Knob State Park	Flush	☐	☐	☐	☐	✓	✓
Pine Lake State Park	Flush	☐	✓	✓	☐	✓	✓
Prairie Rose State Park	Flush	☐	✓	✓	☐	✓	☐
Preparation Canyon State Park	Vault	☐	☐	☐	☐	✓	☐
Red Haw State Park	Flush	☐	☐	✓	☐	✓	✓
Rice Lake State Park	Vault	☐	☐	✓	☐	✓	☐
Rock Creek State Park	Flush	☐	✓	✓	✓	✓	✓
Springbrook State Park	Flush	☐	✓	✓	☐	✓	✓
Stone State Park	Flush	✓	☐	☐	☐	✓	☐
Trappers Bay State Park	N/A	☐	☐	☐	☐	✓	✓
Twin Lakes State Park	Flush	☐	✓	✓	☐	✓	✓
Union Grove State Park	Flush	☐	✓	✓	☐	✓	✓
Viking Lake State Park	Flush	☐	✓	✓	☐	✓	✓
Walnut Woods State Park	Flush	☐	☐	✓	☐	✓	✓
Wapsipinicon State Park	Flush	☐	☐	✓	☐	✓	✓

Iowa

State Park Name	Hiking # of miles	RV - Full Hookups	RV - Partial Hookups	Tent	Primitive	Cabin	Yurt	Lodge
			Camping			Lodging		
Waubonsie State Park	8	☐	☑	☑	☑	☑	☐	☑
Wildcat Den State Park	2	☐	☐	☐	☑	☐	☐	☐

State Park Name	Restrooms	Visitor/ Nature Center	Swimming	Paddling	Store	Picnic	Fishing
Waubonsie State Park	Flush	☐	☐	☐	☐	☑	☐
Wildcat Den State Park	Flush	☐	☐	☐	☐	☑	☐

KANSAS

By Roxie Yonkey

I compare Kansas to a loaf of multi-grain bread. A bread loaf looks ordinary on the outside, but a look inside portrays the bread's real quality. Like a loaf, Kansas has a plain reputation. However, a look inside displays surprising diversity.

Kansas arose in adversity, and so did the state parks. Ironically, floods drowned the land during the 1930s and 1950s drought years. The federal government-built dams to provide protection from both droughts and floods, with recreation as a side benefit. Like the differing grains in a loaf of bread, the parks also showcase Kansas' geologic diversity. The allegedly flat state is full of hills—and even a section of the Ozarks.

Strange rock formations arise beside the Smoky Hill River. Little Jerusalem Badlands State Park is a maze of eroded Niobrara Chalk. The primordial Western Interior Sea laid down the chalk and deposited numerous fossil monsters within it. Watch for them in the buttes around Cedar Bluff State Park.

Rocktown, eroded Dakota Sandstone towers, looms over Wilson Reservoir. Rounded sandstone engraved with flowing water marks dots the ground in Rock City near Minneapolis. Their cousins inhabit Mushroom Rock State Park near Carneiro.

Delight in the sense of place along the Flint Hills Trail and Prairie Spirit Trail. Native peoples traversed the area, followed by Santa Fe Trail traders and settlers. That multi-grain loaf features sunflower seeds. Wild sunflowers decorate the state's landscape in the late summer and early fall. Families and photographers delight in commercial sunflower fields' gigantic blooms. Enjoy the waving wheat in the late spring and early summer before the combines mow down the wheat in the seasonal harvest dance.

Like the inside of a loaf of bread, Kansas offers more than meets the eye. I invite you to savor these slices of Kansas.

Kansas State Park Facts & Important Information

- Kansas contains 28 state parks.
- Kanopolis is the first state park. The Kansas Legislature established it in 1948, but the State Park and Resources Authority (SPRA) began in 1955.
- The state built Meade State Fishing Lake in 1926, but the area didn't become a state park until 1962.
- The SPRA and the Kansas Fish and Game Commission merged in 1987, becoming the Kansas Department of Wildlife and Parks.

- Kanopolis Reservoir flooded the only site where Jelinite amber, the Kansas State Gem, is found. The drowned site made the amber the world's rarest type of the gem.
- Kanopolis intended to be the Kansas state capital. Instead, Topeka kept the capital and Kanopolis received a state park.
- Eisenhower State Park is known for its equestrian trails. Ironically, Eisenhower injured his knee during equestrian practice at West Point. The injury nearly ended his military career before it started.
- Little Jerusalem holds the largest population of Great Plains wild buckwheat, found only within the chalk bluffs prairie of western Kansas.
- The Scott riffle beetle inhabits Big Springs in Historic Lake Scott State Park, and nowhere else in the world.
- El Dorado State Park is the state's largest and most visited.
- Mushroom Rock State Park is the state's smallest with 5 acres of bizarre mushroom-shaped rocks.
- All park visitors must purchase daily or annual park passes. Kansans may buy annual state park passes with their car registrations. Camping requires an additional permit.
- Anglers and hunters 16 and over must possess the appropriate licenses.
- Boaters under 21 must complete a Kansas-approved boater education course.
- Restrained pets are welcome in Kansas state parks, but leashes must be 10 feet or less. The parks forbid pets in swimming areas and in public structures.

A note about accessibility

All Kansas state parks are ADA compliant except for Sand Hills State Park. For specific information visit the state park. In practice, that means each park has accessible features, not that every activity is accessible.

Kansas State Parks Map

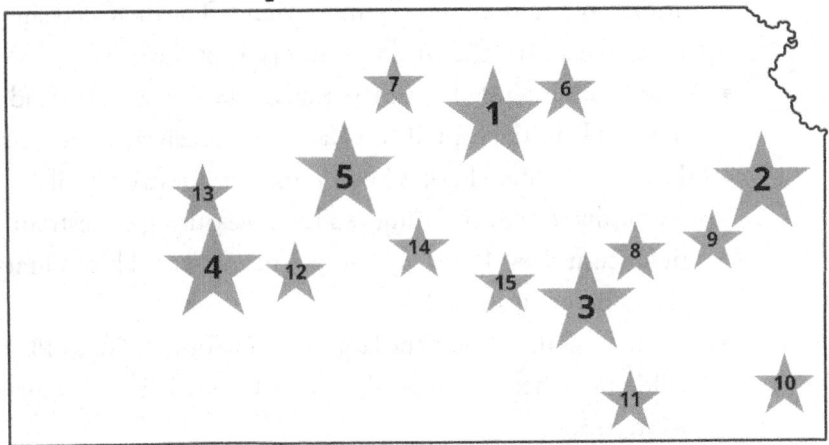

1. Milford State Park 2. Hillsdale State Park 3. Cross Timbers State Park 4. Historic Lake Scott State Park 5. Wilson State Park 6. Tuttle Creek State Park 7. Glen Elder State Park 8. Eisenhower State Park 9. Flint Hills Trail State Park 10. Crawford State Park 11. Elk City State Park 12. Cedar Bluff State Park 13. Little Jerusalem Badlands State Park 14. Kanopolis State Park 15. El Dorado State Park

Region: North

Milford State Park

Escape everyone except the fish at the 65,200-acre Milford Reservoir or party in the crowds at Nudie Beach, where clothing is *not* optional. Or enjoy something between pure solitude and friendly crowds at the state's largest lake. The Corps of Engineers dammed the Republican River to create the reservoir. The park is about 10 minutes north of Interstate 70's western Junction City exit.

Of course, water recreation takes center stage on the lake. Join the Southwind Yacht Club or watch their races.

Summertime is the park's busiest season, but each season offers opportunities. Bald eagles inhabit the park in the winter, attracted by its open water. Attend Eagle Day each third Saturday of January to learn more about the eagles and join an eagle viewing tour. During the spring, watch for migratory birds and listen for bull elk bugling in the fall.

Unwrap beauty on one of the park's four trails. The easy Wildlife Viewing Tower Trail goes to a 21-foot-tall viewing platform. Visit near dawn and dusk or stargaze at night. Look for geodes and deer on the 2.2-mile Crystal Trail and watch bald eagles from November through March. The Eagle Ridge Equestrian Trail provides over 8 miles of horseback riding.

Equestrians should camp at the park's Eagle Ridge Campground, which features a corral.

Cross the lake on the Highway 82 causeway to the Kansas Landscape Arboretum. The arboretum is most beautiful in the fall, but don't miss it in springtime when the crabapple trees bloom.

The Kansas Department of Wildlife and Parks (KDWP) annually ranks Milford as one of the state's best for blue catfish, crappies, smallmouth bass, wipers, and white bass. Plus, the lake shelters channel catfish and largemouth bass. Fishing is best from mid-March into June. Fishing improves after September's first cold front.

Milford holds the current Kansas record for smallmouth bass at 6.88 pounds. The reservoir also has hosted some of the nation's most prestigious fishing tournaments.

Fish on the wall and snakes crawling in cages greet guests inside the Milford Nature Center. Nevertheless, don't let the potential horror stories stop you because all the dangers are locked away.

Outside, animals in rehab or with permanent injuries live in habitats where visitors can view them. Look for the bald eagles. In the playground, adventurous folks can climb on a spider.

Look for the Milford Fish Hatchery's fish runs on the other side of the nature center. It's one of the nation's few warm water "intensive-culture" hatcheries. Watch for the feeding frenzy when the keepers toss fish food into the runs. Call the hatchery for an appointment to see inside.

Unwrap your inner thrill-seeker on motorcycles and ATVs at the School Creek Off-Road Vehicle Area on the lake's west side. With nearly 300 acres of trails, beginners to experts will find a free experience worth trying.

When you want to get away, head for Milford.

Tuttle Creek State Park

Tuttle Creek State Park is only minutes from Manhattan, and it offers the perfect retreat from city life. Steep hillsides surround Tuttle Creek Reservoir's forested shores, which surround the state's second-largest lake at 12,500-acres.

The Randolph Bridge on the reservoir's northern end is one of the state's most beautiful. The 14.75-mile Randolph Equestrian Trail passes below the bridge's east end. Corrals are nearby. The 6-mile Fancy Creek Mountain Biking Trail attracts cyclists from around the world. The trail runs through a hilly cedar forest and native grasslands and challenges riders with rock outcrops and ridges.

The park's three walking trails are all easy. The 1.25-mile paved Western Heritage Trail parallels the Blue River. The gravel Cedar Ridge trail winds through forest and tallgrass prairie on its 0.75-mile course. The natural surface of Cottonwood Trail is only half a mile.

Anglers will enjoy fishing for channel catfish and flathead in the lake and in the river above and below it. The state stocks trout in the lake during the fall and winter. Families should try the 18-hole disc golf course, volleyball courts, horseshoe pits, and archery range. The Fancy Creek Shooting Range is open on the first and third weekends of each month.

Retreat to Tuttle Creek.

Glen Elder State Park

Experience the legend of Waconda Lake at Glen Elder State Park. For millennia, people came to the area for the healing waters of Waconda Springs. "Wakonda" means "Great Spirit." The tribes considered the springs sacred. Later, visitors stayed in a resort beside the spring. The resort company also bottled the mineral water and shipped it throughout the nation.

And then the government decided to dam the Solomon River to prevent floods. Waconda is lost beneath the reservoir, but a replica portrays the spring. A buoy in the lake marks its site. Learn more on the easy 2.5-mile Waconda Springs Replica Trail and at the Waconda Education and Visitor Center. The park's Hopewell Church is a popular wedding venue.

The Chautauqua Fishing Pond is accessible to individuals with disabilities and children. (Special creel and length limits are in effect.) The park stocks the pond with trout in the winter. A modern, accessible fish cleaning station is open from April to October at the east dump station.

Cawker City stands on the reservoir's west end. Add to the World's Largest Ball of Sisal Twine and browse at Eyegore's Curiosities and Monster Museum.

At Glen Elder, you're in for a legendary experience.

Region: East

Hillsdale State Park

From the air, Hillsdale Reservoir looks like a rabbit's head with a carrot in its mouth. Hillsdale State Park includes the rabbit's "mouth" and "chin" plus other enclaves on top of the rabbit's "head." Ironically, Rabbit Ridge Campground lies at the "carrot" tip. The 12,000-acre park and wildlife area are almost three times larger than the 4,580-acre lake. It's about an hour south of Kansas City between Spring Hill and Paola.

Before you head to the lake, pick up some delicious cider at Louisburg Cider Mill 15 minutes southeast.

Boaters should play in the largest section, the rabbit's head. Rock Creek and Bull Creek form the lake's "ears," and they provide a refuge for canoeists and kayakers. Wildlife is more prevalent beside the creeks.

The Corps of Engineers left seventy-five percent of the standing timber in the lake to provide fish and wildlife habitat. While this provides an advantage for anglers, boaters should beware.

Crappie are anglers' most frequent target at Hillsdale. However, trophy-size largemouth bass and walleyes swim in Hillsdale's water. Ever-hungry catfish also prowl the lake. The 51-mile shoreline provides plenty of opportunities to catch the angler's next meal.

Hunters can compete at the shooting range beside the reservoir's outlet on Big Bull Creek. The range provides 50-, 100-, and 200-yard ranges for rifle and pistol shooting. Shotgun shooters can aim for trap and skeet targets.

Birders should look for bald eagles, shorebirds, finches, warblers, sparrows, and hawks. Eagles nest on Rock Creek Arm (the west ear) and Little Bull Creek Arm (the east ear).

Remote control aviation has a home at Hillsdale as well. Fly your aircraft with the RC Barnstormers Club at their field south of the dam.

The same air that supports birds and planes drives sailboats. Launch yours from Windsurfer Beach on the reservoir's southeast side, where the east ear joins the head. Swimmers and paddlers also use the beach, so it can be crowded.

The Saddle Ridge Equestrian Area adjoins Windsurfer Beach. The campground is equipped for those who prefer galloping on trails instead of walking. Camp in 37 sites and ride about 32 miles of marked trails. The area is not accessible, though.

Those who hike or ride bikes have 21 miles divided between five trails. The Bluebird Trail is the longest at 7.7 miles. Allow 2.5 hours for an easy walk beside wildflowers and among birds in season. The 1.6-mile Hidden Springs Trail is more challenging. Allow about 40 minutes for the hilly, rocky hike. The rocks can be slippery when wet. You may or may not see a rabbit.

Whether you're Alice following the White Rabbit down the hole or James Stewart's character enjoying his invisible rabbit Harvey, Hillsdale is a place to know. After all, you can't be late for that important lake date.

Eisenhower State Park

Eisenhower State Park sits in tallgrass prairie on the Flint Hills' eastern edge, under an hour south of Topeka. Originally, Melvern State Park surrounded Melvern Reservoir, but in 1990, the Kansas Legislature renamed the park for the state's most famous son, Dwight Eisenhower. Many of the park's amenities received Eisenhower-themed names.

Equestrians enjoy the 1,785-acre park's facilities and riding areas. The 20-mile Crooked Knee Horse Trail sounds like Ike's knee after his injury. The park allows hikers and cyclists on the trail's Blue and Orange loops, but it's best suited to horses. The hooves chew up the natural-surface trail and render it difficult for two-legged and two-wheeled travelers. Beware of ticks, and wear orange during hunting season.

The Corps of Engineers' Coeur d' Alene Park has two gravel nature trails, the Overlook Trail and the Breakwater Trail. The Tallgrass Heritage Trail runs 2.2 miles from Arrow Rock Park to Coeur d' Alene. Its mowed grass section crosses several hills. The track extends nearly two miles through Arrow Rock on a packed gravel surface suited for hikers and gravel grinding cyclists.

Archers will enjoy the two-mile, 20-target archery trail.

You'll like Ike; we promise.

Flint Hills Trail State Park

As its name indicates, the Flint Hills Trail traverses the Flint Hills. The name does not explain the region's significance. It's the last stand of the tallgrass prairie. In wet years, the tallgrass can reach 7 feet tall. In the late summer wind, the grass looks like a green ocean tossed by the pervasive winds.

The 118-mile trek extends from Osawatomie in the east to Herington in the west. It's the nation's eight-longest rail-to-trail. Riding it straight through would consume an estimated 29 hours, but don't do it. Stop in the friendly communities along the way.

All non-motorized travel is welcome, and the trail requires no permit. Some stretches are accessible to electric wheelchairs.

Before you go, check kanzatrails.org/flint-hills-trail for updates. Points of interest include Bleeding Kansas and Civil War sites, Native American and Black history. During quiet times, wildlife may approach the trail. Watch for rock outcroppings.

Be prepared to lift a bike over the former railroad embankments at some places, and at times, the gravel is large chunks left over from the railroad. Pack a flat tire repair kit just in case.

You'll love being up close and personal with the Flint Hills and its people.

Region: South

Cross Timbers State Park

At Cross Timbers State Park, the Chautauqua Hills create a fascinating landscape. The hills are the northern finger of the Cross Timbers ecoregion that reaches into north central Texas. The region's dense hardwood stands alternate with stretches of open savanna. The forested floodplains house the state's most diverse flora and fauna. All of those trees ensure shaded campsites.

The park surrounds 2,800-acre Toronto Lake, named for the city immediately north of its shores. It's a subtle battleground where the eastern deciduous forest and prairie attempt to conquer each other. The Osage tribe called this home before removal dragged them to Oklahoma. Settlers came slowly because the land's thin soils did not grow crops. They saw the region as a boundary between Euro-American civilization and the frontier.

Blackjack and post oak trees dominate the forested areas. The one-mile Ancient Oak Trail showcases 14 trees that germinated as far back as the 1720s. They were growing before the United States declared its independence. Interpretive signs explain the trees' stories.

Hackberries, hickory trees, and ash trees also dot the landscape. The mix of deciduous trees provides a palette of fall colors each year. Fall color displays depend on the year's weather patterns. A warm wet spring, favorable summer weather, and sunny fall days with cool nights combined produce the most spectacular shows.

Ancient Oaks is for hikers only, but Cross Timbers' other trails are open to mountain bikers as well. Choose four connecting trail loops on the Chautauqua Hills Trail. The shortest loop is 1.5 miles long, and the longest is 11 miles. The yellow loop and the western red loop allow backcountry camping by special permit on the yellow loop.

The 1.25-mile Overlook Trail is full of sandstone outcroppings and steep ravines. After a strenuous climb, the trail's final loop overlooks the reservoir. Look for wildflowers in the spring.

Not all the park's trails are on land. The mile-long Blue Water Trail's maps and floating signs guide paddlers through Mann's Cove on the reservoir's northeast side. If you didn't bring your kayak or canoe, borrow one from the park.

Fish for white crappie, white bass, flathead and channel catfish in the lake and Verdigris River. Seek black bass, bluegill, and sunfish within Cross Timbers' brush piles. The Toronto Point Area has an accessible fishing pier. Boat ramps have been constructed around the reservoir, on Walnut Creek and the Verdigris River to provide boat access.

Between activities, enjoy a leisurely picnic on one of the park's stone tables. At night, look for the stars.

The adjacent 4,700-acre Toronto Wildlife Area is open for public hunting in season. Look for white-tailed deer, turkey, and bobwhite quail. Migratory birds seek the park's marshes. Bring binoculars to see flocks of shorebirds.

The combination of abundant trees, hills, refreshing lake vistas, trails, and wildlife will ensure you are anything but cross at Cross Timbers.

Crawford State Park

The Ozark Plateau extends into Kansas' southeast corner, and Crawford State Park sits on its edge. The Corps of Engineers built most of the state's eastern park reservoirs, but Crawford is an exception. The Civilian Conservation Corps (CCC) built 150-acre Crawford State Fishing Lake in the 1930s. (Locals call the reservoir Lake Farlington.) A sculpture of a CCC worker stands near the park's entrance, 15 minutes northeast of Girard.

The Deer Run Trail connects the 530-acre park to the Farlington Fish Hatchery. It breeds walleye, catfish, and other species. Call 620-362-4166 for a tour appointment. April and June are the best times. The hatchery's proximity ensures prime fishing stocks for anglers.

After the Civil War, the Secretary of the Interior sold Cherokee lands to James Joy, a railroad tycoon. The sale offended the settlers, and they threatened to burn the railroad. Soldiers established an outpost on Drywood Creek. Its remnants remain along the Deer Run Trail.

Lakeview Café sits on the lake's northwest shore. It hosts live music every Friday night from May through September.

Enjoy redbud blooms in the spring and leaf colors in the fall. The Kansas Ozarks are calling you.

Elk City State Park

Table Mound, a big bluff in the northern part of Elk City State Park, is the area's most recognized feature. But it is far from the only hill. Elk City lies within the Osage Cuestas. A cuesta is a hill or ridge with a gentle slope on one side, and a steep slope on the other. The scenery includes rolling meadows and hardwood forests. Dogwoods bloom in the spring and spectacular colors paint the landscape in the fall.

The park covers the west side of Elk City Lake between Elk City and Independence, where catfish rule. In 1998, Ken Paulie of Independence caught the world's largest flathead catfish. The whopper weighed 123 pounds and measured more than five feet long. Fish that large won't taste good; throw them back and let them grow more. Look for them in the reservoir's shady places.

Watch the anglers challenge Paulie's record atop the 2.75-mile Table Mound Hiking Trail. The trail generally follows the lake's eastern shore. Geology geeks will enjoy the rock formations. At the end, scramble to the bluff's top through a crack.

The gear on the half-mile Exercise Trail will help work out the kinks after a day on the water.

Come to Elk City State Park; they'll set the table for you.

Region: West

Historic Lake Scott State Park

People have enjoyed Ladder Creek Canyon, now home to Historic Lake Scott State Park, for millennia. The springs attracted game, and provided water for crops. More than 26 archaeological sites are in and around the park. One of them, El Cuartelejo, was the northeastern most pueblo. The Pin, wel, ene (Picuris) tribe escaped Spanish domination in New Mexico to live peacefully with the Diné (Apache) people for 14 years before the Spanish forced them to return.

Herbert and Eliza Steele settled in the canyon. They grew vegetables using the pueblo's irrigation ditches, and the park preserves their homestead. When the Steeles saw prairie dogs unearthing corn, they contacted archaeologists who revealed the pueblo. The family dreamed that their homestead would become a state park. Their dream became reality in 1928.

Visit Big Spring via a short nature trail and look for the Scott riffle beetle. The spring is the beetle's only home. The springs flow between the Ogallala Aquifer and the Niobrara Chalk formations. The Ogallala forms a long ridge called the Devil's Backbone at the park's southern end.

The park's most visible wildlife are 13-lined ground squirrels, wild turkeys, black-billed magpies, and turkey vultures, while the bobcats are shy. Fill your birding list with Lazuli buntings, Say's phoebes, common poorwills, and black-headed grosbeaks. In the summer, nesting rock wrens inhabit the canyon walls. Yellow-breasted chats also nest there. A large amount and variety of reptiles call the park home.

Beavers dam Ladder Creek. Find the beavers' on-shore work, pointed logs carved with teeth marks.

Scott State Fishing Lake, dammed in 1930, is the park's centerpiece. Bluffs surround the 100-acre spring-fed lake, providing welcome respite from the High Plains' frequent winds. Groves of hackberry, ash, elm, willow, walnut, and cedar trees adorn its banks. Enjoy the unique sound of fluttering cottonwood leaves below the majestic trees as old as the lake. Fish for crappie, walleye, bluegill, channel catfish, and largemouth bass.

A concessionaire sells camping and fishing supplies next to the swimming beach and playground. Rent canoes and paddleboards seasonally.

Battle Canyon is a mile south of the park. The Northern Tsistsis'tas (Cheyenne) fought the US Army there during their flight from an Oklahoma reservation. The Battle of Punished Woman's Fork was the last battle in Kansas. A trail leads from the cairn-style monument to the battlefield. The tribe protected their non-combatants in a cave at the canyon's end.

Learn more about El Cuartelejo and the battle at the El Quartelejo Museum and Jerry Thomas Gallery and Collection in Scott City. ("El Cuartelejo" is the Spanish spelling and "El Quartelejo" is the English spelling of a term meaning "the quarters.")

Book a tour of Duff's Buffalo Ranch through the museum from May to October. Guests learn about the Kansas state mammal and its history in the area.

The park is on the Western Vistas Historic Byway, which connects many Wild West sites. Make your own history at Lake Scott.

Cedar Bluff State Park

Cedar Bluff State Park is well named because cedar trees dot the 150-foot-high limestone bluffs around Cedar Bluff Reservoir. Drive to the top of the bluffs for a spectacular view.

The park lies along the reservoir's north shores. The Bluffton area is more developed, while the Page Creek unit offers more solitude.

Bluffton's shoreline is almost completely accessible with a covered, accessible fishing dock. Beyond swimming and picnicking, Bluffton's guests can play sand volleyball or basketball, pitch horseshoes, and ride the BMX track.

The Smoky Hill Trail passed north of the reservoir. The Butterfield Overland Despatch's Bluffton Station stood nearby, and Bluffton's campgrounds bear trail-related names.

Threshing Machine Canyon wears graffiti from early explorers. In 1867, three freighters were hauling a threshing machine when they camped too close to the bluffs. Warriors killed the freighters and burned the machine. To learn more, walk the 1.75-mile Butterfield Hiking Trail. WaKeeney's Trego County Historical Museum preserves machine parts.

Page Creek is a haven for water sports. Shade trees and shower houses welcome primitive campers.

The park is on the Smoky Valley Scenic Byway. It connects to Interstate 70 at the WaKeeney and Ogallah exits. The road is noted for its spring wildflowers. Ness City, home of the ornate stone Old Ness County Bank, is at the byway's southern end.

Find a haven at Cedar Bluff.

Little Jerusalem Badlands State Park

Little Jerusalem Badlands looks like a set from the 1997 movie Starship Troopers. Its pinnacles, hoodoos and canyons seem otherworldly. The badlands are the state's least-visited park, so people probably won't obscure its vistas. The 330-acre park experience begins with a picnic area at the entrance where limestone chunks stand ready to carve. The chunks demonstrate how fragile the park's formations are.

A short, paved trail segment extends from the parking lot past interpretive panels and ends at the picnic shelter. The park's two trails split from the paved trail behind the shelter. Both are paved with crushed rock. The easy Overlook Trail runs a quarter mile and ends at a bench. Up to the Life on the Rocks Trail's first overlook, it features the same gentle grades as the Overlook Trail. The rest of the 1.5-mile trail is more difficult. The half-mile jaunt ends in another overlook. This view includes the park's highest spires.

The Western Interior Sea laid down the Niobrara Chalk in the late Cretaceous Period. Terrifying beasts swam these seas. Watch for their fossils, but do not disturb them. Keystone Gallery on Highway 83 between Oakley and Scott City leads regional fossil-hunting tours.

Explore space and time at Little Jerusalem.

Region: Central

Wilson State Park

Wilson State Park will persuade you that Kansas is far from flat. The park's cliffs, rocks, and rugged shoreline create unique scenery. Blend the rocks with wildlife to experience a nature lover's delight.

Because the Saline River renders the water too salty for drinking, Wilson is Kansas's only lake that's not part of a municipal water supply. While the river may be salty, the grass allows mud and silt to filter out before reaching the lake. Waist-deep waders can see their feet in the reservoir.

Anglers will enjoy the 9,000-acre reservoir's white bass, walleye, and striped bass population. Wilson Lake holds the Kansas record for walleye (29 inches and 13.16 pounds) and striped bass (44 inches and 44 pounds).

The Rocktown Trail is my favorite. The 3-mile trail undulates through rolling hills to Rocktown on the shores of Wilson Lake. Rocktown's red Kansas sandstone spires rise 15 to 30 feet from the narrow sand beach. Before you start, pick up a self-guided trail brochure at the trailhead.

For the best experience, leave the trailhead in time to reach Rocktown shortly before sunset. The setting sun illuminates the rock spires and marks a trail on the water. The sun's trail beckons visitors to follow it out to space.

Make sure you leave the shore with time to spare. Instead, I approached the trailhead in the dark, and only saw the trailhead sign as a shadow blocking the stars.

Beautiful Rocktown is not the only worthwhile park trail.

The park turned a disaster into a walking trail in the Otoe area. A flood destroyed Otoe's facilities, so the agency built the Cedar Trail, a one-mile hard-surfaced accessible walking path near the reservoir.

Bikers will adore the Epic-rated Switchgrass Mountain Biking Trail. The 24.5-mile trail feels wild and remote, but riders can shorten it with 12 cutoffs. The course is primarily easy to moderate, but short sections are rocky or sand-choked. The trail includes arduous climbs, cliffs, and sharp drops, but most technical areas are short. Allow 2-5 hours, depending on your skill. Before you go, check the Switchgrass Facebook page for updates.

In Kansas wind is generally abundant, but Wilson's Lucas Park is special. Why? Because ravines on the reservoir's north shore funnel wind onto the lake. The ravines force the wind to create waves up to 4 feet high. The conditions make the area a prime spot for kite flying, sailing, and windsurfing.

The Wilson Wildlife Area sprawls across the reservoir's upper end. Most of it consists of rolling hills. Look for waterfowl, upland birds, songbirds, deer, and fur bearers inhabiting the area.

The park hosts the free Lovegrass Music Festival each August.

Post Rock Scenic Byway passes the park between Wilson and Lucas. Visit the World's Largest Czech Egg, then savor top-notch chicken-fried steak at the Midland Railroad Hotel and outstanding cream pies at Made from Scratch Café in Wilson. Lucas's famed quirkiness emanates from the Garden of Eden and spreads throughout the town. Even the public toilet is an artwork in Lucas.

Kansas is both hilly and quirky; Wilson proves the fact.

Kanopolis State Park

Kanopolis State Park is the state's oldest, and it seems timeless. The Corps of Engineers began flooding Horsethief Canyon 75 years ago, but the canyon's history far precedes the reservoir. Experience its history on the park's 30 miles of trails.

The 1.5-mile Buffalo Track Canyon Trail follows Bison Creek. It sheltered bison and wild horses. Before you go, pick up a trail brochure. The trail begins at Sentinel Rock, which marks the Horsethief Canyon entrance. Near the trail's end, look for caves, and the Mortar and Pestle. Water plunges into the mortar-shaped bowl, and it carries hard materials to shape the sandstone like a pestle would.

Prefer to drive? Explore the area's historic sites on the Kanopolis Lake Legacy Tour. View petroglyphs, historic ranches, Smoky Hill Trail sites, Fort Harker, and more. However, drive this route only when it's dry.

The lake's most popular fish species are saugeye, white bass and channel catfish. However, the Kanopolis seep stream holds the state brown trout record. The fish measured 21.5 inches and weighed 4.62 pounds.

Engineers predicted that topsoil loss from farming would silt up the lake by 1998. The engineers were wrong. Improved soil conservation practices have saved the lake, although some portions are now shallower.

Take a time out of time in Kanopolis.

El Dorado State Park

El Dorado State Park holds 4,500 acres on El Dorado Lake's southern shores. The largest park delivers a diverse set of activities. Start with an orientation look in the gazebo southeast of the dam.

Wildlife watchers will see greater prairie chickens "booming" and dancing in the spring, while bald eagles soar in the winter.

Anglers' targets are in the riprap near the dam and the railroad. Look for crappie and largemouth bass near the lake's timber fish attractors. Smallmouth bass, channel and flathead catfish, drum, and walleye all swim in the lake.

The City of El Dorado's Linear Trail joins the Walnut River Trail. The combination welcomes hikers, cyclists, and wheelchair users. The trail tours the campground, crosses the Walnut River three times, and provides access to the Walnut River swimming beach.

The Walnut Ridge Trail also connects to the Linear Trail. Its course traverses thick timber stands. Whitetail deer are abundant, especially in the spring.

El Dorado's Double Black Diamond Bike Trail challenges riders with diverse terrain from Flint Hills uplands to Walnut River bottomlands.

Jump in the lake after the hikes or ride for a cooling dip, and savor the park's diversity.

Roxie Yonkey has written about Kansas for decades, and has won numerous awards for her work. She loves to delve into the state's little-known stories, the ones you never heard in history class. Even so, many of these stories surprised and delighted her. She writes extensively about the state on her website, RoxieontheRoad.com, and on social media as @roxieontheroad.

Kansas State Parks Amenities

Please confirm availability of amenities with the state park system. For more information on Kansas State Parks, visit their website at ksoutdoors.com/State-Parks

A few notes about the amenities:
- RV – Full Hookups include access to electricity, water, and sewer at the campsite.
- RV – Partial Hookups include access to electricity and water, but not sewer.
- Tent: Tent only sites available.
- Primitive: Camping in remote areas without amenities like bathrooms, picnic tables, trash cans, or any other man-made structures.
- Restrooms: Indicates the highest functional type of restroom available.
- Paddling: Boat access; this could be kayaking, canoeing, and/or powered boats.
- Swimming: Selected if swimming is available, either at a beach or a pool.

Eisenhower State Park has yurts available for rental.

Kansas

State Park Name	Hiking # of miles	RV - Full Hookups	RV - Partial Hookups	Tent	Primitive	Cabin
Cedar Bluff State Park	4.8	✓	✓	✓	✓	✓
Cheney State Park	7	✓	✓	✓	✓	✓
Clinton State Park	30.8	☐	✓	✓	✓	✓
Crawford State Park	8.5	✓	✓	✓	✓	✓
Cross Timbers State Park	14.8	✓	✓	✓	✓	✓
Eisenhower State Park	28.5	✓	✓	✓	✓	✓
El Dorado State Park	23.3	✓	✓	✓	✓	✓
Elk City State Park	16.1	✓	✓	✓	✓	✓
Fall River State Park	5.9	✓	✓	✓	✓	✓
Flint Hills Trail State Park	117	☐	☐	☐	☐	☐
Glen Elder State Park	1.1	☐	✓	✓	✓	✓
Hillsdale State Park	54	✓	✓	✓	✓	☐
Historic Lake Scott State Park	4.3	✓	✓	✓	✓	✓
Kanopolis State Park	27.4	✓	✓	✓	✓	✓
Kaw River State Park	3.3	☐	☐	☐	☐	☐
Little Jerusalem Badlands State Park	3	☐	☐	☐	☐	☐
Lovewell State Park	N/A	✓	✓	✓	✓	✓
Meade State Park	1	☐	✓	✓	✓	☐
Milford State Park	11.5	✓	✓	✓	✓	✓
Mushroom Rock State Park	2	☐	☐	☐	☐	☐
Perry State Park	47	☐	✓	☐	☐	✓
Pomona State Park	2.4	✓	✓	✓	✓	✓
Prairie Dog State Park	1.5	✓	✓	✓	✓	✓
Prairie Spirit Trail State Park	51	☐	☐	☐	☐	☐
Sand Hills State Park	14	✓	✓	☐	☐	☐
Tuttle Creek State Park	21.5	✓	✓	✓	✓	✓
Webster State Park	3	✓	✓	✓	✓	✓
Wilson State Park	27.5	✓	✓	✓	✓	✓

Midwest State Park Adventures

State Park Name	Restrooms	Visitor/ Nature Center	Swimming	Paddling	Store	Picnic	Fishing
Cedar Bluff State Park	Showers	✓	✓	✓	✓	✓	✓
Cheney State Park	Showers	✓	✓	✓	✓	✓	✓
Clinton State Park	Showers	✓	✓	✓	✓	✓	✓
Crawford State Park	Showers	✓	✓	✓	✓	✓	✓
Cross Timbers State Park	Showers	✓	✓	✓	☐	✓	✓
Eisenhower State Park	Showers	✓	✓	✓	☐	✓	✓
El Dorado State Park	Showers	✓	✓	✓	✓	✓	✓
Elk City State Park	Showers	✓	✓	☐	☐	✓	✓
Fall River State Park	Showers	✓	✓	✓	☐	✓	✓
Flint Hills Trail State Park		☐	☐	☐	☐	☐	☐
Glen Elder State Park	Showers	✓	✓	✓	✓	✓	✓
Hillsdale State Park	Showers	✓	✓	✓	✓	✓	✓
Historic Lake Scott State Park	Showers	✓	✓	✓	✓	✓	✓
Kanopolis State Park	Showers	✓	✓	✓	✓	✓	✓
Kaw River State Park		☐	☐	☐	☐	☐	☐
Little Jerusalem Badlands State Park	Vault	☐	☐	☐	☐	✓	☐
Lovewell State Park	Showers	✓	✓	✓	✓	✓	✓
Meade State Park	Showers	✓	✓	✓	☐	✓	✓
Milford State Park	Showers	✓	✓	✓	✓	✓	✓
Mushroom Rock State Park	Vault	☐	☐	☐	☐	☐	☐
Perry State Park	Showers	✓	✓	✓	✓	✓	✓
Pomona State Park	Showers	✓	✓	✓	✓	✓	✓
Prairie Dog State Park	Showers	✓	✓	✓	☐	✓	✓
Prairie Spirit Trail State Park		☐	☐	☐	☐	✓	☐
Sand Hills State Park		✓	☐	☐	☐	✓	☐
Tuttle Creek State Park	Showers	✓	✓	✓	✓	✓	✓
Webster State Park	Showers	✓	✓	✓	✓	✓	✓
Wilson State Park	Showers	✓	✓	✓	✓	✓	✓

MICHIGAN

By Veronica Bareman

Michigan loves diversity, and even our state parks join in! From the Great Lakes' sandy beaches to the Upper Peninsula's rugged forests, Michigan's diverse and endless beauty is on display in our state parks every day of the year!

Our long history of state parks and tourism begins at Mackinac Island. In 1895, the Federal Government transferred ownership of Fort Michilimackinac and parts of Mackinac Island to Michigan. Michigan subsequently created the Mackinac Island State Park Commission, and the earliest version of our State Park system was born.

But it took a few years longer for the system to catch momentum. With the auto industry booming, Michigan's growing number of residents could suddenly travel and explore the state. Local leaders recognized the need for public spaces where travelers could enjoy Michigan's beauty. By 1919, Michigan established the State Park system that became the roots of what we love today.

The system has since grown to include a wide assortment of parks with a range of terrains and personalities. With parks open 365 days a year, visitors are welcome to explore Michigan's beauty in whatever way suits them best. Care to explore the dark skies in our gorgeous Upper Peninsula? Does hiking and camping in nature's beauty soothe your soul? Are you a lighthouse lover, a beachcomber, or a sun worshipper? Michigan will meet your need for any adventure you can dream up!

The only thing you'll need to set out on your Michigan State Park adventure is a yearning to explore and a Recreation Passport, which will grant you entry. You can purchase a passport online, at DNR offices, or at many local retailers. The money derived from these sales goes back to the parks and is used to maintain and improve our shared spaces.

Welcome to Michigan! We hope you will connect with nature, bask in the glory of the state's beauty, and learn about the importance of protecting our natural resources. Whether you're seeking a peaceful retreat, an outdoor adventure, or a place to connect with nature, our state parks have something for everyone.

Michigan State Park Facts & Important Information

- The Michigan State Park System comprises a network of 103 state parks and recreation areas covering over 357,000 acres of land, including freshwater beaches, wetlands, forests, and more.
- Michigan's largest state park covers 60,000 acres.
- The state parks in Michigan attract over 28 million visitors each year.

Michigan

- Over 3,200 miles of hiking trails are available for visitors to explore the state parks.
- Many of Michigan's state parks offer camping opportunities, ranging from rustic campsites to modern RV camping.
- Several state parks in Michigan are known for their lighthouses, including Tawas Point State Park and Grand Haven State Park.
- The state parks in Michigan are home to various unique wildlife species, such as bald eagles, loons, and sandhill cranes.
- Many of Michigan's state parks include historically significant features, including military outposts, early Native American Petroglyphs, and over a dozen lighthouses

A note about accessibility

With an intentional approach to accessibility, Michigan's state parks pride themselves on making our natural beauty accessible for everyone! Consider Interlochen State Park, where an accessible kayak ramp and fishing pier will be unveiled within days of this printing—or Rifle River State Park, where you'll find a fully-accessible hunting blind. In addition, many of our state parks have beach access mats that help wheelchair users get close to the water.

Because accessibility can mean many things to travelers, contact the park directly if you have questions about your needs. The Michigan DNR website is a great place to start, with a list of parks' accessible activities and facilities.

Michigan State Parks Map

1. Fort Wilkins Historic State Park 2. Petoskey State Park 3. Mackinac Island 4. Holland State Park 5. Sanilac Petroglyphs Historic State Park 6. Porcupine Mountains Wilderness State Park 7. Tahquamenon Falls State Park 8. Wilderness State Park 9. Silver Lake State Park 10. Tawas Point State Park 11. Hartwick Pines State Park 12. Fort Custer Recreation Area 13. Saugatuck Dunes State Park 14. Maybury State Park 15. Belle Isle Park

Upper Peninsula Region

Fort Wilkins Historic State Park

The Fort Wilkins Historic State Park sits at the top tip of the Keweenaw Peninsula in Michigan's Upper Peninsula and is a fascinating destination for history buffs and nature lovers. The park nestles between Lake Superior and picturesque Lake Fanny Hooe.

The park's namesake, Fort Wilkins, was established in 1844 to protect the interests of the US government during the Copper Rush. The fort was abandoned in 1859 and restored in the 1930s, then added to the National Register of Historic Places in 1970. Fifteen of the fort's original buildings are ADA-accessible and open to wandering. The park has re-enactors on site to give visitors a glimpse into life on the northern frontier during the mid-1800s.

Feel like fishing? Cast your line out on Lake Fanny Hooe, where you can reel in a variety of game fish, such as perch, crappie, walleye, and bass. The lake is long and narrow, with a few deep spots. Take note that there is also an ADA-accessible fishing dock on the lake.

Lake Superior is only a quarter of a mile away and offers fishing, boating, and paddling. Because of the inherent dangers associated with this area of Lake Superior, local officials highly encourage extreme caution on the big lake and to consider a guided tour if you choose to kayak.

Lighthouse lovers will love the view of the Copper Harbor Lighthouse, built in 1866, which sits across the harbor from the State Park. Photo opportunities are plentiful, but a Copper Harbor Lighthouse boat tour will give you the best view.

The park offers modern campground facilities split into East and West areas. Laundry machines are available in the East campground, and you will have easy access to Lake Fanny Hooe from both sites for swimming, paddling, and fishing. Both campers and day visitors will enjoy the picnic area, the playground, the swimming beach, and the boat launch that will accommodate boats up to 26 feet in length. The campsites are only ¼ mile off the Lake Superior shoreline, which provides stunning views of the lake.

Finally, hikers will love the 2.5 miles of hiking trails in the park that range from easy to strenuous. And after a satisfying day hike, make time for the stunning dark sky opportunities available at the nearby Keweenaw Dark Sky Park, headquartered at the Keweenaw Mountain Lodge, about 15-20 min up the road and open to the public. On a clear night, you can gaze up into the heavens and see the Milky Way. Sometimes the Northern Lights even make an appearance.

Fort Wilkins Historic State Park is a great place to spend a day with family and friends, enjoying both the stunning natural beauty and the fascinating historical treasures of the Upper Peninsula.

Special Note: The West campground will be closed from early to mid-May 2023 for improvements. The East campground will remain open for semi-modern camping, but 19 sites will be closed from May through June to allow the grass and landscaping to recover.

Porcupine Mountains Wilderness State Park

Porcupine Mountains Wilderness State Park spans nearly 60,000 acres, making it the largest state park in Michigan. Located in the Porcupine Mountains of Michigan's Upper Peninsula, the park is known for its rugged beauty, abundant wildlife, and opportunities for outdoor recreation.

With over 115 miles of hiking trails, you can choose your adventure. Go easy, or plot a more strenuous route for a real challenge. With walk-in, tent, and partial hookup sites, this park suits the solo backpacker or the RV'ing family.

Keep an eye out for a wildlife sighting. Black bears and deer, moose, and wolves are frequently spotted. Look skyward, and you may be lucky enough to spot America's symbol, the Bald Eagle, soaring majestically through the sky.

Bring your boat or kayak and use the boat launch to dip into Lake Superior for paddling and fishing. If you play in the water, consider local safety recommendations closely. The Great Lakes can behave more like an ocean than a lake, which means they can be dangerous if you're not using appropriate caution.

Finally, Porcupine Mountains Wilderness State Park is a favorite for the wintertime outdoor adventurer. This park is terrific for winter camping, dog sledding, snowshoeing, downhill and cross-country skiing, and snowmobiling.

Tahquamenon Falls State Park

Tahquamenon Falls State Park covers 50,000 acres in Michigan's Upper Peninsula, making it the second biggest state park in Michigan. The two waterfalls, Upper Falls and Lower Falls are known for their distinctive dark-colored water, earning them the nickname "Rootbeer Falls." The coloring comes from the tannins leaching from the cedar swamp that feeds into the falls.

Because most of this park consists of wild and undeveloped land, a variety of wildlife resides within it. Look out for black bears, deer, moose, wolves, and coyotes. There are also over 200 species of birds in the park, including bald eagles and ospreys. Listen closely, and you may even hear the haunting cry of a loon.

This park is a nature lover's dream, with over 21 miles of hiking trails and multiple camping options. Whether you lay your head on your pillow in a fully-outfitted RV in one of the modern campsites or choose to hike in and out with what you can carry, you will not be disappointed.

Tahquamenon Falls State Park is a beautiful and diverse park that offers a variety of activities for visitors of all ages. Whether you're looking to hike, camp, fish, boat, or relax and enjoy the scenery, Tahquamenon Falls State Park is a great choice!

Northwest Region

Petoskey State Park

If you love rock hunting, look no further than Petoskey State Park, where you can hunt to your heart's content for Michigan's State Rock, the Petoskey Stone. This distinctive stone is a fossilized coral with a pattern of interlocking hexagons reminiscent of the coral's skeletal structure. The stone gets its name from the city of Petoskey, where you will most commonly find them. Ask any Michigander about a Petoskey stone, and they'll know what you're talking about!

But stones aren't the only outstanding feature of Petoskey State Park. Once you stop peering beneath your feet for treasure, look up, and you'll see one mile of beach area that looks out over the crystal-clear waters of Lake Michigan.

Are you a hiker and up for a fun climb? Then you'll enjoy the Old Baldy Trail, a half-mile loop that takes you to the top of Old Baldy Dune. You'll climb stairs from the trailhead to reach the observation deck near the top. When you arrive, enjoy gorgeous, scenic views of Lake Michigan from above. Look closely on a clear day; you might get a peek at the Frankfort pier and lighthouse on the northern horizon. Trust me when I tell you it's worth the effort to reach the peak. The Old Baldy Trail is the perfect climb for those who prefer a leisurely hike with a view.

For a slightly longer hike, check out the Portage Trail, which takes you through a wooded dune area. The trek is a one-mile loop, perfect for a midday jaunt.

One feature that makes Petoskey State Park incredibly accommodating is its dog-friendly nature. Pets are welcome in most park areas if they are always on a six-foot leash and under the owner's control. Because of the Piping Plover habitat along the beach, dogs are prohibited on the lakeshore. Piping Plovers are small shorebirds that nest and feed along beaches like this one. Because they are a threatened species, we must do all we can to protect and care for them. Unfortunately, our pets don't always understand that, so keeping your dog away from their habitat is necessary and important.

Camping at Petoskey State Park is made easy with two modern campgrounds. If you're an RV camper, expect sites with cement pads and partial hookups. If tent camping is your scene, you will also find plenty of tent-friendly sites available. This park even offers two mini-cabins available for rent!

If you'd like to venture out of the park, Harbor Springs and Petoskey are just a stone's throw away. Both areas have dining options, shopping, and picturesque harbors. Be sure to check out the nearby Oden Fish Hatchery, one of the oldest in the state, where you can learn about rainbow trout and brown trout and how the hatchery stocks them in state waters.

For beautiful nature, stunning sunsets, and leisurely hiking, you can't beat Petoskey State Park.

Wilderness State Park

Wilderness State Park is located on the tip of Michigan's Lower Peninsula and boasts 26 miles of shoreline along Lake Michigan. After checking out the shoreline, head inland to explore the dense coniferous and hardwood forest areas. Keep an eye peeled for open meadows and lovely wildflowers as you wander. You may even surprise some wildlife basking in the sun.

With over 30 miles of hiking trails to choose from, you'll have no problem finding the perfect trail for you! Wilderness State Park is also a designated dark sky preserve. What this means is that the area meets the qualifications required to provide optimal viewing of the nighttime sky. Because artificial light is limited here, you can enjoy a look at the Milky Way or spot a shooting star. If you're a photographer, then nighttime skies provide a special kind of beauty to capture on film.

Camping facilities range in this park from full hookup for the RVer who roughs it in style to the backpacker who treks in and out by foot. Either way, while you're exploring the over 10,000 acres in this park, be sure to carry a map and pay close attention to the trail signs. Getting lost in nature is great. Being lost is not.

Silver Lake State Park

Michigan is home to gorgeous sand dunes; you simply cannot leave our state without climbing one. And there is no better place to try it out than at Silver Lake State Park!

Silver Lake is home to a 450-acre area that allows off-road vehicles to drive, race, and play on the dunes. If you plan to bring your Jeep, your 4-wheeler, or your side-by-side to the dunes, be sure to study up on local safety regulations and laws. And then have fun! If you don't have your own ORV, take a tour with Mac Woods Dune Rides for a hosted good time.

But it doesn't take an engine to truly appreciate this state park and all it has to offer. Adjacent to the designated ORV area is a pedestrian area where you can climb the dunes on foot. When you reach the top, take in the magnificent view of Lake Michigan. Slide down on your way back to get a real feel for the shifting sand beneath you!

Silver Lake State Park also features the iconic Little Sable Point Lighthouse. She's located at the southern portion of the park and is easily accessible on a paved walkway to the base, where you can tour the inside.

Silver Lake State Park is not only stunning, but full of opportunities for adventure. Plan on bringing a little sand home with you after your visit!

Northeast Region

Mackinac Island and Fort Mackinac Historic Park

If you have not been to Mackinac Island or the Fort Mackinac Historic Park, you have not experienced one of Michigan's greatest treasures.

Michigan

Mackinac Island is off the uppermost Eastern shore of Michigan's Lower Peninsula in the Straits of Mackinac, which connects Lake Huron to Lake Michigan. Visitors must take a ferry from either the Upper Peninsula (UP) out of St. Ignace or the Lower Peninsula (LP) out of Mackinac City to reach the island.

Once you arrive on the island, prepare to step back in time to when the sound of horses and carriages instead of engines fills your ears. Mackinac Island has had a motor vehicle ban in place since 1898. After the first few automobiles showed up on the island and frightened the horses, the village leaders created the automobile ban, which is still in effect today!

Savvy travelers will bring a bike when visiting the island, but if you're traveling light, you can tour the island on a rental bike or a horse and carriage tour. And touring the island is a must! You can make your way around the entire island on M-185, the only state highway in the US that does not allow motorized vehicles.

Mackinac Island is about 8 miles long and 2 miles wide and is home to several historic sites, including Fort Mackinac and the Mackinac Island State Park. Approximately 80% of the island is comprised of state park land. Hiking trails and scenic areas make up most of this land.

A horse-drawn tour will take you to the main attractions on the island, including the much-photographed Arch Rock. But if you want to travel at your speed and explore off the beaten path, I recommend bringing or renting a bike or wearing comfortable walking shoes and packing a water bottle.

Fort Mackinac is visible in the distance from Main Street on Mackinac Island. The fort is on a bluff overlooking the downtown area. It is a large, imposing structure with a white brick exterior topped by a line of wooden fence slats that point toward the sky like sharp teeth. The fort also contains several buildings, including barracks, a powder magazine, and a hospital. Plan a tour of the fort to learn about the island's history and those who lived there. Fort Mackinac has stood strong since 1780 and is Michigan's only Revolutionary War-era fort.

Because Mackinac Island is committed to preserving its natural forest, no camping is permitted. Still, many options exist for staying overnight in hotels and Bed and Breakfasts. And an overnight stay on Mackinac is almost necessary to enjoy everything this park offers.

Make time during your visit to enjoy the Richard & Jane Manoogian Mackinac Art Museum, where you can enjoy a collection of artworks that spell out the history of the area and the island.

Finally, every June for the past 75 years, the Mackinac Island Lilac Festival takes place. This 10-day celebration is about the lilacs and their historical connection to Mackinac Island. You don't want to miss it!

Tawas Point State Park

On Michigan's East coast, on a sand spit in Saginaw Bay, sits Tawas Point State Park. The sand spit borders Tawas Bay. This State Park and its bay within a bay is like a pearl in the clamshell of Lake Huron.

Tawas Point is a nature-lovers playground. Visitors can enjoy fishing, paddling, biking, hiking, and birdwatching in the summer. Keep an eye out for sailboats; Tawas Bay has a reputation as one of the country's best sailing areas. Protected waters and the natural air currents create nearly perfect sailing conditions.

The Monarch migration occurs each autumn when the butterflies travel from their summer homes up North down through the States and into their winter homes in Mexico. Tawas Bay becomes the short-term home for thousands of Monarch butterflies during the migration.

Don't miss a visit to the magnificent Tawas Point Lighthouse. True lighthouse connoisseurs will marvel that she still utilizes her tower's original 4th-order Fresnel lens. Although she is no longer the main working lighthouse, she still stands tall against the summer sky.

Stay for a few days in a Yurt, a Mini Cabin, or a Camper Cabin rental. Or bring your camper or tent to enjoy partial hookup and amenities such as electricity, water, and on-site flush toilets.

Hartwick Pines State Park

The majestic centuries-old pine trees are one feature among many that make Hartwick Pines State Park unique.

History shows that, at one time, ancient pine trees just like this, covered most of Michigan. Hartwick Pines is the perfect place to peek into our past and see how the area might have appeared to early settlers. It is no wonder Michigan played a significant role in the timber era.

Stop at the fully accessible visitor's center and logging museum in the park to get an idea of what a nineteenth-century logging camp looked like and see some of the tools and equipment used to harvest these behemoth trees. Forty-nine acres of the original virginal forest remain, and 9,000 additional acres are designated for hiking, mountain biking, cross-country skiing, and camping.

The modern Hartwick Pines Campground has everything from full hookup pull-through sites to smaller, tent-friendly sites. Four ADA sites are also available. Because this state park lies at just about the center of the upper portion of the state, it makes a perfect stop on the way up to the magnificent Mackinac Bridge and Mackinac Island, and Fort Mackinac Historic Park.

Southwest Region

Holland State Park

Holland State Park is the park that lies closest to my heart. You see, I live in this area of the state and have spent more hours here than in any other park!

What are my favorite parts? The soft and silky sand that shifts beneath my feet while walking down the beach. Of course, swimming in the unsalted and shark-free lake is just the right way to spend a hot summer's day. After a swim, I love to walk down the pier while listening to the sound of water crashing on either side. Anglers often line the pier's edges, hoping to reel in the big catch!

If I'm not feeling energetic, I find a bench or park my beach chair somewhere along the channel that connects inland Lake Macatawa to Lake Michigan; the perfect location to watch boats of all shapes and sizes make their way in and out of the channel. And, of course, our local star, lighthouse Big Red, shines the brightest at the south end of the channel. (Pictured on front cover.)

Visit the park on any summer day, and you will have an adventure. You never know what you may find, from a view of kites flying high against the blue sky to families frolicking in the waves and building castles in the sand or children swinging and climbing on the play equipment located near the parking area. A day at the beach at Holland State Park is a picture of summer perfection.

If accessibility is your concern, know that Holland State Park offers a beach walkway that will take visitors close to the water but not quite into it. In addition, they offer a beach wheelchair that is free to use. This beach chair has giant, inflated tires that make sand travel possible for everyone. The beach also has an ADA-accessible beach house with modern restrooms.

Campers will love the accommodations available at the two Holland State Park Campgrounds: a modern beach campground with sandy lots and the other more wooded and grassy. Both campgrounds have electricity and water on site. The modern sandy campground offers full hookups on 31 sites.

And the fun doesn't stop when the weather cools and you've tucked away your swimsuits. One of my favorite times to camp at the state park is during the fall festival, when the campground transforms into a Halloween wonderland at the end of September. Campers are encouraged to bring their décor and spooky up their lot.

The park puts on the dog yearly and provides a haunted scavenger hunt, donuts and cider, crafting opportunities, and even site-to-site trick-or-treating. If you can only camp for one weekend, make this your choice!

Finally, visitors who bring their electric vehicles to the park can rest on the beach while their vehicle charges on one of the available electric charging stations. Holland State Park is one of the first in Michigan to receive EV charging stations.

The fact is simple. No matter what time of year you visit, you will leave Holland State Park with a smile.

Fort Custer Recreation Area

Fort Custer Recreation Area is a beautiful park that covers over 3,000 acres. Located in the lower half of Michigan and near the mid-area of the state, it is easily reached from anywhere in Michigan and is a popular destination for those coming in from the states below.

Wildlife is abundant here. Waterfowl love to call this park home, primarily because of the large land area and many water sources. Fort Custer is home to three lakes and the Kalamazoo River. Fishing enthusiasts can wet their lines in many locations throughout the park.

Hikers will find plenty to explore, with over 25 miles of hiking trails through forest land and remnant prairie areas. History lovers will also find inspiration here.

Fort Custer began as farmland. During World War II, the Federal Government acquired the land and created Camp Custer, a military training center for the US Army. In 1971, the land became the property of the State of Michigan, which designated this land space for public use.

Camping is available with over 200 sites, giving visitors plenty of time to relax and enjoy the surrounding beauty. Any time you spend at Fort Custer Recreation Area will be relaxing and educational.

Saugatuck Dunes State Park

West Michigan is a treasure trove of beaches and parks that cozy up to the stunning shores of Lake Michigan. The view of the lake from the top of the dune is one of my favorite experiences in West Michigan, and Saugatuck Dunes does not disappoint.

The park is largely undeveloped, making it a delightful place to spend time climbing the 200-foot-high dunes, discovering the wooded areas surrounding them, and hiking some or all of the over 14 miles of trails, broken down into four different trail routes.

This park's 300-acre natural area boasts more than just dunes. It is also the habitat for multiple rare and endangered and threatened birds, plants, fish, and amphibians, among them the Bald Eagle (threatened), the Creek Chubsucker (endangered), the Pitcher's Thistle (threatened), and the Spotted Turtle (threatened).

After exploring the natural areas in Saugatuck Dunes, make your way to the nearby Felt Manion, which sits adjacent to the State Park. This picturesque old estate has a rich and compelling history and is worth exploring. The National Register of Historic Places added the Felt Mansion in 1996.

But most visitors find this state park's 2.5-mile stretch of Michigan lakefront the most compelling. Go ahead and take a dip!

Southeast Region

Sanilac Petroglyphs Historic State Park

Sanilac Petroglyphs Historic State Park may not be Michigan's biggest state park. It may not offer modern camping facilities or a swimming hole, but it makes up for that by having one of our state's most extraordinary historical displays.

You can find this small state park near Cass City in the thumb area of Michigan. Yes, Michiganders really do use their hand as a map of their state, so imagine me pointing to my thumb to show you the location of this state park.

The Sanilac Petroglyphs Historic State Park is home to Michigan's most extensive known collection of Native American Petroglyphs. But what is a petroglyph? Petroglyphs are images carved into rock that early civilizations used to teach and tell stories.

When you arrive at the state park, you will traverse a limestone trail for about a quarter of a mile to reach the covered collection. When you arrive, close your eyes and inhale deeply. Imagine Native American hands carving these figures into the stone with their rudimentary chisels and hammers. This display is marvelous and vital to helping us understand those who came before us. Can't you feel the history laid out before you?

This fantastic collection of rock carvings is called ezhibiigaadek asin, or "written on stone," in the Anishinabeg language. The Anishinaabeg Nation is a group of indigenous people that inhabit areas from as far north as Canada and down through several states in the US. This people group remains active today and is organized into several other groups, including Naakowe, Mississauga, Odishwaagaamii'ininiwag, Amikwaa, Boodiwaadmi, Ojibwe, and Odaawa.

A partnership between the Michigan Department of Natural Resources (DNR) and the Saginaw Chippewa Indian Tribe of Michigan works to manage this park. This state park is just one of the twelve museums and historic sites maintained and interpreted by the DNR's Michigan History Center based in Lansing.

After you've explored the display of petroglyphs, continue to enjoy the trail that winds through some of the beautiful, wooded areas of the state park. You will find dense foliage and even cross a branch of the Little Cass River. Interpretive signs are placed along the trail to help you make your own connection to the park and its stories.

Be aware that this is a self-guided trail through the woods, so it will have uneven surfaces, rocks, and roots. Because this trail is close to the Little Cass River, it can become quite muddy or even flood and become impassable.

The Sanilac Petroglyphs Historic State Park is open year-round for hiking on the trails. The historic petroglyphs collection on display is open from Memorial Day through Labor Day each summer. Still, checking the DNR website before visiting is always a good idea to be aware of any unexpected closures.

Michigan's history and beauty are fully displayed at this magnificent state park. I have no doubt that you will enjoy your time here and likely take some new knowledge home with you.

Maybury State Park

Maybury State Park is a quaint and lovely day-use park near Detroit in Wayne County. Maybury has a unique and fascinating history. You may typically expect a state park to have roots as farmland, but that's not the case here.

In 1919, this park was home to a Tuberculosis sanitarium. Yikes! And this wasn't just your run-of-the-mill town hospital. The sanitarium consisted of 40 buildings and was almost entirely self-sustaining as they could generate their own power and residents grew their own food. When antibiotics arrived on-scene many years later, the sanitarium was no longer needed to quarantine people with this contagious disease, and it was closed.

In 1975, the State of Michigan DNR took over the land, and Maybury State Park was born. Today you can enjoy a thousand acres of lush, green forest and open meadows. Take a tour down the 6 miles of hiking trails, or try biking on one of the two designated biking trails. You can even enjoy the equestrian trail on horseback.

The park has a playground and plenty of space for cross-country skiing and picnicking. You can cast your line into the 8-acre, spring-fed fishing pond and reel in bass or bluegill. Don't miss a stop at the educational working farm on site to visit the over 100 animals, play on the farm-themed playground and learn about agriculture.

The park now offers a track chair that will slog through the sand, snow, and even water, making this park incredibly accessible!

Belle Isle Park

In a state surrounded by water, one should not be surprised that we have islands. If you study closely, you will find many islands around Michigan, some tiny, some larger, and all unique.

Belle Isle Park is no exception. This park is situated right off the shore of our biggest city, Detroit. It is 2.5 miles long and spans 982 acres! Locals love pronouncing that Belle Isle is bigger than New York City's Central Park. And yep. We get to enjoy it right here in Michigan!

A day on Belle Isle is chockfull of natural beauty, no matter how you spend your time. Kayaking float your boat? No problem. There are two accessible kayak launches. Care for a hike? Choose one of the two easy hiking trails. The island also offers an aquarium, a conservatory (greenhouse), a lighthouse, a swimming beach, a giant slide, a nature center, outdoor gardens, a Great Lakes museum, and even a golf course. Yes, this park is truly a nature-lovers playground.

You can access Belle Isle Park by vehicle, public transportation, biking, or walking across the MacArthur Bridge. No matter how you get there, you won't want to leave.

Veronica Bareman is an author, blogger, and award-winning Photographer. Also known as the Hip Grandma with a Camera, Veronica is an online influencer, a brand ambassador, and a freelance writer, contributing images and articles to multiple online and print publications. A Holland, Michigan native, her book 100 Things to Do in Holland Before You Die *hits the shelves Fall 2023. Veronica passionately lives life to the fullest in her middle years, and the only thing she likes more than traveling and having adventures is her big family with five kids and two grandkids. You can learn more about Veronica at www.hipgrandmalife.com and follow her on social media @hipgrandmalife.*

Michigan State Parks Amenities

Please confirm availability of amenities with the state park system. For more information on Michigan State Parks, visit their website at www.michigan.gov/dnr/places/state-parks

A few notes about the amenities:
- RV – Partial Hookups include access to electricity and water, but not sewer.
- Tent: Tent only sites available. In Michigan, these are called Rustic Sites and offer few, if any, amenities.
- Restrooms: Indicates the highest functional type of restroom available.
- Paddling: Boat access; this could be kayaking, canoeing, and/or powered boats.
- Swimming: Selected if swimming is available, either at a beach or a pool.

Notes about individual state parks:
- Algonac State Park and Bay City State Park will both be adding full hookup sites in late 2023/early 2024.
- Backcountry camping is available at Craig Lake State Park, Porcupine Mountains Wilderness State Park, Tahquamenon Falls State Park, and Wilderness State Park
- Teepees & Pop-up Campers available at Bewabic State Park and Cheboygan State Park.
- Mackinac Island State Park has an on-site hotel.

Michigan

State Park Name	Hiking # of miles	Camping RV - Full Hookups	Camping RV - Partial Hookups	Tent	Primitive	Lodging Cabin	Yurt	Lodge
Algonac State Park	57	☐	☑	☑	☐	☐	☐	☐
Aloha State Park	0	☑	☐	☐	☐	☐	☐	☐
Bald Mountain Recreation Area	15	☐	☐	☐	☐	☑	☐	☐
Baraga State Park	0.75	☑	☑	☑	☐	☑	☐	☐
Bass River Recreation Area	7	☐	☐	☐	☐	☐	☐	☐
Bay City State Park	7.15	☐	☑	☐	☐	☐	☐	☐
Belle Isle Park	7.5	☐	☐	☐	☐	☐	☐	☐
Bewabic State Park	2	☐	☑	☑	☑	☐	☐	☐
Brighton Recreation Area	10.4	☐	☑	☑	☐	☑	☐	☐
Brimley State Park	0	☐	☑	☑	☐	☐	☐	☐
Burt Lake State Park	1	☐	☑	☑	☐	☑	☐	☐
Cambridge Junction Historic State Park	0	☐	☐	☐	☐	☐	☐	☐
Cheboygan State Park	6.05	☐	☑	☑	☐	☐	☐	☑
Clear Lake State Park	6.05	☐	☑	☐	☐	☑	☐	☑
Coldwater Lake State Park	4.5	☐	☑	☐	☐	☑	☐	☐
Craig Lake State Park	0	☐	☐	☐	☐	☐	☑	☐
Dodge #4 State Park	15	☐	☐	☐	☐	☑	☐	☐
Duck Lake State Park	1	☐	☐	☐	☐	☐	☐	☐
Fayette Historic State Park	5	☐	☑	☑	☐	☐	☐	☐
Fisherman's Island State Park	2.5	☐	☐	☑	☐	☑	☐	☐
Fort Custer Recreation Area	25.6	☐	☑	☑	☐	☐	☐	☑
Fort Michilimackinac State Park	2.5	☐	☐	☐	☐	☐	☐	☐
Fort Wilkins Historic State Park	2.5	☐	☑	☐	☐	☑	☐	☐
Grand Haven State Park	0	☐	☐	☐	☐	☐	☐	☐
Grand Mere State Park	2.5	☐	☑	☑	☐	☑	☐	☐
Harrisville State Park	4	☐	☑	☑	☐	☐	☐	☑
Hartwick Pines State Park	1.2	☑	☐	☐	☐	☐	☐	☐
Highland Recreation Area	4	☐	☑	☑	☐	☑	☐	☐
Historic Mill Creek Discovery Park	23.4	☐	☑	☑	☐	☑	☐	☐
Hoeft State Park	4	☐	☑	☑	☐	☐	☐	☑
Holland State Park	2.8	☑	☑	☐	☐	☐	☐	☐
Holly Recreation Area	7.7	☐	☑	☑	☐	☑	☐	☑
Indian Lake State Park	2	☐	☑	☑	☐	☑	☐	☐
Interlochen State Park	7.2	☐	☑	☑	☐	☑	☐	☐
Ionia State Recreation Area	12.5	☐	☑	☑	☐	☑	☐	☐
Island Lake Recreation Area	0	☐	☐	☐	☐	☑	☐	☐
Lake Gogebic State Park	3.3	☐	☑	☑	☑	☑	☐	☐
Lake Hudson Recreation Area	5	☐	☐	☑	☐	☑	☐	☐
Lakeport State Park	54	☐	☑	☑	☐	☑	☐	☑
Laughing Whitefish Falls State Park	2.5	☐	☐	☐	☐	☐	☐	☐
Leelanau State Park	8.5	☐	☐	☑	☐	☐	☐	☐
Lime Island State Recreation Area	0	☐	☐	☑	☐	☑	☐	☐
Ludington State Park	22.5	☐	☑	☑	☐	☐	☐	☐
Mackinac Island State Park	29.4	☐	☐	☐	☐	☑	☐	☐
Maybury State Park	6	☐	☐	☐	☐	☐	☐	☐
McLain State Park	4	☐	☑	☑	☑	☑	☐	☐
Mears State Park	1	☐	☐	☐	☐	☐	☐	☐
Menominee River Recreation Area	6	☐	☐	☐	☐	☐	☐	☐
Meridian-Baseline State Park	1.4	☐	☐	☑	☐	☐	☐	☐

Midwest State Park Adventures

State Park Name	Restrooms	Visitor/Nature Center	Swimming	Paddling	Store	Picnic	Fishing
Algonac State Park	Flush	☐	☐	☑	☐	☑	☑
Aloha State Park	Showers	☐	☑	☑	☑	☑	☑
Bald Mountain Recreation Area	Vault	☐	☑	☑	☐	☑	☑
Baraga State Park	Flush	☐	☑	☑	☐	☑	☑
Bass River Recreation Area	N/A	☐	☐	☑	☐	☐	☑
Bay City State Park	Showers	☑	☑	☐	☐	☑	☑
Belle Isle Park	Flush	☑	☑	☑	☑	☑	☑
Bewabic State Park	Flush	☐	☑	☑	☐	☑	☑
Brighton Recreation Area	Flush	☐	☑	☑	☐	☑	☑
Brimley State Park	Flush	☐	☑	☑	☐	☑	☑
Burt Lake State Park	Showers	☐	☑	☑	☑	☑	☑
Cambridge Junction Historic State Park	N/A	☑	☐	☐	☐	☐	☐
Cheboygan State Park	Flush	☐	☑	☐	☐	☑	☑
Clear Lake State Park	Showers	☐	☑	☐	☐	☑	☑
Coldwater Lake State Park	Showers	☐	☑	☑	☐	☑	☑
Craig Lake State Park	N/A	☐	☑	☐	☐	☐	☐
Dodge #4 State Park	Flush	☐	☑	☑	☐	☑	☑
Duck Lake State Park	Flush	☐	☐	☑	☐	☑	☑
Fayette Historic State Park	Flush	☑	☑	☑	☑	☑	☑
Fisherman's Island State Park	Vault	☐	☐	☑	☐	☑	☑
Fort Custer Recreation Area	Flush	☐	☑	☑	☑	☑	☑
Fort Michilimackinac State Park	Vault	☐	☑	☑	☐	☑	☑
Fort Wilkins Historic State Park	Flush	☐	☑	☑	☑	☑	☑
Grand Haven State Park	Flush	☑	☐	☐	☑	☑	☐
Grand Mere State Park	Showers	☐	☑	☑	☑	☑	☑
Harrisville State Park	Flush	☐	☑	☑	☐	☑	☐
Hartwick Pines State Park	Vault	☐	☑	☑	☐	☑	☑
Highland Recreation Area	Showers	☐	☑	☑	☑	☑	☑
Historic Mill Creek Discovery Park	Flush	☑	☐	☑	☑	☑	☑
Hoeft State Park	Flush	☐	☑	☐	☐	☑	☐
Holland State Park	Flush	☐	☐	☐	☑	☑	☐
Holly Recreation Area	Flush	☑	☑	☑	☑	☐	☐
Indian Lake State Park	Flush	☐	☑	☑	☐	☑	☑
Interlochen State Park	Flush	☐	☑	☑	☑	☑	☑
Ionia State Recreation Area	Flush	☐	☑	☑	☐	☑	☑
Island Lake Recreation Area	Vault	☐	☑	☑	☑	☑	☑
Lake Gogebic State Park	Flush	☐	☑	☑	☐	☑	☑
Lake Hudson Recreation Area	Vault	☐	☑	☑	☐	☑	☑
Lakeport State Park	Flush	☐	☑	☑	☐	☑	☑
Laughing Whitefish Falls State Park	Vault	☐	☐	☐	☐	☑	☐
Leelanau State Park	Vault	☐	☐	☐	☑	☑	☐
Lime Island State Recreation Area	Vault	☐	☐	☐	☐	☑	☐
Ludington State Park	Flush	☐	☑	☑	☑	☑	☑
Mackinac Island State Park	Flush	☑	☐	☑	☑	☑	☑
Maybury State Park	Flush	☐	☐	☐	☐	☑	☑
McLain State Park	Flush	☐	☐	☐	☑	☑	☑
Mears State Park	Flush	☑	☐	☑	☑	☑	☑
Menominee River Recreation Area	Flush	☐	☐	☐	☐	☑	☑
Meridian-Baseline State Park	Vault	☐	☐	☑	☐	☐	☐

Michigan

State Park Name	Hiking # of miles	RV - Full Hookups	RV - Partial Hookups	Tent	Primitive	Cabin	Yurt	Lodge
Metamora-Hadley Recreation Area	6	☐	✓	✓	☐	☐	☐	☐
Mike Levine Lakelands Trail State Park	34.7	☐	☐	☐	☐	✓	☐	☐
Mitchell State Park	2.5	☐	✓	✓	☐	☐	☐	☐
Muskallonge Lake State Park	1.5	☐	✓	✓	☐	☐	☐	☐
Muskegon State Park	11.5	☐	✓	✓	☐	✓	✓	☐
Negwegon State Park	10.4	☐	☐	☐	✓	☐	☐	☐
Newaygo State Park	4	☐	✓	✓	☐	☐	☐	☐
North Higgins Lake State Park	11.6	☐	✓	☐	☐	✓	☐	☐
Onaway State Park	0	☐	✓	☐	☐	✓	☐	☐
Orchard Beach State Park	3.5	✓	✓	✓	☐	✓	☐	☐
Ortonville Recreation Area	12.5	☐	☐	✓	☐	✓	☐	☐
Otsego Lake State Park	0	☐	✓	☐	☐	✓	☐	☐
Hoffmaster State Park	4.1	☐	✓	✓	☐	☐	☐	☐
Palms Book State Park	0	☐	☐	☐	☐	☐	☐	☐
Petoskey State Park	2	☐	✓	✓	☐	✓	☐	☐
Pinckney Recreation Area	61.7	☐	✓	✓	✓	✓	✓	☐
Pontiac Lake Recreation Area	1.9	☐	✓	✓	☐	☐	☐	☐
Porcupine Mountains Wilderness State Park	115.1	☐	✓	✓	☐	✓	✓	✓
Port Crescent State Park	5.55	☐	✓	✓	☐	✓	☐	☐
Proud Lake Recreation Area	20	☐	✓	✓	☐	✓	☐	✓
Rifle River Recreation Area	14	☐	✓	✓	☐	✓	☐	☐
Rockport Recreation Area	0	☐	☐	☐	☐	☐	☐	☐
Sanilac Petroglyphs Historic State Park	1	☐	☐	☐	☐	☐	☐	☐
Saugatuck Dunes State Park	13	☐	☐	☐	☐	☐	☐	☐
Seven Lakes State Park	4.95	☐	✓	✓	☐	☐	☐	☐
Silver Lake State Park	0	☐	✓	✓	☐	☐	☐	☐
Sleeper State Park	3.48	☐	✓	✓	☐	✓	☐	☐
Sleepy Hollow State Park	16	☐	✓	✓	☐	✓	☐	☐
South Higgins Lake State Park	0.5	✓	☐	☐	☐	✓	☐	☐
Sterling State Park	3.75	✓	✓	☐	☐	☐	☐	☐
Straits State Park	1	☐	✓	☐	☐	✓	☐	☐
Sturgeon Point State Park	0	☐	☐	☐	☐	☐	☐	☐
Tahquamenon Falls State Park	21.5	☐	✓	✓	☐	✓	☐	✓
Tawas Point State Park	1.5	☐	✓	✓	☐	✓	✓	☐
Thompson's Harbor State Park	6	☐	☐	☐	☐	☐	☐	☐
Tippy Dam Recreation Area		☐	☐	✓	☐	✓	☐	☐
Traverse City State Park	3.8	☐	✓	✓	☐	✓	☐	✓
Twin Lakes State Park	39.5	☐	✓	✓	☐	☐	☐	☐
Van Buren State Park	18	☐	✓	✓	☐	✓	☐	☐
Van Riper State Park	5	☐	✓	✓	☐	☐	☐	☐
Wetzel State Recreation Area	4.5	☐	☐	☐	☐	☐	☐	☐
Hayes State Park	6	☐	✓	✓	☐	✓	☐	☐
Warren Dunes State Park	5.74	☐	☐	✓	☐	☐	☐	☐
Warren Woods State Park	0.51	☐	☐	☐	✓	✓	☐	☐
Waterloo Recreation Area	59.4	☐	✓	✓	☐	☐	✓	☐
Watkins Lake State Park and County Preserve	5	☐	☐	☐	☐	✓	☐	✓
Wells State Park	32.79	☐	✓	✓	✓	✓	☐	☐
Wilderness State Park	33.59	✓	✓	✓	☐	☐	☐	☐
Willia G. Milliken State Park	0.4	☐	☐	☐	☐	☐	☐	☐

Midwest State Park Adventures

State Park Name	Restrooms	Visitor/Nature Center	Swimming	Paddling	Store	Picnic	Fishing
Metamora-Hadley Recreation Area	Flush	☐	☐	☐	✓	☐	✓
Mike Levine Lakelands Trail State Park	Vault	☐	☐	☐	☐	☐	☐
Mitchell State Park	Flush	✓	✓	✓	☐	✓	✓
Muskallonge Lake State Park	Flush	☐	✓	✓	☐	✓	✓
Muskegon State Park	Flush	☐	✓	✓	✓	✓	✓
Negwegon State Park	Vault	☐	☐	✓	☐	☐	✓
Newaygo State Park	Vault	☐	✓	✓	☐	✓	✓
North Higgins Lake State Park	Showers	☐	✓	✓	☐	✓	✓
Onaway State Park	Showers	☐	✓	✓	☐	✓	✓
Orchard Beach State Park	Flush	☐	☐	☐	☐	✓	✓
Ortonville Recreation Area	Flush	☐	☐	✓	☐	✓	✓
Otsego Lake State Park	Showers	☐	✓	✓	✓	✓	✓
Hoffmaster State Park	Flush	✓	✓	☐	☐	✓	☐
Palms Book State Park	Flush	☐	☐	☐	✓	✓	✓
Petoskey State Park	Showers	☐	✓	✓	✓	✓	☐
Pinckney Recreation Area	Showers	☐	✓	✓	☐	✓	✓
Pontiac Lake Recreation Area	Flush	☐	✓	✓	☐	✓	✓
Porcupine Mountains Wilderness State Park	Showers	✓	✓	✓	✓	✓	✓
Port Crescent State Park	Flush	☐	✓	✓	☐	✓	✓
Proud Lake Recreation Area	Flush	☐	☐	✓	☐	✓	✓
Rifle River Recreation Area	Flush	☐	✓	✓	☐	✓	✓
Rockport Recreation Area	N/A	☐	☐	✓	☐	☐	✓
Sanilac Petroglyphs Historic State Park	Vault	☐	☐	☐	☐	✓	☐
Saugatuck Dunes State Park	Vault	☐	✓	☐	☐	☐	☐
Seven Lakes State Park	Flush	☐	✓	✓	✓	✓	✓
Silver Lake State Park	Flush	☐	✓	✓	✓	✓	✓
Sleeper State Park	Flush	☐	✓	✓	✓	✓	✓
Sleepy Hollow State Park	Flush	☐	✓	✓	✓	✓	✓
South Higgins Lake State Park	Showers	☐	✓	✓	✓	✓	✓
Sterling State Park	Flush	☐	✓	✓	☐	✓	✓
Straits State Park	Flush	☐	☐	✓	☐	✓	☐
Sturgeon Point State Park	Vault	☐	☐	☐	✓	✓	☐
Tahquamenon Falls State Park	Showers	✓	☐	✓	✓	✓	☐
Tawas Point State Park	Flush	☐	✓	✓	✓	✓	☐
Thompson's Harbor State Park	Vault	☐	☐	☐	☐	☐	✓
Tippy Dam Recreation Area	Vault	☐	✓	✓	✓	☐	✓
Traverse City State Park	Flush	☐	✓	✓	☐	✓	✓
Twin Lakes State Park	Showers	☐	✓	☐	☐	☐	☐
Van Buren State Park	Flush	☐	✓	✓	✓	✓	✓
Van Riper State Park	Flush	☐	✓	✓	☐	✓	✓
Wetzel State Recreation Area	N/A	☐	☐	☐	☐	☐	✓
Hayes State Park	Flush	☐	✓	✓	☐	✓	✓
Warren Dunes State Park	Flush	☐	✓	☐	✓	☐	✓
Warren Woods State Park	Vault	☐	☐	☐	☐	☐	☐
Waterloo Recreation Area	Flush	✓	✓	✓	✓	✓	✓
Watkins Lake State Park and County Preserve	N/A	☐	☐	☐	☐	☐	☐
Wells State Park	Vault	☐	✓	✓	☐	✓	✓
Wilderness State Park	Vault	☐	✓	✓	☐	✓	✓
Willia G. Milliken State Park	Flush	☐	☐	☐	☐	✓	✓

Michigan

State Park Name	Hiking # of miles	RV - Full Hookups	RV - Partial Hookups	Tent	Primitive	Cabin	Yurt	Lodge
Wilson State Park	0	☐	✓	✓	☐	✓	☐	☐
Yankee Springs Recreation Area	28.7	☐	✓	✓	☐	✓	☐	☐
Young State Park	6.5	☐	✓	✓	☐	✓	☐	☐

State Park Name	Restrooms	Visitor/ Nature Center	Swimming	Paddling	Store	Picnic	Fishing
Wilson State Park	Flush	☐	✓	✓	☐	✓	✓
Yankee Springs Recreation Area	Flush	☐	✓	✓	✓	✓	✓
Young State Park	Flush	☐	✓	✓	✓	✓	✓

MINNESOTA

By Dustin & Kelly Ratcliff

Minnesota is known as the land of 10,000 lakes, though we actually have over 11,000 and our state park system is as robust. Outdoor enthusiasts of all interest levels and abilities will find a reason to love any of our 66 state parks. The state parks are scattered throughout Minnesota allowing nature lovers to find a state park close to home or within a few hours' drive.

Stop by the park ranger's office of each park for a bird checklist, maps, and other park literature.

Annual or day state park passes are available for purchase at any of the state parks. Several times throughout the year Minnesota will have a "free state park day".

There are three programs to be aware of. The Hiking Club Trails and Passport Stamps are two engaging reasons to visit and explore all the state parks. Both programs have a small fee. The Junior Park Naturalist Program is free.

For the Hiking Club, you will take 68 trails. You'll receive a logbook with the information needed for each state park. Complete the hike and look for the password at the designated spot on the route, typically halfway through the hike. Record the password and earn rewards for free nights of camping at a state park.

For the Passport Club, you'll receive a book of information and a log to record the passport stamps that are available when you stop by the park office of each state park.

The Junior Park Naturalist Program is designed to get kids interested in service projects. The programs are hosted by park rangers and give kids opportunities for some hands-on learning about bugs, birds, and plants that are found outdoors.

Fishing within Minnesota state parks is free if you are fishing from shore or a boat, as long as the lake is completely within the state park.

You may not pick wildflowers or plants, but you may pick edible mushrooms.

Remember, to leave no trace when visiting any state park, in any state!

Minnesota State Park Facts & Important Information

- We have a wonderful state park system in Minnesota made up of the following:
    - 66 state parks
    - 9 recreation areas
    - 9 waysides
    - 4,466 campsites
    - 244 horse campsites
    - 104 group camps
    - 108 water access sites
    - 644 archaeological and historic cemetery sites
    - 306 buildings on the National Register of Historic Places
- Minnesota's is the country's second oldest state park system, establishing Itasca State Park on April 20, 1891.
- The newest state park, Lake Vermillion State Park, was established in 210.
- The largest state park is St. Croix and the smallest is Franz Jevne.
- Just 1% of the land in Minnesota is designated as state park land. This ranks us 29th compared to other states.
- Annual Fee: $35 for unlimited use
- Camping costs range from $20-$80 per night and require a reservation

A note about accessibility

Some Minnesota state parks offer wheelchair accessibility for both trails and lodging. You'll want to verify with each state park beforehand to find out how accessible they will be for your needs.

We suggest checking out the link in the Amenities section for state parks that specifically mention and detail the accessibility, and also calling for more detailed information.

Minnesota State Parks Map

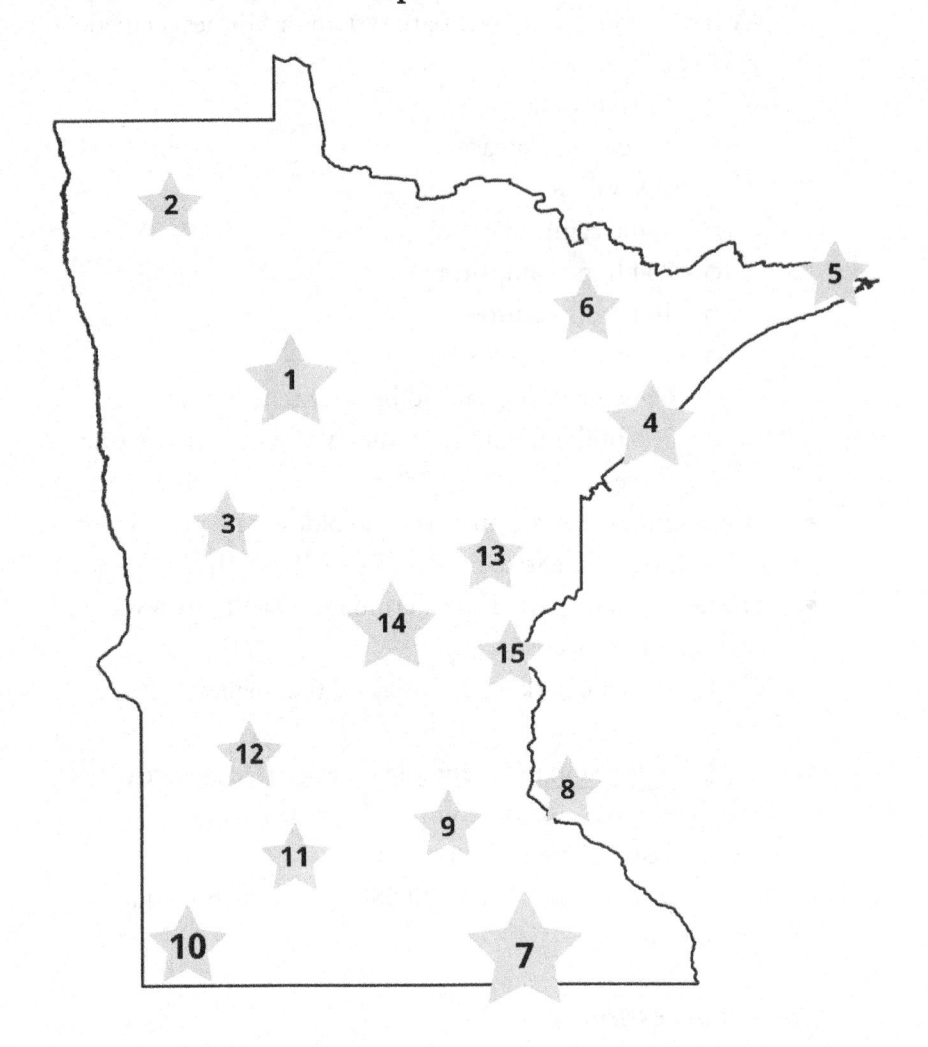

1. Itasca 2. Lake Bronson 3. Maplewood 4. Gooseberry Falls 5. Grand Portage
6. Lake Vermillion-Soudan Underground Mine 7. Forestville/Mystery Cave 8. Frontenac
9. Nerstarand Big Woods 10. Blue Mounds 11. Upper Sioux Agency 12. Minneopa
13. Banning 14. Charles A. Lindbergh 15. Interstate

Region: Northwest

Itasca State Park

Established in 1891, Itasca State Park is Minnesota's oldest state park. There are over 100 lakes in this state park alone.

Itasca State Park is especially unique, as it's the Mississippi Headwaters' birthplace. This state park was created specifically to protect the forests and the waters surrounding the mighty Mississippi River.

The Mississippi River begins here in Itasca, flowing through 10 states and eventually emptying into the Gulf of Mexico. Look for interpretive markings throughout the park.

The park itself is designated as a National Register Historic District along with many other historic sites within the 32,000 acres.

Before you start your adventure at Itasca State Park, visit the 13,000-square-foot Visitor Center to learn more about the history and importance of the Mississippi River.

Learn about how Native Americans lived along the Mississippi River for over 6,000 years, utilizing the river for transportation, food, and water.

Don't miss your chance to actually walk across the Mississippi River. At the north end of Lake Itasca, take the accessible 0.5 loop that takes you through the first quarter mile of the river.

Visitors can walk across the headwaters on large stepping stones that rest in shallow water. For adults, the water will come below your knees. Take a selfie next to the Mississippi Headwaters Monument.

As always, we recommend an early start getting to the headwaters as there will be fewer visitors. This park receives over a million visitors a year.

This portion of the park also contains a gift shop and cafe nearby. As a matter of fact, there are three gift shop locations within Itasca.

This state park truly offers an up north feeling, as it's full of red and white pine trees that have been here for centuries.

Head to Preacher's Grove, a lake surrounded by these gorgeous tall trees, and then imagine how Northern Minnesota once looked being mostly covered by these trees. You can easily access the area from the road and is a really quick hike. You don't need to spend a lot of time here but it's a beautiful view.

We highly suggest experiencing taking a cruise on the Wilderness Drive, a scenic and hilly drive that can be enjoyed by car or bike for a beautiful overview of the park. This is about a 16-mile drive. It would be especially beautiful to drive in the fall.

Climbing the Aiton Heights Fire Tower will be worth the 100 steps for a stunning panoramic view of Lake Itasca.

Visitors can also take a narrated boat tour of the Mississippi River where you'll have a pretty good chance of spotting eagles and our state bird, the loon.

Bring your bikes or rent them to enjoy the 16 miles of paved biking. If you prefer hiking, there are 49 miles of trails taking you through the most scenic portions of the park.

Stay at the historic Douglas Lodge. It's been welcoming guests since 1905 and also features a restaurant that focuses on Minnesota ingredients.

Lake Bronson State Park

Lake Bronson is your park if you're looking for a quiet, remote state park. Located in Northern Minnesota, Lake Bronson is just 20 miles south of the Canadian Border. Set on 352 acres, Lake Bronson is a quaint state park that feels a bit cozy. The nearest town is about 20 miles away.

We mentioned that Minnesota is home to more than 10,000 lakes but ironically, Lake Bronson is the only lake in the area and it's manmade.

In the 1930s there was a drought that caused the wells in the area to go dry. The solution was to build a dam that created Lake Bronson in 1936. This became a nice water recreation area for visitors and provides easy access for swimming, canoes, and kayaks.

This state park is quite flat. This is a result of Agassiz, the glacial lake that covered this area into North Dakota and Canada.

This makes the trails a bit flat too so it is a nice, casual camping or hiking experience.

We love the observation tower on the property. The view from the tower really shows off the two different landscapes that are present in this state park- prairie and forest.

Maplewood State Park

Farmland surrounds the area, yet suddenly there is a tree-covered state park that spans nearly 10,000 acres. This park includes 8 major lakes and lots of ponds.

Maplewood is on the eastern edge of the Red River Valley and the hills are a result of the Alexandria Glacial Moraine.

You'll find two landscapes in this park- western prairie and eastern forests with vegetation and animals in each of the areas.

There are lots of beautiful flowers throughout the park as well. Wildflower lovers will love it here. Learn about the flora through interpretive trail signs.

Enjoy a scenic 5-mile drive through the park to see prairie restoration. If you love to canoe, paddleboard, or kayak, you'll especially enjoy Beers Lake.

With over 20 miles of hiking trails, trails range from hilly to mostly flat. Hike up to Hallaway Hill for a panoramic view of the area.

The state park is also popular with horseback riders as it's 1 of 13 state parks to offer trails for horseback riding.

This park is especially beautiful in the fall with the forest of hardwood trees which include sugar maple, basswood, American elm, and oak. Imagine the hills and valleys covered in fall splendor!

Region: Northeast

Gooseberry Falls State Park

The North Shore in Minnesota is home to 8 state parks that are all stunning. Known as the gateway to the north, Gooseberry Falls is nestled along Scenic Byway Highway 61.

Don't miss the Joseph N. Alexander Visitor Center where you can learn more about Lake Superior and Minnesota's North Shore.

Gooseberry Falls State Park is arguably one of the most visited and favorite state parks in the state. It was the first state park to be built on the North Shore.

Some people just stop by to see Gooseberry Falls some spend a day or more at this park alone.

The neat thing about this particular park is that it's free to park and view Gooseberry Falls. A state park pass is not required for entry to this portion so if you decide not to explore this state park, you can at least see her crowning glory as you make your way up or down the North Shore of Lake Superior.

Gooseberry River flows to Gooseberry Falls. The Falls are made up of Upper, Middle, and Lower falls. Take the time to hike a 3-mile loop to all the different viewing areas as the falls are stunning from every angle. There are a total of five waterfalls in the park.

Chose a winding paved path or take paved steps to go up or down the falls. Enjoy beautiful views of Lake Superior along the way. There are three bridges that cross the river and take you to various spots in the park. The Catwalk Bridge just below Hwy 61 will give you an amazing birds-eye view of the upper falls. You can reach the fifth waterfall from this bridge.

Get up close and personal with the falls by dipping your toes in the water or hopping across enormous rocks. You can also walk around and above the falls on various trails and bridges. Be very careful to not get too close to the rushing waters.

The water flowing over these falls can be described as rootbeer with tones of caramel and cream. This color is a result of tannins found in the water created by bark, oak leaves, and trees.

In addition to the falls, there are over 18 miles of trails to take in that take you along the Gooseberry River and along the Lake Superior Shoreline.

Visitors can access the Superior hiking Trail and the Gitchi-Gami State Trail from here as well. If you love biking take the Gooseberry Loop of the Gitchi-Gami Trail. It's a paved 14-mile loop with spectacular views and takes you through Split Rock Lighthouse State Park.

Don't miss hiking to Agate Beach. From the visitor's center, it's about a mile's walk or you can drive closer and hike in. If you love rock hunting you'll love this spot!

This state park is popular with fishermen as well. We often see anglers in quieter parts of the waterfalls.

If you weren't already in love with Lake Superior, a visit to Gooseberry Falls will ensure it happens.

Grand Portage State Park

Grand Portage State Park sits on the Canadian border. The Pigeon River separates the United States from Canada. The High Falls of the Pigeon River is aptly named for a 120-foot and is the tallest waterfall in Minnesota.

The Grand Portage Band of Ojibwe has shared this land with the Minnesota State Park System for all to enjoy. Don't miss the visitor center to learn about the culture of Ojibwe.

From the visitor center, pavement leads to a beautiful boardwalk to High Falls. It's a wooded and peaceful walk where visitors are often met with wildlife. Interpretive signs teach about the life and survival of the Ojibwe Tribe on this land.

When you approach the falls, take steps to three viewing decks to observe the falls for fantastic views of High Falls.

There are two additional trails to take. A 4.5-mile advanced trail takes you to the middle falls. Visitors can picnic on another trail that is a half-mile walk round trip.

This is a day park only so no camping. Near the state park but worth a stop is the Grand Portage National Park to learn about the North American Fur Trade of the Anishinabe.

Lake Vermillion State Park

Underground tours of an obsolete iron ore mine make this state park unique. The Soudan Mine is the oldest and deepest underground mine in Minnesota. After the mine became obsolete in the 1960s, the US Steel Corporation donated it to the State of Minnesota which then combined the land with Lake Vermillion State Park.

Three types of mine tours are available. One takes you down in the mine and requires a hard hat. Take a walking tour to see what life was like for the miners. The last tour dives into scientific discovery. Stop at the museum with a gift shop for cool rock gifts.

If you love biking, the Mesabi Bike Trail can be accessed within the state park and is 150 miles long.

Lake Vermillion is the fifth largest lake in Minnesota. There are over 10 miles of continuous lakeshore and many islands on the lake. It's quite popular for fishing. For unique lodging rent a houseboat!

The habitat of this state park is quite diverse because of the lakeshore and the forest creating a paradise for birds and birdwatchers alike! Bears and timberwolves, deer, and beavers, are just some of the animals that can all be spotted.

Region: Southeast

Forestville/Mystery Cave State Park

The region of this state park is known as the Driftless Region, meaning the landscape was unscraped by glaciers. In Minnesota, we call this area "bluff country". It's beautiful and unique and lends itself as a beautiful backdrop for fly fishing, horseback riding, canoeing, tubing, hiking, and biking.

The South Branch of the Root River runs through this state park and is excellent for trout fishing. Preston is known as Minnesota's Trout Capitol. The Root River is a tributary to the Mississippi River.

The Root River and its bluff landscape are something to see and are unique to southeast Minnesota. The river water is clear and moves slowly (perfect for tubing) and must be experienced.

Mystery Cave is a highlight and separate from the main portion of the state park. The Mystery Cave is the longest cave in Minnesota, covering 13 miles underground, and is a popular destination in Minnesota.

Multiple cave tour options include scenic, lantern, geology, photography, and wild caving tours. Tours are seasonal and reservations are recommended.

The beautiful turquoise lake is located within this cave with waters so blue you'll forget your surroundings.

Both kids and adults will enjoy any of the guided tours where you will see all kinds of fossils and stalactites and underground pools that are so blue you wonder if you're in Minnesota. Dress warm as it stays 48°F degrees year round!

History lovers will enjoy a walk over the historic Carnegie Steel Bridge to the restored Historic Forestville, a living history village operated by the Minnesota Historical Society inside the state park. Step back in time with period-styled tours of an 1800's farmstead, store, sawmill, grist mill farm, and learn about the challenges of the time period. Check out the old graveyard with tombstones dating to the 1800s.

Learn how the town evolved from settler-colonists and how the development of the Southern Minnesota Railroad bypassed Forestville and turned it into a ghost town.

This state park is a favorite amongst equestrians. You'll need to pay attention to where you're walking as trails that are shared with horses can lead to messy encounters if you don't watch where you're walking.

Hikers of all levels will find a trail to their liking. It's more challenging but you can hike up to Overlook Trail for views of the bluffs.

The quarter-mile river trail runs parallel to the Root River and takes you along the sheer limestone cliffs. This is a great area to fly fish and also enjoy a small swimming beach.

Hike to Big Springs where you'll see unbelievably clear waters of the Canfield Creek and South Branch Root River.

If you are bringing your bikes to this park there are no paved trails within the state park but a very popular Root River Biking Trail about 12 miles from the state park.

Frontenac State Park

This state park is located on the river bluffs of Lake Pepin and is near the Mississippi River. Lake Pepin's habitat offers bluff land, prairie, floodplain forest, and hardwood forest. This means that it attracts birds of all kinds and birdwatching has been popular here as there are more than 260 species of birds recorded. Bring binoculars for your visit!

A glacier river once ran through this region leaving most of Frontenac underwater, save for the park's bluff. Visit the landmark that is still on this bluff today called the In-Yan-Teopa. It's viewed as a sacred site by some Native Americans.

Hiking is lovely in this state park due to the bluffs and valleys. Many of the trails overlook Lake Pepin and give access to views of the Mississippi River. For a challenging hike take the lower bluffs trail which includes hills and a lot of steps.

Hike to the limestone quarry that would have been active in the 1890s.

Head to the wildlife observation blind on the southeastern edge of Pleasant Valley Lakelet for a quiet opportunity for wildlife and bird viewing.

Believe it or not, rattlesnakes are native to this part of Minnesota. You will see signs warning of what the Timber rattlesnake looks like in case you encounter a snake during your time in Frontenac.

Nerstrand Big Woods State Park

There are two highlights in this state park: the Big Woods and a small waterfall.

This hardwood forest of the Big Woods that once covered most of southeast Minnesota is protected in this state park. You'll find the Big Woods full of elm, basswood, sugar maple, and red oak trees here. The trees make up beautiful canopies of leaves in the summer months and of course, are beautiful with the color change in the fall.

If you love flora, this is the state park for you. Head here in the spring for wildflower viewing. You'll also find the dwarf trout lily which can only be found in this state park. The best months to spot the dwarf lily are between April and May.

Take a short hike to Hidden Falls where you'll find crystal-clear water and a creek. It's a unique waterfall that is beautiful when frozen in the winter or flowing the rest of the year!

Most of the hiking is pretty flat so we consider this an easy park to hike and great for families or lower hiking abilities. The terrain is not great for strollers.

Nerstrand is one of 26 state parks in Minnesota to offer free loaners for geocaching.

Region: Southwest

Blue Mounds State Park

Blue Mounds State Park is set in the beautiful and unique southwest corner of Minnesota. You'll first notice a landscape change of tall grass prairie and pink quartz rocks, and then you'll notice bison.

Yes, a herd of bison calls this state park home. The bison are free to roam 533 acres that contain tall grass native to the area. This park is one of two Minnesota state parks that is revitalizing the bison in their native lands that were once hunted to near extinction.

If the bison feel like it, they'll make an appearance during your visit, perhaps visible to visitors from one of three observation decks. Remember, they have 533 acres to roam. Another viewing option is to take a 90-minute prairie and bison tour. It's recommended to reserve tickets in advance. It is wheelchair accessible.

The tallgrass prairie and wildflowers you'll find here once covered most of North America. Thankfully a restoration project is helping to restore, preserve and protect the native tallgrass prairie and wildflowers. The tallgrass also attracts western bird species.

The pink Sioux Quartzite, formed at the bottom of an ancient sea, is what makes the state park a stunning and unique feature of this part of the southwestern corner of Minnesota.

There is a pink quartzite cliff that is 100 feet in some areas and a mile long and is not to be missed.

The ruggedness of this landscape is so interesting combined with lush grass and trees that grow around it. It makes for wonderful hiking views. It's also a popular winter hiking spot for outdoor enthusiasts.

Visit the historic Cliffline Quarry off the interpretive center. Yell into the quarry and listen for your echo. You'll also see the blue mounds that the park was named for. The pink quarry looks stunning against clouded or clear skies.

If you make your way into the neighboring towns of Luverne or Pipestone you will see the pink quartzite buildings as it was once a popular building material.

A hike to Eagle Rock Vista is the highest point in the park and allows you to see into the neighboring town of Luverne as well as peer into the corners of Iowa and South Dakota.

This is another region of Minnesota that does not have a natural lake and there is no swimming at this state park.

Late summer is a beautiful time to hike the Mounds, Upper, and Lower Cliffline trails. Rock climbing the rugged Sioux quartzite is a popular activity. A permit for rock climbing in the state park is required.

For unique lodging, consider renting one of the three tipis for overnight camping. They're near a stream and overlook one of the viewing areas for the bison.

Another unique feature of this park is the prickly pear cacti which will bloom in June and July.

Upper Sioux Agency State Park

The landscape of this portion of Minnesota is quite unique to the state. Upper Sioux Agency State Park sits on a plateau left behind from a glacial retreat. As the last glacier in this region receded the meltwater created Lake Agassiz and as that dried up, it left a huge valley with a tiny river that eventually became the Minnesota River. Visitors can learn more about the unique geology in the interpretive center.

The current landscape is made up of grasslands and wetlands, woods, and the Minnesota River valley provides some ruggedness to enjoy via hiking, horseback riding, picnicking, and fishing.

This park preserves the site of the Yellow Medicine Agency that was established to carry out the terms of the Treaty of the Traverse Des Sioux of 1851. The Yellow Medicine Agency was destroyed during the U.S.-Dakota War of 1862.

Don't miss the historical buildings that are on the National Register of Historic Places.

With both the Yellow Medicine River and the Minnesota River running through it, this park really highlights recreational activities in the Minnesota Scenic River Valley.

Tipis are available for rent if you are looking for unique lodging.

Minneopa State Park

This was the third designated state park in Minnesota. This park is divided into two sides by Highway 68. One side of Highway 68 features a bison drive. In addition to Blue Mounds State Park, bison herds have also been returned to their native land at Minneopa. The other side of the highway features a waterfall at Minneopa Creek.

Drive through the 325-acre bison range. Keep your eyes peeled if you don't obviously see them in their habitat. Sometimes they're lying down and relaxing in the distance or grazing somewhere less obvious while other times they will parade in front of your vehicle and stop traffic.

While you're on this side of the state park, drive up to the Seppman windmill. This is a wind-driven German-styled historic grist mill that overlooks the nearby Minnesota River Valley.

On the waterfall side of the park, find the falls at Minneopa Creek. Minneopa in Dakota language means "water falling twice". A walking bridge takes you over the first falls where you can take a set of limestone stairs to reach the basin of the second waterfall.

This park has nice picnic areas as well. This would be a park that would be easy to enjoy for a quick dose of nature.

Region: Central

Banning State Park

Banning is known for its pink sandstone quarry. In 1892 when quarrying began operations they would move the quarried stone by railroad to Duluth. In 1894 quarrying was affected by The Great Hinckley Fire that burned more than 350,000 acres, or 400 square miles of the area.

Once quarrying resumed the next challenge was the manufacturing trend that moved from the use of sandstone to steel. The quarry was basically abandoned by 1905. As you can imagine, Banning became a ghost town.

It wasn't until 1959 that the Pine County Historical Society acquired the town of Banning. It was an incredibly scenic area that became a state park in 1963.

This stunning state park stretches 10 miles and is surrounded by the Kettle River. Not only is this park beautiful for those that want to soak in the beauty but it's also for those who love adventure.

The Kettle River has rapids of varying degrees that make them some of the most challenging in the state! If you like to canoe or kayak, explore the Blueberry Slide Rapids, Mother's Delight Rapkids, or the Dragon's

Minnesota

Tooth Rapids, Little Banning, and Hell's Gate. Some have rapids up to class IV.

Banning State Park is one of five state parks that allow rock climbing and permits are required.

The Kettle River was the state's first designated "Wild & Scenic State River" in 1975.

Take a self-guided hike on the historic trail of the Sandstone Quarry. On the quarry loop, you'll pass by and be able to explore the ruins of a historic building that stands today.

You may notice stone potholes near the kettle river. This is a result of glacial melting and the force behind the waters that carried debris that left the potholes.

There is also solitude to be found on one of the many beautiful hiking trails or babbling brooks. Don't miss a hike to Wolf Creek Falls, a small 12-foot waterfall. If you take this hike in the winter you could walk behind the frozen falls. With 17 miles of hiking trails, this park offers a trail for all skill levels all with amazing views to take in.

Park next to the picnic area and take a 3.4-mile roundtrip hike to Quarry Loop Trail, Deadman's Trail, High Bluff, and Wolf Creek Trails.

Bring your bike and hit the bike trail over Wolf Creek. The paved trail connects with the Willard Munger State Trail taking you all the way to Duluth if you dare.

This park is covered in beautiful "up north" trees with birch, aspen, Norway, and eastern white pines dominating the park.

This park has a cave that is not open to visitors as it is home to different bat species that call the cave home for hibernation.

Bird lovers will enjoy looking for 184 bird species that have been sighted in the park.

The park is especially spectacular in the fall.

Charles A Lindbergh State Park

Located in Little Falls, Charles A. Lindbergh State Park sits along the Mississippi River and is named for the famous aviator. His childhood home is across the street on the banks of the Mississippi River and tours are operated by the Minnesota Historical Society.

The Lindbergh family donated their 110-acre farm to the state in 1913 when it was turned into a state park.

Before or after going into the state park area, visit the historic site that is located just across the road from the state park. It's an easy 10-minute walk from the campground.

Visit the limestone water tower that sits inside the park. This was built of limestone in 1939. It's not used today but once held 5,000 gallons of water.

There are nice picnic areas in the park, both sheltered and open. Head over to the footbridge to overlook Pike Creek which empties into the Mississippi. Canoe or kayak rentals are available as well.

Enjoy the other footbridge from the campground. There are 7 miles of hiking trails along the banks of the Mississippi.

This park is pretty flat and is popular for snowshoeing in the winter.

Interstate State Park

Located along the St. Croix River and just outside Taylors Falls, a popular Minnesota destination is Interstate State Park. This is the second oldest Minnesota state park and the first state park to span two states. Directly across the St. Croix River is the Wisconsin Interstate State Park.

Stop by the visitors center to learn more about the unique geography and geology that makes this state park so unique.

Visitors will notice a plethora of tall, white pine trees that line the St. Croix River. The greenery offers a beautiful contrast to the brown basalt cliffs. Tourism in the area began in the 1800s as people came out to watch the lumberjacks struggle to move the trees downstream to Stillwater.

Explore the views from the cliffs, hiking trails, or by canoe or kayak. Climbing is allowed here too, a permit is required.

Hike 5 miles of different trails. For a stunning view, head to Angle Rock where the river makes a 90-degree turn.

This park is famous for its glacial potholes. There are over 200 potholes in the state park. Some of the potholes are so big they have names including one that is 60 feet deep.

Dustin and Kelly Ratcliff are the writers and owners behind a Midwest Travel Blog, Dining Duster. Dustin and Kelly love to dine, drink and discover the Midwest and beyond. They love trying new, plant-based foods at local restaurants, visiting breweries and wineries, and also love taking in historical home tours, botanical gardens, and state parks.

Learn more at diningduster.com and follow Dustin and Kelly on social media @diningduster

Minnesota State Parks Amenities

Please confirm availability of amenities with the state park system. For more information on Minnesota State Parks, visit their website at www.dnr.state.mn.us/state_parks/index.html

A few notes about the amenities:
- RV – Full Hookups include access to electricity, water, and sewer at the campsite.
- RV – Partial Hookups include access to electricity and water, but not sewer.
- Tent: Tent only sites available.
- Primitive: Camping in remote areas without amenities like bathrooms, picnic tables, trash cans, or any other man-made structures.
- Restrooms: Indicates the highest functional type of restroom available.
- Paddling: Boat access; this could be kayaking, canoeing, and/or powered boats.
- Swimming: Selected if swimming is available, either at a beach or a pool.

Yurts are available for rental at Afton and Glendalough State Parks.

Minnesota

State Park Name	Hiking # of miles	Camping RV - Full Hookups	Camping RV - Partial Hookups	Tent	Primitive	Lodging Cabin	Lodge
Afton State Park	20	☐	☐	☑	☑	☑	☐
Banning State Park	17	☐	☑	☑	☐	☑	☐
Bear Head Lake State Park	14	☐	☑	☑	☐	☑	☐
Beaver Creek Valley State Park	8	☑	☐	☑	☐	☑	☐
Big Stone Lake State Park	3	☑	☐	☐	☐	☐	☐
Blue Mounds State Park	13	☑	☐	☐	☐	☐	☐
Buffalo River State Park	12	☑	☐	☑	☐	☐	☐
Camden State Park	15.8	☑	☐	☑	☐	☐	☑
Carley State Park	5	☐	☑	☑	☐	☐	☐
Cascade River State Park	18	☑	☐	☑	☐	☐	☐
Charles A. Lindbergh State Park	7	☑	☐	☑	☐	☐	☐
Crow Wing State Park	18	☑	☐	☑	☐	☐	☐
Father Hennepin State Park	4.5	☑	☐	☑	☐	☐	☐
Flandreau State Park	8	☑	☐	☑	☐	☐	☑
Forestville/Mystery Cave State Park	20	☐	☐	☐	☐	☐	☐
Fort Ridgley State Park	9	☑	☐	☑	☐	☑	☑
Fort Snelling State Park	18	☐	☐	☐	☐	☑	☐
Franz Jevne State Park	2.5	☐	☑	☐	☑	☐	☐
Frontenac Stae Park	13	☑	☐	☑	☑	☐	☑
George H. Crosby Manitou State Park	24	☐	☐	☐	☑	☐	☐
Glacial Lakes State Park	16	☑	☐	☑	☐	☑	☑
Glendalough State Park	9	☐	☐	☑	☑	☑	☐
Gooseberry Falls State Park	20	☐	☐	☑	☐	☐	☑
Grand Portage State Park	4	☐	☐	☐	☐	☐	☐
Great River Bluffs State Park	9	☐	☐	☑	☐	☐	☐
Hayes Lake State Park	13	☑	☐	☑	☐	☑	☐
Hill Annex Mine State Park	0	☐	☐	☐	☐	☐	☐
Interstate State Park	4	☑	☐	☑	☑	☐	☐
Itasca State Park	49	☑	☐	☑	☑	☑	☑
Jay Cooke State park	50	☐	☐	☑	☐	☑	☐
John A. Latsch State Park	0.5	☐	☐	☐	☐	☐	☐
Judge C.R. Magney State Park	9	☐	☐	☐	☐	☐	☐
Kilen Woods State Park	5	☐	☑	☑	☑	☐	☐
La qui Parle State Park	7	☑	☐	☑	☑	☑	☐
Lake Bemidji State Park	11	☑	☐	☑	☐	☑	☐
Lake Bronson State Park	14	☑	☐	☑	☑	☐	☐
Lake Carlos State Park	14	☑	☐	☑	☑	☑	☐
Lake Louise State Park	11.6	☑	☐	☐	☑	☐	☐
Lake Maria State Park	14	☐	☐	☐	☑	☑	☐
Lake Shetek State Park	14	☑	☐	☑	☐	☑	☐
Lake Vermillion-Soudan Underground Mine SP	5	☐	☑	☐	☑	☑	☐
Maplewood State Park	25	☑	☐	☑	☑	☑	☐
McCarthy Beach State Park	18	☑	☐	☑	☑	☑	☐
Mille Lacs Kathio State Park	35	☑	☐	☑	☑	☑	☐
Minneopa State Park	4.5	☑	☐	☑	☐	☑	☐
Monson Lake State Park	1.2	☐	☑	☑	☐	☐	☐
Moose Lake State Park	5	☐	☑	☑	☐	☑	☐
Myre-Big Island State Park	16	☐	☑	☑	☑	☑	☐
Nerstrand Big Woods State Park	11	☑	☐	☑	☑	☐	☐
Old Mill State Park	7	☐	☑	☐	☐	☐	☐
Rice Lake State Park	5	☑	☐	☑	☑	☐	☐
St. Croix State Park	5	☑	☐	☑	☑	☑	☐
Sakatah Lake State Park	5	☑	☐	☑	☑	☑	☐
Savanna Portage State Park	27	☑	☐	☑	☑	☑	☐
Scenic State Park	14	☑	☐	☑	☑	☑	☐
Schoolcraft State Park	2	☐	☐	☑	☑	☐	☐
Sibley State Park	18	☑	☐	☑	☑	☑	☐
Split Rock Creek State Park	4.5	☐	☐	☐	☐	☐	☐

Midwest State Park Adventures

State Park Name	Restrooms	Visitor/Nature Center	Swimming	Paddling	Store	Picnic	Fishing
Afton State Park	Flush	✓	✓	☐	✓	✓	✓
Banning State Park	Flush	☐	☐	✓	✓	☐	✓
Bear Head Lake State Park	Flush	☐	✓	✓	☐	✓	✓
Beaver Creek Valley State Park	Flush	✓	☐	☐	☐	✓	✓
Big Stone Lake State Park	Flush	✓	✓	✓	☐	✓	✓
Blue Mounds State Park	Flush	✓	☐	☐	✓	✓	✓
Buffalo River State Park	Flush	☐	✓	✓	☐	✓	✓
Camden State Park	Flush	☐	✓	✓	✓	✓	✓
Carley State Park	Flush	☐	☐	✓	☐	✓	✓
Cascade River State Park	Flush	☐	☐	✓	☐	✓	✓
Charles A. Lindbergh State Park	Flush	✓	☐	✓	☐	✓	✓
Crow Wing State Park	Flush	✓	☐	✓	✓	✓	✓
Father Hennepin State Park	Flush	✓	✓	✓	✓	✓	✓
Flandreau State Park	Flush	☐	✓	✓	☐	✓	✓
Forestville/Mystery Cave State Park	Flush	✓	✓	✓	✓	✓	✓
Fort Ridgley State Park	Flush	☐	☐	✓	✓	✓	✓
Fort Snelling State Park	Flush	✓	✓	✓	☐	☐	✓
Franz Jevne State Park	Vault	☐	☐	✓	☐	☐	✓
Frontenac State Park	Flush	✓	☐	✓	✓	✓	✓
George H. Crosby Manitou State Park	Vault	☐	☐	✓	☐	☐	✓
Glacial Lakes State Park	Flush	☐	✓	✓	✓	✓	✓
Glendalough State Park	Flush	☐	✓	✓	✓	✓	✓
Gooseberry Falls State Park	Flush	✓	☐	✓	✓	☐	☐
Grand Portage State Park	N/A	✓	☐	☐	✓	✓	✓
Great River Bluffs State Park	Flush	☐	☐	✓	✓	☐	☐
Hayes Lake State Park	Flush	☐	✓	✓	✓	✓	✓
Hill Annex Mine State Park	Flush	✓	☐	☐	✓	☐	☐
Interstate State Park	Flush	✓	☐	✓	✓	✓	✓
Itasca State Park	Flush	✓	✓	✓	✓	✓	✓
Jay Cooke State park	Flush	✓	☐	☐	✓	✓	✓
John A. Latsch State Park	Flush	☐	☐	☐	☐	✓	☐
Judge C.R. Magney State Park	Vault	☐	☐	☐	☐	✓	✓
Kilen Woods State Park	Flush	☐	☐	✓	☐	☐	✓
La qui Parle State Park	Flush	✓	✓	✓	☐	☐	✓
Lake Bemidji State Park	Flush	✓	✓	✓	✓	✓	✓
Lake Bronson State Park	Flush	✓	✓	✓	✓	✓	✓
Lake Carlos State Park	Flush	✓	✓	✓	✓	✓	✓
Lake Louise State Park	Flush	☐	✓	✓	☐	✓	✓
Lake Maria State Park	Flush	✓	☐	☐	☐	✓	✓
Lake Shetek State Park	Flush	✓	✓	☐	✓	☐	✓
Lake Vermillion-Soudan Underground Mine SP	Flush	✓	✓	✓	✓	✓	✓
Maplewood State Park	Flush	☐	✓	☐	☐	✓	✓
McCarthy Beach State Park	Flush	☐	✓	☐	✓	✓	✓
Mille Lacs Kathio State Park	Flush	✓	✓	✓	✓	✓	✓
Minneopa State Park	Flush	✓	☐	☐	☐	✓	✓
Monson Lake State Park	Flush	☐	✓	☐	☐	☐	✓
Moose Lake State Park	Flush	☐	✓	✓	☐	☐	✓
Myre-Big Island State Park	Flush	☐	✓	✓	✓	✓	✓
Nerstrand Big Woods State Park	Flush	✓	☐	☐	✓	✓	☐
Old Mill State Park	Flush	☐	✓	☐	✓	✓	✓
Rice Lake State Park	Flush	✓	☐	✓	✓	✓	✓
St. Croix State Park	Flush	✓	✓	☐	✓	✓	✓
Sakatah Lake State Park	Flush	✓	✓	✓	☐	✓	✓
Savanna Portage State Park	Flush	☐	✓	✓	☐	✓	✓
Scenic State Park	Flush	✓	✓	✓	✓	✓	✓
Schoolcraft State Park	Vault	✓	☐	✓	✓	✓	✓
Sibley State Park	Flush	✓	✓	✓	☐	✓	✓
Split Rock Creek State Park	Flush	✓	✓	✓	✓	✓	✓

Minnesota

State Park Name	Hiking # of miles	Camping RV - Full Hookups	Camping RV - Partial Hookups	Tent	Primitive	Lodging Cabin	Lodge
Split Rock Lighthouse State Park	12	☐	✓	✓	✓	☐	☐
Temperance River State Park	22	✓	☐	✓	✓	☐	☐
Tettegouche State Park	23	☐	✓	✓	✓	☐	☐
Upper Sioux Agency State Park	18	☐	✓	✓	✓	☐	☐
Whitewater State Park	10	✓	☐	✓	✓	✓	☐
Wild River State Park	35	✓	☐	✓	✓	✓	☐
William O'Brien State Park	12	✓	☐	✓	☐	✓	☐
Zippel Bay State Park	6	✓	☐	✓	☐	☐	☐

State Park Name	Restrooms	Visitor/ Nature Center	Swimming	Paddling	Store	Picnic	Fishing
Split Rock Lighthouse State Park	Flush	✓	✓	✓	✓	✓	✓
Temperance River State Park	Flush	☐	☐	☐	✓	✓	✓
Tettegouche State Park	Flush	✓	☐	☐	✓	✓	✓
Upper Sioux Agency State Park	Flush	✓	☐	☐	☐	✓	✓
Whitewater State Park	Flush	✓	✓	✓	✓	✓	✓
Wild River State Park	Flush	✓	☐	☐	☐	✓	✓
William O'Brien State Park	Vault	✓	✓	✓	✓	✓	✓
Zippel Bay State Park	Vault	☐	✓	✓	☐	☐	☐

MISSOURI

By Matthew and Thena Franssen

The Show-Me State really does pull out all the stops for our state parks. Outdoor enthusiasts and campers will agree that no two state parks in Missouri are the same. What makes Missouri state parks unique and amazing is that everyone is welcome and is certain to find something that they love and enjoy. From roaring rivers to tranquil prairies, the landscape seamlessly shifts before your eyes.

Whether you're hoping to spend a night, weekend, or week exploring Mother Nature's beauty, any state park in Missouri will gladly welcome you with stunning views, epic sunsets, and some of the best nature viewing.

We've lived in Missouri for almost our entire lives and have yet to tire of the landscapes and adventures. With over 150,000 acres to see and explore, how could we?

From hiking and biking all over the state to climbing and scaling some of the largest rocks you'll ever see, the beautiful countryside in Missouri was made to be explored.

Even though our section will cover just a handful of some of the top parks in Missouri, don't let that stop you from diving in and researching the rest. Combined, there are over 92 state parks and historical sites. The history that lies in the state of Missouri deserves to be explored and recognized.

History and nature can be found in every portion of the state. Hike the countryside, bike the trails, swim with the fish, canoe or kayak the waters, spend the day birdwatching, sit around the campfire, plan a fun trail ride, or arrive for a day visit and a picnic. All of these activities are an option when planning a trip to the parks in Missouri.

One thing we've learned throughout our time exploring the sites of Missouri is that there's never a bad time. Not only are the state parks clean and filled with friendly workers, but those who visit are pleasant and just as excited to be exploring as you.

The next time you're ready to get "back to nature," let the Missouri state parks welcome you with open arms. You'll find multiple state parks you love and enjoy, from picnics to hiking, camping to swimming!

Missouri State Park Facts & Important Information
- Established in 1917, there are 92 historic sites and state parks.
- Combined, the state parks and historic sites cover more than 150,000 acres.
- Missouri state parks have over 3,500 campsites available, where most are now reservable 12 months in advance.
- Over 1,000 miles of trails within the state park system can be used for hiking, biking, and more.
- Over 18 million people visit Missouri's historic sites and state parks annually.
- The state park system employs over 14,000 people, and many volunteers also assist.
- Camping reservations at any Missouri State Park can be made 12 months in advance.

A note about accessibility

Each park will vary depending on ADA accessibility. Look for the signage around the state parks and trails indicating ADA.

There are particular cabins, lodge rooms, and campsites that are ADA-compliant. Research the MO state park website or call ahead to confirm before arrival.

Missouri State Parks Map

1. Long Branch State Park 2. Finger Lakes State Park 3. Meramec State Park
4. Bennett Spring State Park 5. Echo Bluff State Park 6. Mark Twain State Park
7. Thousand Hills State Park 8. Arrow Rock State Historic Site 9. Katy Trail State Park
10. Route 66 State Park 11. Castlewood State Park 12. Ha Ha Tonka State Park
13. Roaring River State Park 14. Johnson's Shut-Ins State Park 15. Elephant Rocks State Park

Region: Northeast

Long Branch State Park

Long Branch State Park is perfect for anyone who loves water, water sports, or boating. While we're not ranking state parks, it's safe to say this one is at the top of our list. The main reason we keep going back to this location is because of the water views and the spacious campsites that are available right on the water. There's nothing like waking up to that view and sunrise over Long Branch Lake.

With the focal point of this state park being Long Branch Lake, it's an excellent place to park and camp for the night and wake up to crazy sunrises and views. Please be aware that not all campsites are located on the water, but all are within walking distance to see the lake without issue.

This state park is quite famous for visitors and locals because fishing and swimming are easy to access and do. Anyone looking for a relaxing day can easily park and soak up the sun on the beach. The beach section and the lake activities are open daily to the public and can be used for day use by campers staying overnight.

If you're looking for an overnight stay and camping experience, the campground here is also top-notch. There are basic and electric campsites available to reserve, and there are also eight non-reservable campsites that can be booked on a first-come, first-serve basis. (Side-note: some non-reservable campsites offer the best water views!)

Check out their family camping spots for larger groups if you're camping with a group. They're not water views, but they are close enough to the lake.

The campground is in a secluded area from the beach. This makes it an excellent distance to enjoy the day playing in the water, return to a quiet campsite, and enjoy sitting around the campfire.

Even though the campsite and the beach aren't close together, the camp does have an amazing view of the lake. Enjoy a cup of coffee while watching the boats as they pass. You'll see many birds, boats, and possibly even some bald eagles while standing on the shore.

There is a marina that is open daily that offers gas for the boats and snacks and other goodies for visitors. Along with those items, fishermen can get live bait, and campers can also get charcoal and propane at the marina.

Firewood for the campfire ring can be purchased at the campground when you check in or from the host. The campground host is right by the check-in station and will have a sign posted as to whether they're on duty for the night.

Long Branch State Park also has a few boat-in camping spots available, which are unique and reservable through the park reservation system.

Mark Twain State Park

The view of Mark Twain Lake is enough to take your breath away, and when you pair that with the abundance of outdoor activities, you'll be planning your next visit right away.

Plan a few hours to walk and explore the trails and bluffs overlooking the lake, giving stunning views. Walking through the woods on the trails will have you seeing deer and turkeys and hearing all the sounds of birds and nature. There are multiple hiking trails totaling more than 6 miles to see some of the best bluff views around.

This state park is perfect for fishing, boating, and camping and is popular for picnics and day use. A frisbee disc golf course was recently added, and a public beach area is open and accessible. There is no lifeguard on duty, and there is a change house at the beach area.

Buzzards Roost Picnic Area is always active with people eating, playing games, having weddings, and family reunions. The green space is great for tossing a ball, relaxing, or just taking in all the wildlife you'll see at any given time. The facility is often rented for celebrations and gatherings.

Bring your tent or camper to book one of the lovely campsites, or book a camper cabin if you need a place to stay. The six cabins are newer and are reservable through the online reservation system. The camper cabins do not have water or bathrooms, but a modern bathhouse is nearby. There is one cabin that is handicap accessible.

Three campgrounds offer basic and electric sites that can be reserved up to 12 months in advance. Camping spots booked on the weekend do require a two-night minimum stay. This campground is popular during summer.

Thousand Hills State Park

With 17 miles of shoreline, this state park is popular with all who love water sports and activities. Swimmers come here during the hot summer month for the beach area, and fishermen love coming to the marina for fresh bait to fish the day away.

The history of this state park is also worth noting because it's believed to be over 1,500 years old and once was used as a Native American ceremonial ground. For this reason, it's listed on the National Register of Historic Places.

Campsites are reservable and offer modern toilets and hot showers. While there are no full-hook-up campsites, many offer electric options.

Seven cabins are available for rent for those who want to stay overnight without their camper or tent. The cabins do have electricity, kitchens, and bathrooms.

The other unique factor about this state park is that it has a dining lodge where delicious food is served. It gets pretty popular, so getting reservations is always a good idea if you plan to eat there for dinner.

On any given hot summer day, you'll see visitors water skiing, boating, swimming, or fishing. The on-site marina makes it an ideal place to spend the day on the water.

Region: Central

Finger Lakes State Park

Most people think of quiet when it comes to state parks, and while Finger Lakes State Park does offer this, it's also a popular place for off-road motorcycle and ATV trail riding.

The unique landscape of portions of this state park deserves to tell a bit of the backstory about the history. While the almost 1200 acres of this park are now divided into trails, camping, hiking, and more, it was once the location of Mark Twain Mine, where over 1.2 million tons of coal were removed. This action created the terrain that draws in bikers and riders from all over the state.

While the trails are a big bonus and challenge for experienced riders, there is also a motocross track that showcases the riding skills of professional riders from all over the US. These races and rides are open to the public and often draw a good crowd on motocross weekends.

If you're looking for more of the "typical" park experience, stop by the check-in station to plan your visit. The name of this park stems from the shape of the lake that is available to enjoy during your adventures. Kayak and canoe rentals are available for half-day and full-day lake exploration. There is also a beach for families to chill and enjoy. (with a change house located close by) Locals will also use this beach access for the day and swim in the lake.

The campground is situated at the backside of the park and offers basic and electric campsites for rent. Firewood can be purchased at the campground and during check-in, and new modern showers and restrooms are available for use.

In addition to all the fantastic activities listed above, there are shelters for picnics, an enjoyable bicycle path for the kids to use, endless trails with a beautiful waterfall, and a firing range outside the state park gates. (Side note: You will hear the firing range at the campsites or when you're hiking the trails.)

For extra added security, the front gate to the park does close and locks at a certain point daily, which requires a code to get in. This is important to remember in case you're arriving at a later time!

Arrow Rock State Historic Site

Arrow Rock State Historic Site is a historic site, but the campground within this state parks system is one of the cutest and cleanest parks you'll visit. We had to include it on this list because it would be a shame not to plan a visit here while exploring the best that Missouri has to offer. Fun fact? The ENTIRE town of Arrow Rock has been listed as a National Historic Landmark for a good reason. The streets and buildings are riddled with history, and you can easily spend an entire day talking to the locals about the town and how it has developed and changed over the years.

The state park is a mixture of nature and history, and to be noticed. You can spend the days walking the street, exploring the antique shops, or visiting the visitor center to learn more about the area's history. This center has many displays that showcase the area and how it has transformed over the years.

If spending the night at the campground, take a loop on the trail to get a view of the entire area. We also had one of the most incredible experiences here when it was dark at night with the abundance of lightning bugs creating quite a glorious glow.

The town of Arrow Rock is tiny but offers large and fun activities for all. One of the other big draws to the area is Lyceum Theatre which has live productions on stage. The small town of Arrow Rock gets bustling between shows, shopping, and nature activities.

Be sure to grab a bite to eat at J. Huston Tavern while you're there. It's been dubbed the oldest continuously running restaurant west of the Mississippi River - and it doesn't disappoint!

Katy Trail State Park

Katy Trail State Park is perfect for anyone who likes to explore nature on foot or bike. It's the ideal trail that allows views of the woods, river, bluffs, and more - all on the same trip! On any given day, you'll find people biking, hiking, running, and overall enjoying mile after mile of this developed trail. Pets on leashes are also welcome, making it a fun adventure full of variety.

It's not only a trail that creates the perfect way to explore nature but also a great way to walk and be a part of the past. Even though motorized vehicles are prohibited, electric bicycles can be used on the trail.

This beautiful state park trail is 240 miles long and allows people to use it and see some of the state's best views. The trail will show a variety of landscapes, but it is typically close to the Missouri River in one capacity or another.

We've walked, ran, and pedaled hundreds of miles on this trail and see something new and exciting every single time. On the weekends, there are kids on training wheels and groups running and training for their next marathon or event. During the fall months, a tram runs along the trail, taking people on a short trip to see the leaves changing colors. It's quite a stunning site surrounded by yellow, red, and orange leaves.

With the length of the trail, it's important to note that it is only open from sunrise to sunset. While no camping or campgrounds are located along the trail, some private options may be reservable.

Many people think that the trail was just created to get from one place to another, but it was previously a railroad track that has since been turned into a trail. Along the trail be sure to take note of the railroad depots along the way, as there are four that have been restored and are lovely to view. Along the 240 miles of this trail, 26 trailheads offer parking and the ability to start at the trail at many different intervals.

This state park has an equestrian section but only in a specific area. The area allowing for horses is from Clinton to the Sedalia State Fairgrounds and Tebbetts to Portland. Besides that area, you'll only see people on foot or pedaling.

The Katy Trail does hook up to the MKT trail and goes through Columbia, Missouri. This is a fun option and trip that offers the chance to get off the beaten path and get a delicious bite to eat or a fun drink along the way. You can also stop at fun eateries in Rocheport, Missouri, along with Columbia.

… Missouri

Region: St. Louis (East)

Meramec State Park

Meramec State Park is a beauty to behold. The park combines springs, hiking trails, lovely bluffs, and a cave or two lurking around.

Right when you enter the park, be sure to stop at the visitor center. Here you'll find a ton of great information about the Meramec River and all the different types of fish and wildlife found in the water and around the park.

The Meramec River has become quite a destination for locals and tourists as people from all over the state will come here to swim (at their own risk), float, and even load up on various floating trips and spend the day enjoying the calmness that the water of the river has to offer. You'll see canoes, kayaks, rafts, or even people on individual floats on the river on almost any given day. Everyone who has floated on the river says it's an experience, and if it's something of interest, just know that the weekday floats are calmer and less crowded than the weekend floats. Since many campgrounds use the Meramec River for floating drop-off points, the water can get full quickly in various sections. Buses full of people will pull up to start their float trip at multiple points on the river.

With over 13 miles of hiking trails, there is reason to start early and explore. You'll have the chance to get up close and personal with beautiful flowers, nature, and more. Pack your hiking boots and a walking stick and enjoy the scenery. It's a good idea to have a map handy as the trails can go pretty deep into the woods.

If you're feeling like an adventure, do your best and try to locate as many of the 40 caves scattered throughout. If you can take the tour of the Fisher Cave, do so! It's led by a tour guide and a fun way to get inside a cave and see how the inside varies and changes with each step. Plus, having a guide with fun facts and information is always a plus.

Spending a weekend here isn't a challenging stretch at all. The campground offers electric hookups, a few with full hookups, and modern facilities for restrooms and showers. A laundry area is also located at the campground, and some cabins are available for rent for those who don't have other means of lodging. (They are fully stocked cabins to be able to show up and unwind)

The on-site conference center and motel also offer lodging and meeting opportunities for larger groups.

Make sure to grab a bite to eat at the restaurant. You'll also find firewood, camping supplies, and anything else you might have forgotten for your state park trip located right inside the park.

Route 66 State Park

Visiting this state park is like stepping back in time. Stop by the visitor center to view the displays and memorabilia that are a perfect throwback to Route 66. There are many exhibits and items to look at, and then grab something fun for yourself at the gift shop.

While there isn't overnight camping at this park, this is the perfect place for walking and biking. The paved trails allow even the youngest riders to find confidence peddling the day away.

Not only does this park give you a chance to be secluded from the hustle and bustle of the nearby city and towns, but it still puts you close enough to be able to stop here for a picnic and hike and do all the other fun activities scattered about nearby. We stopped at this park when the kids were young, and it was perfect for letting them run around without worries.

A fun fact is that over 40 different types of birds have been viewed and identified in this park alone! Bring your binoculars and see how many you can spot.

Castlewood State Park

Castlewood State Park is it if you're looking for a beautiful state park for a day visit or a family gathering. Not only does it have reservable picnic shelters that can host large gatherings, but it also offers fantastic views of the Meramec River.

This state park once was the hot spot for weekenders looking for dancing, partying, and activities on the water. Back in the early 1900s, there was also a large hotel and cabins for those who wanted to get out of the hustle and bustle of the city to find a place to relax. During popular times, you'd find more than 10,000 people enjoying the river and sandbar in this location.

Now this state park is a hot spot for outdoor enthusiasts. The trails that wind through the state park are perfect for mountain bikes and hikers, and many consider these trails to be some of the best bike trails in and around the St. Louis area.

The playground is also great for the kids to get out and stretch their legs if you're visiting the park for the day.

Region: Lakes (Southwest)

Bennett Spring State Park

Anyone who loves to fish has been to Bennett Spring State Park for a time or two. And who can blame them? The springs offer some of the most transparent and coolest waters, making catching rainbow trout fun and relaxing.

With more than 100 million gallons of spring water gushing daily, it's no wonder this is one of Missouri's best trout fishing locations.

For those who don't like to spend their day fishing, this state park offers many other unique activities that can entertain everyone in your family or party. The swimming pool is a great way to swim the day away during those hot Missouri summer days. Just know the pool is also open to the public, so it can and will fill quickly. (Don't forget that you can also stand in the cool springs and fish to cool down on a hot day!)

Due to the popularity of this state park, there are plenty of lodging options to consider. While camping might be the most plentiful, there is a lodge that rents rooms, duplex cabins, single cabins, and even a four-plex unit for larger parties.

Many visitors give rave reviews about Bennett Spring State Park because you don't have to leave for anything once you arrive. What's better than a trip where you can fully relax once you get there?

The dining lodge on-site is within walking distance of all the various types of lodging, making it super simple to walk right up for your breakfast, lunch, or dinner. Check out their breakfast and dinner buffets if you're there on the weekend.

Remember that fishing tags are needed for anyone who is going to fish, but they can be purchased at the store. While there, be sure to get educated about the different fishing zones, as some rules apply when casting a line.

If you are pulling a camper or looking for a place to pitch a tent for the night, you'll find five campground options within this park. Family campsites are also available for larger groups.

The camp store is perfect for last-minute needs, and the campground hosts are friendly and can answer any questions. You can also purchase firewood upon check-in as well. This state park has no minimum night stay requirement, and it fills up quickly during trout season.

Ha Ha Tonka State Park

Ha Ha Tonka State Park is one of the most unique destinations in the entire state of Missouri. Not only are there caves, streams, wildlife, a natural bridge, and even sinkholes scattered throughout the park, but the history of Ha Ha Tonka is one to learn more about before arriving.

Beginning in the early 1900s, a businessman started building his dream castle using locally quarried sandstone carried by mule and railroad. The construction halted about one year later once the businessman was killed in one of the first automobile accidents in the entire state of Missouri. The family continued building the castle, which was completed in 1922.

During the 1940s, the castle property was used as a hotel until chimney sparks burned the interior of the entire castle. The nearby carriage house also burned on that same day, and in 1976, the water tower was burned by vandals.

The castle ruins are lovely to look at and take pictures of, and many scenic overlooks exist. Stroll down the hiking path to the bottom of the bluff to view the beautiful waters underneath.

Make sure to arrive and be prepared to walk to look at everything. There is parking all around the park, but it fills up quickly with people looking for a fun history-filled day. If you are looking for a great campground that is close, Lake of the Ozarks State Park offers plenty of camping options. (and stunning lake views)

Roaring River State Park

Anyone who visits Roaring River State Park remembers the beauty that it offers. This is just one of the reasons it's the most visited state park in Missouri.

Now a serene and peaceful area, the land was once used by outlaws and others as hideouts during the Civil War. Following the conclusion of the Civil War, the land was purchased by a wealthy businessman who ultimately turned the 2400 acres over to the state.

People now come from all over to spend their days fishing for trout, hiking, and enjoying the scenic views. The landscape of this park is unique because it's located in the hills of the Ozarks. This makes for great hiking trails and a fun getaway for families.

Picnic shelters are available to stop and have a fun lunch, or there are plenty of lodging options. The campground offers hookups with water and electricity and group camping.

There are 26 rustic cabins for rent and a hotel and restaurant on site. Dogs are allowed in some of the cabins, but not all.

A stop at the on-site nature center is a great way to grab some historical books and view a few live animals.

Region: Southeast

Echo Bluff State Park

With over 450 acres, Echo Bluff State Park is the true meaning of natural beauty. What used to be the location of a summer camp for kids, the lovely state park is now open for families to enjoy and make their memories.

This is one of the newest additions to the state park system, and it's quite a stunning site. The campground is located in a valley, with paved camping spots and paved roads that are perfect for the kids to bike and explore. In addition to great camping spots, there are platforms for the tent campers to keep them and their tents off the ground.

Keep your eyes peeled for the wild horses visiting the state park. Typically, 3-4 in a group will sometimes make their appearance, and it is quite a sight to see. Our trip didn't result in seeing the horses, but we did see remnants of their visit when we woke up in the morning.

This park is great for overnight stays because of the lovely lodge and cabin options available for rent. The lodge offers beautiful rooms and a great open restaurant for breakfast, lunch, or dinner. We walked to the lodge from the campground and enjoyed a delicious coffee for breakfast.

Show the kids the massive playground area because it's one of the best. You might as well pack a picnic and spend several hours alone at the playground - it's that good. After the kids have run amok and expelled their energy, walk to see the Sinking Creek. Skipping rocks on the water at the creek was one of our kid's favorite memories.

There is also an excellent blufftop shelter that can be used for family gatherings, picnics, or just a way to sit and relax as you walk around the park.

Johnson's Shut-Ins State Park

Johnson's Shut-Ins State Park is the perfect day use or weekend getaway. Booking a spot at the campground will give you an unparalleled view of the starry skies, but book quickly because this campground is extremely popular.

One whole section of the campground is for equestrian camping, and this is fun and a great way to bring the horses to enjoy the trails.

One of the biggest draws to this state park is the chance to swim in the shut-ins. Think of it like rapids on a minor scale with cold and clear water. The area is a "swim at your own risk" area, and caution should be taken as there are deep parts, and the various water levels can rise quickly when it rains. Our camping trip there was during a stormy time, and the rapids were closed to the public because of flooding issues.

In addition to swimming, the hiking trails are worth your time. There are six trails of varying distances, with one of those trails being an equestrian trail. Our hike led us into the woods and we found a picture-perfect little spot to cool down.

Stopping here for the day for a picnic has plenty of options. Fourteen covered shelters are first come, first serve. There is also a playground that offers great fun for the kids.

Elephant Rocks State Park

There's no way to describe the look of Elephant Rocks State Park, but I'll do my best. Think huge, unique, and jaw-dropping. Made from granite that is over 1.5 billion years old, the rocks are a sight to see. They are massive rocks that lie next to one another, creating extraordinary paths and the ability to walk from the top of one stone to the next.

The Braille Trail is a fantastic trail that is created to ensure everyone can see and be a part of the rocks. The trail goes through the rocks instead of on top of them, making it an accessible option.

When your party isn't walking and leaping over and on the rocks, there are plenty of picnic tables and areas to sit down and enjoy a bite.

While there are no camping or overnight options at this park, plenty of exploring will keep you there for hours easily.

Be sure to get to the highest rock you can and stop to enjoy the view that goes for miles! It's a good idea to stay close to the kids as some stones are significant and could be dangerous if someone were to slip and fall.

Thena and Matthew are the brains behind the popular camping blog: hodgepodgehippie.com and are valuable members of the Midwest Travel Network. In addition to their love of camping and travel, they enjoy exploring nature, hiking, and tandem-biking together all over towns in the Midwest. Their love for all things that the Midwest has to offer is strong! Above all, Thena and Matthew hope that travel brings memories, happiness, and excitement and that this book helps you find and explore towns, parks, and activities waiting outside your door.

Learn more about Thena and Matthew (and their fun family travels) at HodgePodgeHippie.com

Missouri State Parks Amenities

Please confirm availability of amenities with the state park system. For more information on Missouri State Parks, visit their website at mostateparks.com

A few notes about the amenities:
- RV – Full Hookups include access to electricity, water, and sewer at the campsite.
- RV – Partial Hookups include access to electricity and water, but not sewer.
- Tent: Tent only sites available.
- Primitive: Camping in remote areas without amenities like bathrooms, picnic tables, trash cans, or any other man-made structures.
- Restrooms: Indicates the highest functional type of restroom available.
- Paddling: Boat access; this could be kayaking, canoeing, and/or powered boats.
- Swimming: Selected if swimming is available, either at a beach or a pool.

Echo Bluff State Park has an on-site lodge.

Midwest State Park Adventures

State Park Name	Hiking # of miles	Camping RV - Full Hookups	Camping RV - Partial Hookups	Camping Tent	Lodging Cabin	Lodging Yurt	Lodging Hotel/Resort
Annie and Abel Van Meter State Park	3.5+	☐	☑	☑	☐	☐	☐
Arrow Rock State Historic Site	1+	☑	☑	☑	☐	☐	☐
Bennett Spring State Park	11+	☑	☑	☑	☑	☐	☑
Big Lake State Park		☐	☑	☑	☑	☐	☐
Big Oak Tree State Park	2+	☐	☐	☐	☐	☐	☐
Big Sugar Creek State Park	3+	☐	☐	☐	☐	☐	☐
Bryant Creek State Park	4+	☐	☐	☐	☐	☐	☐
Castlewood State Park	22+	☐	☐	☐	☐	☐	☐
Crowder State Park	14+	☑	☑	☑	☐	☐	☐
Cuivre River State Park	38+	☑	☑	☑	☐	☐	☐
Current River State Park	6+	☐	☐	☐	☐	☐	☐
Don Robinson State Park	6+	☐	☐	☐	☐	☐	☐
Dr. Edmund A Babler Memorial State Park	13+	☐	☑	☑	☐	☐	☐
Echo Bluff State Park	6+	☑	☑	☑	☑	☐	☐
Edward "Ted" and Pat Jones-Confluence Point State Park	>1	☐	☐	☐	☐	☐	☐
Elephant Rocks State Park	1+	☐	☐	☐	☐	☐	☐
Finger Lakes State Park	11+	☐	☑	☑	☐	☐	☐
Graham Cave State Park	4+	☐	☑	☑	☐	☐	☐
Grand Gulf State Park	>1	☐	☐	☐	☐	☐	☐
Ha Ha Tonka State Park	13+	☐	☐	☐	☐	☐	☐
Harry S Truman State Park	3+	☐	☑	☑	☐	☐	☐
Hawn State Park	13+	☐	☑	☑	☐	☐	☐
Johnsons Shut-Ins State Park	19+	☑	☑	☑	☑	☐	☐
Katy Trail State Park	240	☐	☐	☐	☐	☐	☐
Knob Noster State Park	18+	☐	☑	☑	☐	☐	☐
Lake of the Ozarks State Park	40+	☐	☑	☑	☑	☑	☐
Lake Wappapello State Park	17+	☐	☑	☑	☑	☐	☐
Lewis and Clark State Park	0.9	☐	☑	☑	☐	☐	☐
Long Branch State Park	8+	☐	☑	☑	☐	☐	☐
Mark Twain State Park	6+	☐	☑	☑	☑	☐	☐
Meramec State Park	13+	☑	☑	☑	☑	☐	☑
Montauk State Park	2+	☐	☑	☑	☑	☐	☑
Morris State Park	2+	☐	☐	☐	☐	☐	☐
Onondaga Cave State Park	7+	☐	☑	☑	☐	☐	☐
Pershing State Park	8+	☐	☑	☑	☐	☐	☐
Pomme de Terre State Park	3+	☐	☑	☑	☑	☑	☐
Prairie State Park	12+	☐	☐	☑	☐	☐	☐
Roaring River State Park	10+	☑	☑	☑	☑	☐	☑
Robertsville State Park	3+	☐	☑	☑	☐	☐	☐
Rock Bridge Memorial State Park	19+	☐	☐	☐	☐	☐	☐
Route 66 State Park	6+	☐	☐	☐	☐	☐	☐
Sam A Baker State Park	19+	☐	☑	☑	☑	☐	☐
St. Francois State Park	16+	☐	☑	☑	☐	☐	☐
St. Joe State Park	25+	☐	☑	☑	☐	☐	☐
Stockton State Park	12+	☐	☑	☑	☑	☐	☐
Table Rock Lake State Park	12+	☑	☑	☑	☐	☑	☐
Taum Sauk Mountain State Park	13+	☐	☐	☑	☐	☐	☐
Thousand Hills State Park	12+	☐	☑	☑	☑	☐	☐
Trail of Tears State Park	11+	☑	☑	☑	☐	☐	☐

Missouri

State Park Name	Restrooms	Visitor/ Nature Center	Swimming	Paddling	Store	Picnic	Fishing
Annie and Abel Van Meter State Park	Showers	✓	☐	✓	☐	✓	✓
Arrow Rock State Historic Site	Showers	✓	☐	☐	☐	✓	✓
Bennett Spring State Park	Showers	✓	✓	✓	✓	✓	✓
Big Lake State Park	Showers	☐	☐	✓	☐	✓	✓
Big Oak Tree State Park	Vault	☐	☐	☐	☐	✓	✓
Big Sugar Creek State Park		☐	☐	☐	☐	☐	☐
Bryant Creek State Park	N/A	☐	☐	☐	☐	☐	☐
Castlewood State Park	Flush	☐	☐	☐	☐	✓	✓
Crowder State Park	Showers	☐	☐	✓	☐	✓	✓
Cuivre River State Park	Showers	✓	✓	✓	☐	✓	✓
Current River State Park	Flush	☐	☐	✓	☐	✓	✓
Don Robinson State Park	Vault	☐	☐	☐	☐	✓	☐
Dr. Edmund A Babler Memorial State Park	Showers	✓	☐	☐	☐	✓	☐
Echo Bluff State Park	Showers	☐	✓	✓	✓	✓	✓
Edward "Ted" and Pat Jones-Confluence Point State Park	Flush	☐	☐	☐	☐	☐	✓
Elephant Rocks State Park	Flush	☐	☐	☐	☐	✓	☐
Finger Lakes State Park	Showers	☐	✓	✓	☐	✓	✓
Graham Cave State Park	Showers	✓	☐	☐	☐	✓	✓
Grand Gulf State Park	Vault	☐	☐	☐	☐	✓	☐
Ha Ha Tonka State Park	Flush	☐	✓	✓	☐	✓	✓
Harry S Truman State Park	Showers	☐	✓	☐	✓	✓	✓
Hawn State Park	Showers	☐	☐	☐	☐	✓	☐
Johnsons Shut-Ins State Park	Showers	☐	✓	☐	✓	✓	✓
Katy Trail State Park	Flush	☐	☐	☐	☐	☐	☐
Knob Noster State Park	Showers	✓	☐	✓	☐	✓	✓
Lake of the Ozarks State Park	Showers	✓	✓	✓	✓	✓	✓
Lake Wappapello State Park	Showers	✓	✓	✓	☐	✓	✓
Lewis and Clark State Park	Showers	☐	☐	☐	☐	✓	✓
Long Branch State Park	Showers	☐	✓	✓	✓	✓	✓
Mark Twain State Park	Showers	☐	✓	☐	☐	✓	✓
Meramec State Park	Showers	✓	✓	✓	✓	✓	✓
Montauk State Park	Showers	☐	☐	☐	✓	✓	✓
Morris State Park	Vault	☐	☐	☐	☐	☐	☐
Onondaga Cave State Park	Showers	✓	✓	☐	✓	✓	✓
Pershing State Park	Showers	☐	☐	☐	☐	✓	✓
Pomme de Terre State Park	Showers	☐	✓	✓	✓	✓	✓
Prairie State Park	Vault	✓	☐	☐	☐	✓	☐
Roaring River State Park	Showers	✓	☐	☐	✓	✓	✓
Robertsville State Park	Showers	☐	☐	☐	☐	✓	✓
Rock Bridge Memorial State Park	Flush	☐	☐	☐	☐	✓	☐
Route 66 State Park	Flush	✓	☐	☐	☐	✓	✓
Sam A Baker State Park	Showers	✓	✓	✓	✓	✓	✓
St. Francois State Park	Showers	☐	✓	☐	☐	✓	✓
St. Joe State Park	Showers	☐	✓	✓	☐	✓	✓
Stockton State Park	Showers	☐	✓	✓	✓	✓	✓
Table Rock Lake State Park	Showers	☐	✓	☐	✓	✓	✓
Taum Sauk Mountain State Park	Vault	☐	☐	☐	☐	✓	☐
Thousand Hills State Park	Showers	☐	✓	✓	✓	✓	✓
Trail of Tears State Park	Showers	✓	✓	☐	☐	✓	✓

Midwest State Park Adventures

State Park Name	Hiking # of miles	Camping RV - Full Hookups	Camping RV - Partial Hookups	Camping Tent	Lodging Cabin	Lodging Yurt	Lodging Hotel/Resort
Wakonda State Park	15+	✓	✓	✓	☐	☐	☐
Wallace State Park	6	☐	✓	✓	☐	☐	☐
Washington State Park	8+	☐	✓	✓	✓	☐	☐
Watkins Mill State Park	7+	☐	✓	✓	☐	☐	☐
Weston Bend State Park	9+	☐	✓	✓	☐	☐	☐

State Park Name	Restrooms	Visitor/Nature Center	Swimming	Paddling	Store	Picnic	Fishing
Wakonda State Park	Showers	☐	✓	✓	☐	✓	✓
Wallace State Park	Showers	☐	☐	☐	☐	✓	✓
Washington State Park	Showers	☐	✓	✓	✓	✓	✓
Watkins Mill State Park	Showers	✓	✓	☐	☐	✓	✓
Weston Bend State Park	Showers	☐	☐	☐	☐	✓	☐

NEBRASKA

By Tim and Lisa Trudell

Nebraska embraces both nature and history with its state parks. From viewing three states at one time to stargazing at the annual Star Party at Merritt Reservoir State Recreation Area--named an International Dark Sky Park--or hiking trails through dense woods, the Cornhusker State's state parks and recreation areas number more than 75. While some recreation areas are larger than other states' parks, they haven't quite achieved rock-star status, but they're definitely worth visiting.

Across the state, you can hike, fish for trout, bass, bluegill, catfish and more, and camp or relax in a cabin, as well as swim, play on a zipline obstacle course or explore nature on horseback. Nebraska's state parks system has something for everyone.

Proud of its history, Nebraska territory has been home to more than 15 Native American nations. While the Umo Ho (Omaha), Ho-Chunk (Winnebago), iSanti Dakotah (Santee Dakota) and Usni (Cold) Ponca (Northern Ponca) are the state's four primary nations today, the Lakota, Cheyenne, Missouri, Oto, Kansas and Pawnee once lived here. Tribal history can be found across the state, but visitors will find memorials at places such as Ponca State Park and Fort Robinson State Park, the site of the killing of powerful Lakota leader Crazy Horse.

As you explore Nebraska, you'll find the landscape changes, from tall river bluffs along the Missouri River in the east to sandhills and buttes in the west. Once off the interstate, Nebraska's scenery and landscape change from flat to rolling hills and a beautiful sea of prairie grass.

Nebraska State Park Facts & Important Information

- For residents, an annual park pass is $31 and daily permits for $6. For non-residents, an annual park pass is $61 and daily permits for $12.
- The first state park was Chadron State Park in 1921 and the newest one, Mahoney opened in 1992.
- The tallest waterfall in the state can be found at Smith Falls State Park.
- Fort Robinson served as a military outlet and POW camp

A note about accessibility

Information about Nebraska state park accessibility is included in the individual park descriptions.

Nebraska State Parks Map

1. Niobrara State Park 2. Ponca State Park 3. Smith Falls State Park 4. Platte River State Park 5. Eugene T. Mahoney State Park 6. Indian Cave State Park 7. Chadron State Park 8. Fort Robinson State Park

Region: Northeast

Niobrara State Park

From a weekly bison dinner to scenic views, Niobrara State Park offers an array of fun activities and experiences. Located at the confluence of the Missouri and Niobrara rivers, Niobrara State Park features fishing, hiking, and horse trails, as well as biking and picnicking. While at the park, check out the "prehistoric" marker, which celebrates the discovery of fossils of a mosasaurus, a giant lizard that lived in the sea, growing to 30 feet long. The mosasaurus lived in the area about 70 million years ago.

With groomed trails, hiking at Niobrara State Park, a short drive west of the small town of Niobrara, hikers traverse rolling hills with views of rocky bluffs on the South Dakota side of the Missouri River.

Horseback riding enthusiasts enjoy about 120 acres of free-range riding, rather than being restricted to trails. Equestrians can also enjoy camping near their horse, as Niobrara State Park features an equestrian campground on a first come, first served basis. Horses can be kept at a nearby corral. Water must be hauled in via buckets.

The park is perfect for either a weekend getaway or a day visit. With picnic areas situated atop hills, picnickers enjoy dynamic views during their park experience. Sites include grills and covered picnic tables. Of course, day visitors have access to the park's amenities as long-term guests, including a playground and swimming area.

Anglers enjoy fishing both the Niobrara and Missouri Rivers. Taking a boat out on the "Mighty Mo" can result in hauls of catfish, carp, bluegill and trout. The Niobrara River is known for channel catfish, grass pickerel and green sunfish. Shoreline fishing is also available, and results in excellent catches. Of course, State fishing permits are required.

Each Saturday night during the summer, Niobrara State Park hosts a bison cookout. Dinner includes bison burgers and sides such as salad and beans. Diners are entertained by Western poets and storytellers. Reservations are required through the park office (402-857-3373) before noon on the day of the cookout. The dinner requires a minimum of 25 participants.

Open year-round, Niobrara State Park offers winter camping and activities such as cross-country skiing.

Niobrara State Park features lodging, camping with electricity and basic sites.

There are 20 cabins; 12 include two bedrooms, as well as furnished kitchens and screened porches. Seven cabins feature three bedrooms. Each cabin includes air conditioning and heating, bedding, and a grill. The 20th cabin is a ranch house.

Niobrara State Park features 77 electric plus sites, serving 20/30 amps. The park includes drinking water, modern restrooms, and coin-operated showers. The campground also features a dump and fill station. Sites include a grill and picnic table. Wi-Fi access is available near the shower facilities. Reservations are available for half the camper sites.

Offering 30 basic camping sites on hills around the park, campers without reservations need to check in with the park office for availability.

Each site includes a grill and a fire ring. The park's water, restrooms and showers are available.

Ponca State Park

Named for the Ponca people, who once were the dominant Indigenous nation of the area, Ponca State Park ranks as one of the most popular in Nebraska. The state's natural history is celebrated near the entrance with Towers of Time, a stone and water exhibit taking visitors from the Cretaceous period—when Nebraska was part of a prehistoric sea—to contemporary times. Three 27-foot cast stone towers trace the state's animals from sea life, such as giant fish, on to woolly mammoths and saber-toothed tigers, through wildlife that can be found today, including deer, bison, and blue heron. A water fountain and waterfall feature a four-sided fountain celebrating Nebraska's Indigenous Peoples' history.

Located at the confluence of the Big Sioux and Missouri Rivers, Ponca State Park offers an impressive view of three states - Nebraska, Iowa, and South Dakota - along the Overlook Trail. Situated on bluffs high above the waterways, Ponca State Park features more than 20 miles of trails taking hikers and bicyclists through dense woods. Along the Old Oak Trail, which runs 1.9 miles, visitors will find the oldest tree in Nebraska dating back to the 1600s. "Old Oak" is also accessible from the roadway, but requires walking down a set of wooden stairs.

Ponca State Park's wetlands offer majestic views of migratory birds. Birding tours are popular during the spring, as well as summertime naturalist-led programs. During the Halloween season, the park offers haunted hayrack rides along paths featuring "scary" decorations. The holiday season features all sorts of fun activities, including snowman-building contests and the ever-popular New Year's fruitcake toss.

Hunting and fishing are popular year-round activities. With boat launches located at the base of the park, fishing the Missouri River can be accessed by boat or shoreline. Common catches include catfish and walleye. The Eric Wiebe Shooting Complex offers ranges for weapons such as pellet gun, muzzle-loader, .22 rifles and shotgun, as well as tomahawks, archery, and slingshot. Visitors can bring their own archery equipment to the range, but the park prohibits outside firearms and will provide them for educational programs.

Ponca State Park features camping grounds and lodges, which can be reserved. With 27 cabins available year-round, four rustic cabins can be reserved April through mid-November. There are 15 cabins - mini-lodges - with four bedrooms. Each includes a bathroom, kitchen, living room, patio, big screen TV, cable, wireless internet, wood fireplace and gas grill. There are 10 two-bedroom cottages with a full kitchen, electric fireplace, gas grill, wireless internet and cable TV. Two cabins are green, featuring two bedrooms, and were constructed from straw bales. Green cabins include a kitchen, bathroom, big-screen TV, cable, wireless internet and gas grill.

Camping is allowed at Ponca State Park, with electric plus, electric and basic spots offered. Turkey Ridge features 35 electric-plus sites, while Oak Bluff has 37 locations (reservations available). Riverfront has 20 pads available on a first come, first served. Basic camping sites are available on a first-come, first-served basis.

Region: North Central

Smith Falls State Park

Enjoy a cold shower at Nebraska's tallest waterfall when you visit Smith Falls State Park. At 63 feet, Smith Falls is located on the south end of the Niobrara River, and its creek flows into the northern Nebraska river. Smith Falls may be the park's anchor, but the Valentine-area nature site is full of fun and amazing things to do.

Smith Falls' cold temperature results from spring-fed water traveling a small route among the dense shade of trees hugging the shoreline. Accessing Smith Falls requires a walk along a variety of surfaces, from gravel and grass paths to a wooden boardwalk, which takes people within a few feet of the waterfall. The walk through the canyon at the foot of the waterfall offers beautiful views of trees stretching skyward.

Visitors headed to Smith Falls cross the old Verdigre Bridge, which was relocated from the Knox County town along Highway 14. Now a pedestrian bridge crossing the river, the Verdigre Bridge was built in 1910. More than 150 feet long, the bridge was disassembled and transported to the state park in 1996. Reducing its width by 10 feet, the Verdigre Bridge is an outstanding attraction on its own, offering an excellent view as it crosses the scenic river. Stand in the middle of the bridge and soak in the amazing views of the Niobrara River.

Named for homesteader Frederic Smith, Smith Falls State Park is a popular destination for outdoor enthusiasts because it's an excellent spot for canoeing and kayak the scenic Niobrara River. Honored as a National Scenic River, the Niobrara is fairly shallow, offering the perfect environment for wading in the water, as well as conducting river floats. On any given summer day, it's common to see kayaks, canoes, tubes and inflatables floating downriver. Outfitters use the state park as a starting point for their water tours.

Since its opening in 1992, Smith Falls State Park has been a popular destination for campers. Combining the beauty of the area with the impressive night sky views of millions of stars twinkling above, the quiet of the country adds to a wonderful experience.

Don't plan to park an RV or small camper onsite, Smith Falls State Park is strictly basic camping. Reservations are required and can be made online at outdoornebraska.gov or by calling 402-471-1414. Set up a tent at the designated spot and plan for a weekend or week of living like your ancestors did, using primitive services. Smith Falls State Park includes basic restrooms, pay showers and picnic tables.

Fishing is available on the Niobrara River, with anglers nabbing catfish, trout, pike and other species. A state fishing permit is required. Shoreline fishing is popular, as well as dropping a line from a canoe or kayak.

The visitors center, at the north end of the park, with parking available, has maps available and park employees can share additional information about the state park. The center is home to a small collection of photographs, historical information, fossils and more. A modern restroom is available during business hours. The visitors center is open daily May-September.

Region: Southeast

Platte River State Park

Its picturesque waterfall may be the most charming attraction at Platte River State Park, but there's plenty to see and do at the Louisville park, located midway between Omaha and Lincoln. From hiking in densely wooded areas to an archery range and more, Platte River State Park offers beautiful scenery to wonderful nature experiences.

With about 15 miles of trails available, hikers will find themselves traversing the park through its wooded hills offering views of the Platte River, along with signs of wildlife such as deer, coyotes, bobcats, turkeys and all kinds of birds. Of course, the scenic waterfall is found along the hiking trail. While it is small, its beauty outreaches much taller ones. Mountain biking enthusiasts enjoy taking on the challenges of the trails.

Kayakers and canoe handlers enjoy spending the day on the Platte River with launch opportunities from Platte River State Park. Crawdad Creek, which feeds into Jenny Newman Lake, offers learning with a little fun as children can interact with creek inhabitants such as tadpoles, crawdads and minnows. Kids may get a little muddy.

Head to Jenny Newman Lake for fishing and paddle boating. From Memorial Day weekend through Labor Day, enjoy Platte River State Park's spray park.

Would-be cowpokes can try their hand at horseback riding during one-hour guided tours. Follow horseback riding with a little archery or learn about gun safety at the firing range at the Roger G. Sykes Outdoor Heritage Education Complex.

Climb to the top of the observation tower and soak in the picturesque views of the Platte River valley.

Platte River State Park may have some of the widest array of lodging opportunities in Nebraska. From glamping to traditional, campers can enjoy the luxuries of home or rough it with community showers and restrooms. The park was once home to two separate camps—Harriet Harding Campfire Girls Camp and Camp Esther K. Newman.

Glamping cabins feature comfortable beds in cozy bedrooms in tiny house-style cabins. Each of the cabins includes a kitchen and bathroom.

With 21 modern cabins, campers enjoy the benefits of residential-style living with full kitchenettes and bathrooms. While some of the cabins include a screened-in porch, each features a picnic table and a fire ring. Modern cabins, which are available year-round, also include linens.

Visitors step into community camping with a stay at one of the 31 camper cabins. They share shower facilities and restrooms, with four to six cabins in a pod. Visitors also bring their own silverware, dishes and pillows. Camper cabins include bed linens, a refrigerator, table and chairs, air conditioning (except for Whitetail), fire grates for cooking and a picnic table. Camper cabins are excellent choices for anyone looking for an economical stay.

Platte River State Park includes 48 full hookup facilities, with each offering 50-amp service. Pads are 20 feet wide and 50 feet long. There are 15 pull-through pads and five ADA-compliant lots. Reservations are available for 19 of the pads. Campers without reservations need to visit the park office to check availability.

Eugene Mahoney State Park

Long considered the gem of the Nebraska state park system, Eugene Mahoney State Park is situated on hills overlooking the historic Platte River. The Ashland attraction features fishing, horseback riding and hiking, as well as taking on the challenges of a zipline obstacle course. Mahoney offers year-round activities.

Mahoney State Park features six miles of hiking trails that wind through the park, among oak stands between Kiewit and Riverview lodges. A nature trail loop is located near Kiewit Lodge. Paved trails connect attractions, such as Owen Marina, James Conservatory and the Family Aquatic Center. Bicyclists need to contact the visitors center for their routes.

Offering trail rides May-Labor Day, Mahoney State Park's horseback riding includes guided tours along some of the park's attractive scenery. Rides, which cost an extra fee, start at the park's stables.

Traversing the Go Ape obstacle course involves negotiating six rope obstacle courses, each culminating with a zipline ride to the ground. Each course offers a different level of challenges, with the Go Ape course about 40 feet above the ground. Participants must be at least 49 inches tall. Climbers undergo a 20-minute prep before starting the course.

Family fun can be had at the indoor Activity Center, with its slides, tubes and net bridges and ball pits. Venture Climb offers the challenge of rock climbing without leaving the safety of the indoors. Each climber is protected by an automatic or manually-operated rope belay. The 42-foot-tall climbing wall includes a view of the park through floor-to-ceiling windows. The attraction is great for beginners and is ADA-accessible.

Outdoor activities include the Owens Marina, with paddle boats, as well as the Aquatic Center, which features tubes and slides. Miniature golf is the perfect outing for a family of would-be linksters.

Golf enthusiasts enjoy hitting a few golf balls at the John R. Lauritzen Driving Range. Buy a bucket of balls and enjoy driving the ball to your heart's content. The golf attraction is open Memorial Day weekend through Labor Day.

Anglers can fish at both Owen Marina and CenturyLink Fishing Lake. Owen Marina is a catch-and-release lake, while state fishing regulations apply at CenturyLink Fishing Lake. State fishing permits are required.

Opening in 1991, Mahoney State Park may be the most modern of Nebraska's state parks. Between a hotel-style lodge to modern camping hook-ups and quality basic camping, visitors have a variety of options in which to enjoy their stay.

Peter Kiewit Lodge offers a year-round hotel-style experience. Reservations are required for a stay at any of its 40 rooms. With an onsite restaurant, guests don't need to leave the state park during their stay. The lodge is also available for conferences, meetings and other social events.

The Crete Carrier Riverview Lodge is perfect for weekend getaways, as well as meetings and events.

With 57 cabins available, they are able to host a variety of party sizes, with 49 of them featuring two bedrooms. Five cabins have six bedrooms and three others have four sleeping rooms. Each cabin includes air conditioning/heat, a TV and a kitchen.

Indian Cave State Park

Named for the historic cave with petroglyphs, Indian Cave State Park near Shubert combines the beauty of the winding Missouri River with scenic nature trails in southeast Nebraska. With more than 20 miles of trails taking hikers through dense woods and along the river, Indian Cave State Park offers plenty of fun for weekend adventures or seasonal vacations.

The Indian Cave attraction, decimated by a cyclone bomb in 2019, reopened in 2022 with a new, accessible boardwalk. It also includes a staircase. With an 8-foot-wide viewing platform beneath the cave's entrance, visitors can appreciate the historic geological attraction, as well as enjoy views of the Missouri River.

While shoreline fishing is available, Indian Cave State Park includes a concrete boat ramp for easy river access. Once on the water, enjoy fishing for catfish and carp, among other species. Water skiing and tubing are also among the river fun.

History buffs enjoy a walk through Nebraska's past with a visit to the vintage schoolhouse and general store from the old town of St. Deroin.

Visitors can witness classic crafts being made by reenactors during the summer months.

Seasons change, as do activities at Indian Cave State Park. Fall brings out ghouls and goblins as the park is decorated for Halloween with possessed haystacks, scary figures and haunted hayrides. Visitors get involved, too, decorating RVs and campsites. Christmas comes early at Indian Cave State Park, as in July. The park's Christmas in July program features horse-drawn sleigh rides, a visit with Santa Claus and a holiday movie under the stars.

With 22 miles of trails, hikers and bicyclists enjoy impressive views of southeast Nebraska. Wildlife that may be seen include deer, beavers, woodchucks and turkeys, as well as barred owls.

Horseback riders can enjoy 16 miles of riding trails. During the summer, Indian Cave State Park hosts guided horseback rides for children six years and older. Equestrian enthusiasts can camp along the horse trails. With hitches and 12 corrals available, equestrian camping is first come, first served. Riders need to bring their own water. A water wagon is available for horses. The area includes a restroom, grill and picnic tables.

Camping is available for recreational vehicles and basic campers. Indian Cave State Park features 83 electric plus and 51 electric pads between Ash Grove and Hackberry Hollow. The camping areas include showers, modern restrooms, laundry facilities and dump and fill stations, as well as picnic tables and grills. Reservations are available for half of each area.

Basic campsites are available year-round. Showers are available in the basic camping area, as well as a water hydrant and electrical hookups. Grills and ground-level fire rings can also be found.

All campers should check in at the park entrance or office upon arrival. Those camping without reservations need to go to the park entrance booth or office upon arrival to check availability and register to camp. People arriving after hours need to register their nightly camping fees in a raised locked box called an Iron Ranger.

Region: West

Chadron State Park

Located among buttes and canyons in the panhandle, it's appropriate that Chadron became home to the first Nebraska state park. Created in 1921, Chadron State Park is home to charming rock formations, steep hills blanketed by tall ponderosa pines and veritable cottonwood trees. With 974 acres, Chadron State Park is located within a portion of Pine Ridge and the Nebraska National Forest.

With about 100 miles of trails available between Chadron State Park and the national forest, hikers and mountain bikers have their choice of routes and skill levels when traversing the landscape. Bluffs, buttes and forested paths await the most-experienced hiker, as well as the casual walker. The views are the stars of the trails.

If someone prefers to soak in the scenery from atop an equine, horseback trails are located throughout Chadron State Park. Guided tours, taking riders through the backwoods and along the hills of the state park, are available for visitors six years and older. Horseback tours are offered Memorial Day weekend through Labor Day, with reduced hours starting mid-August.

Starry, starry nights await campers with breathtaking views of stars going on for infinity on a clear night. With silhouettes of pines and buttes in the foreground, star gazing at Chadron State Park offers a special experience.

Anglers can fish for trout in Chadron Creek and the park's lagoon. Fishing is also available at nearby lakes such as Whitney Lake, which is about 30 minutes west of the state park. Here, you'll find channel catfish and trout, as well as other species.

Head to Chadron State Park's swimming pool and enjoy an impressive view of the ponderosa pines while playing a game of "Marco, Polo" or just enjoy a little sun on the lounge chairs next to the pool. The swimming pool is open noon-6 p.m. daily Memorial Day weekend through mid-August when it's open only on the weekend.

Visitors to Chadron State Park are encouraged to enjoy paddle boats on the lake or play a game of horseshoe. Other activities at the state park include archery, sand volleyball and disc golf. The park is also home to softball fields, playgrounds and winter sledding hills.

With 22 cabins available, visitors can enjoy air conditioning/heating during their visits. Each cabin features a full kitchen with silverware and cooking utensils, as well as blankets and towels.

With 70 pads available for recreational vehicles and campers, Chadron State Park is an excellent spot for a spring-fall visit. Each pad offers electric services. Amenities at the park include showers, laundry, picnic tables and grills, as well as children's playgrounds.

Basic campers can use one of 18 sites around Chadron State Park. Park officials can often find a few additional spots, if necessary.

Reservations are available for half of the sites, with the rest on a first come, first served basis. Campers without reservations need to stop at the park's office to check availability. After-hour entries require completing camp information and inserting it in the secured box, known as an Iron Ranger.

Fort Robinson State Park

Fort Robinson State Park has lived several lives over the years, beginning as a military outpost during westward expansion. Opened as Camp Robinson in 1873, soldiers served here after the federal government relocated the Red Cloud Indian Agency to the area. The agency worked with Lakota and Dakota (Sioux) Native Americans in the area.

Fort Robinson was the site of the 1877 killing of Chief Crazy Horse, a Lakota tribal leader who was revered by Native Americans. The military said he was killed while resisting arrest. Native Americans have long believed he was murdered by an American soldier. A monument honoring Crazy Horse is located near the site of his death.

The fort also served as a regiment for Buffalo Soldiers (African-American cavalry members).

Nebraska

The role of Fort Robinson evolved during the 1900s. In 1919, the fort's role was reassigned as a quartermaster remount depot, with horse and mule units trained here. During World War II, German prisoners of war were kept there. Following WWII, the fort closed and was eventually turned over to the state.

Besides its history, Fort Robinson State Park has a lot to offer, from trail rides with panoramic views to outstanding fishing. While it's a perfect getaway for a long weekend, it's easy to spend a week exploring one of Nebraska's best state parks.

With more than 20 miles of trails, as well as access to Nebraska National Forest, Fort Robinson State Park provides outstanding riding opportunities. Visitors can also enjoy an Old West stagecoach ride around the park's main area.

Hiking enthusiasts can explore the park's over more than 60 miles of trails. Mountain bikers can challenge the park's terrain with about 20 miles of trails.

Anglers cast lines at 10 ponds and cold-water streams as they seek a bounty of rainbow and tiger trout, big mouth bass and bluegill, among other fish.

Amidst heavenly scenery, the state park offers Jeep tours during the summer. Taking riders among buttes and unique geologic formations, tours offer memorable experiences.

Lodging at Fort Robinson is as unique as its history. Consider staying at the historic enlisted soldiers' quarters or the officer's hall, sleeping between two and 20 people. For large groups or family reunions, Comanche Hall sleeps 60 people. The Historic Lodge has 22 rooms.

Fort Robinson State Park also features cabins with kitchens, baths and bedrooms. Larger cabins also feature living rooms. Each cabin includes blankets, towels, stoves, refrigerators, silverware and cooking utensils.

Campers enjoy full hookups, electric plus, and basic campsites. Red Cloud Campground has 74 full hookup campsites, while Soldier Creek Campground features 77 electric plus. Mare Barn campground offers 20 electric plus, and four with full hookups. The park has 20 basic campsites.

Amenities include modern restrooms, showers, drinking water, a dump and fill station, picnic tables and shelters. A coin-operated laundry is located near Mare Barn.

Camping reservations are available for half of the electrical campsites. All other camping is first come, first served. Visitors without reservations need to stop at the visitor's office.

Tim and Lisa Trudell, residents of southwest Omaha, own the travel blog The Walking Tourists. Lisa was a travel professional for more than 16 years and currently works as an online marketing specialist for an in-home care company. Tim is a freelance writer and an enrolled member of the Santee Dakota Nation. A US Air Force veteran, Tim currently writes for outlets such as Indian Country Today, Nebraska Magazine, Flatwater Free Press, Next Avenue, TravelAwaits, Extended Weekend Getaways, Nebraska Life and Living Here Midwest. He is also the photographer, editor and author of the blog. When not traveling they love to continue to share their love of their city and state. You can follow them at @100ThingsOmaha or thewalkingtourists.com

Nebraska State Parks Amenities

Please confirm availability of amenities with the state park system For more information on Nebraska State Parks, visit their website at www.outdoornebraska.gov

A few notes about the amenities:
- RV – Full Hookups include access to electricity, water, and sewer at the campsite.
- RV – Partial Hookups include access to electricity and water, but not sewer.
- Tent: Tent only sites available.
- Restrooms: Indicates the highest functional type of restroom available.
- Paddling: Boat access; this could be kayaking, canoeing, and/or powered boats.
- Swimming: Selected if swimming is available, either at a beach or a pool.

Midwest State Park Adventures

State Park Name	Hiking # of miles	Camping RV - Full Hookups	Camping RV - Partial Hookups	Tent	Lodging Cabin	Lodge
Chadron State Park	100+	☐	✓	✓	✓	☐
Fort Robinson State Park	20+	✓	✓	✓	✓	☐
Indian Cave State Park	22	☐	✓	✓	✓	☐
Mahoney State Park	2.3	✓	✓	✓	✓	✓
Niobrara State Park	14	☐	✓	✓	✓	☐
Platte River State Park	17	✓	☐	✓	✓	☐
Ponca State Park	22	☐	✓	✓	✓	✓
Smith Falls State Park	5+	☐	☐	✓	☐	☐

State Park Name	Restrooms	Visitor/ Nature Center	Swimming	Paddling	Store	Picnic	Fishing
Chadron State Park	Showers	✓	✓	✓	✓	✓	✓
Fort Robinson State Park	Showers	✓	✓	✓	✓	✓	✓
Indian Cave State Park	Showers	✓	☐	☐	☐	✓	✓
Mahoney State Park	Showers	✓	✓	✓	✓	✓	✓
Niobrara State Park	Showers	✓	✓	☐	☐	✓	✓
Platte River State Park	Showers	✓	✓	✓	✓	✓	✓
Ponca State Park	Showers	✓	✓	✓	✓	✓	✓
Smith Falls State Park	Showers	✓	☐	✓	✓	✓	✓

NORTH DAKOTA

By Alicia Underlee Nelson

State parks look a little different in North Dakota. That's because just one percent of the state's land is classified as forest, according to the North Dakota Game and Fish Department. So while you'll certainly find a few shady woodland trails within our borders, those sun dappled footpaths are only the beginning. North Dakota's State Park system showcases a variety of habitats in its 13 parks.

The most dramatic vistas are out west, where weathered badlands bluffs reveal colorful striations of rust and ochre, black and bone. Rugged, arid, and otherworldly, this almost alien landscape couldn't be more different than the rolling prairies of the east, where songbirds chatter and shy wildflowers peek through the prairie grasses that ripple like the waves on Devils Lake and Lake Sakakawea. These massive bodies of water boast an astonishing 1,875 miles of shoreline and are home to four state parks that make it easy to get out on the water.

The prettiest tree-lined trails connect pristine glacial lakes along the Canadian border and wind through river bottom forests in the eastern and central parts of the state. We North Dakotans are a hardy bunch, so when the snow falls, we just trade our hiking boots, bikes, and watercraft for snowshoes, cross-country skis, kicksleds, and skishoes, which you can rent from several state parks. (Warm weather rentals—including boats, kayaks, canoes, and stand-up paddleboards—are available, too.)

Educational opportunities abound. Visit a reconstructed Native American village, tour a frontier fort, or see historic buildings from the homestead era. Rangers lead guided hikes and paddling excursions and teach you how to identify wildlife, spot wildflowers, and even make syrup. You can appreciate nature from a replica streetcar, behind the wheel of a boat, or while twirling across the floor at a square dance. And when you finally get tired, you can bunk in a cabin, a farmhouse—even a yurt or a covered wagon.

There's so much to do in the North Dakota State Park system. Just pick a spot on the map to choose your first adventure.

North Dakota State Park Facts & Important Information

- You can step onto the North Country National Scenic Trail in Lake Sakakawea State Park and walk all the way to Vermont. A section also runs through Fort Ransom State Park.
- North Dakota is a geocaching hotspot. Hunt for hidden treasures at Cross Ranch, Fort Stevenson, Fort Ransom, Grahams Island, Icelandic, Lake Metigoshe, Lewis and Clark and Turtle River State Parks using geocaching.com, the free geocaching app, or borrow a GPS unit from participating parks.

North Dakota

- Park rangers engage young learners with a YouTube series, printable activity booklets, a passport program, and activities. Find resources at parkrec.nd.gov/take-home-learning.
- Find horse trails, horse camping options, and corrals at Fort Ransom, Fort Abraham Lincoln, Sully Creek and Little Missouri State Parks. A daily permit costs $6 per horse. An annual permit runs $30 per horse.
- The daily entrance fee is $7 per vehicle. Annual single vehicle passes are $35. (Seniors over and veterans with service-related disabilities can apply for discounts.) Annual family permits cost $55.
- Cardholders can check out state park passes from most North Dakota public libraries to visit for free.
- Modern plus campsites contain water, electric, and sewer hook-ups. Modern campsites offer water and electric. Most primitive campsites only include a camping pad, although some offer water or electric. Contact the specific park for details.
- You can put a tent on any campsite type. Some parks also have dedicated tent campgrounds.
- Campsite reservations can be made within 95 days of arrival. Reserve yurts, cabins, and other specialty lodging up to a year in advance.
- Towels and bed linens are not included in your yurt, cabin or specialty lodging reservation. Bring your own.

A note about accessibility

Accessibility at North Dakota state parks is a bit of a patchwork. But many parks are currently working to make even more spaces ADA-compliant.

Generally speaking, visitor centers and at least one comfort station or vault toilet will be open to all guests. All of the public buildings at Fort Abraham Lincoln State Park except the Custer house are ADA-accessible.

Eight of the 13 parks offer at least one ADA-accessible full-service cabin, camping cabin, or yurt. These lodging options are detailed in each park's section. Campsites within the North Dakota State Park system are level, packed gravel and well-manicured grass, so they're navigable for many people with mobility aids, but not truly ADA-compliant

The state's only trak wheelchair is housed at Fort Stevenson State Park. The park also offers a ramp to help guests board boats. Call the park directly at 701-337-5576 to reserve. Contact 701-328-5357 for general accessibility questions.

North Dakota State Parks Map

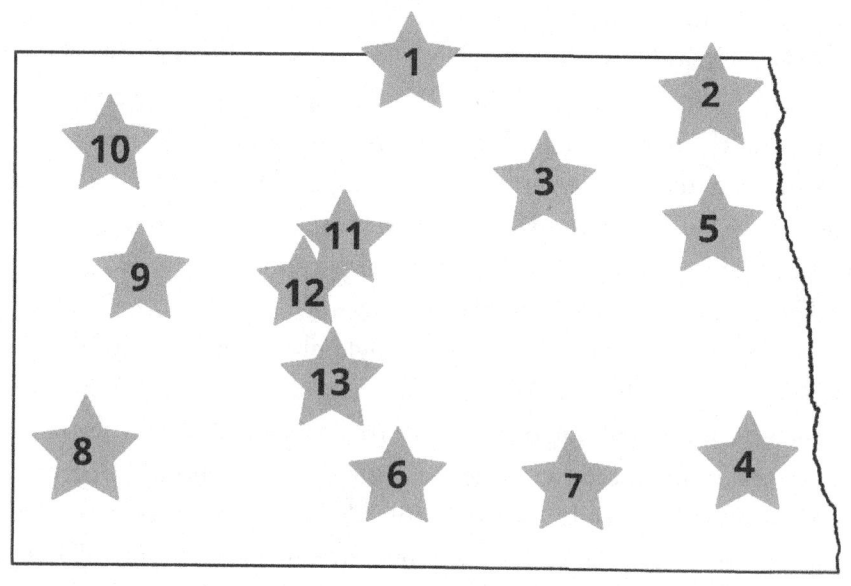

1. Lake Metigoshe State Park 2. Icelandic State Park 3. Grahams Island State Park
4. Fort Ransom State Park 5. Turtle River State Park 6. Fort Abraham Lincoln State Park
7. Beaver Lake State Park 8. Sully Creek State Park 9. Little Missouri State Park
10. Lewis and Clark State Park 11. Fort Stevenson State Park 12. Lake Sakakawea State Park
13. Cross Ranch State Park

Region: North

Lake Metigoshe State Park

You'll find Lake Metigoshe State Park at the very top of the state, just north of Bottineau, hidden in the rolling hills of the Turtle Mountains. This forested enclave is gorgeous in every season. It contains a chain of sparkling glacial lakes that spans the border between North Dakota and Manitoba, so you can launch a boat, kayak, or canoe in the United States soil and sail into Canadian waters.

Rent a canoe or kayak right in the park to explore the water trail anchored by School Section Lake. For an international adventure, take the Eramosh Lake portage and paddle in both the U.S. and Canada. It's quiet except for the occasional splash of a beaver and red-wing blackbirds calling from the cattails.

Lake Metigoshe is much larger (1,544-acres, to be exact) so there's plenty of room for motorized boats. Use the park's two-lane boat ramp and spend the day fishing, tubing, water-skiing, and making waves on a personal watercraft. The park's three fishing docks make it easy to catch northern pike, bluegills, crappies, walleye and perch without a boat. There's also a swimming beach near the playground.

The park offers nearly 14 miles of trails for hikers. Most are relatively flat, so they're open to cyclists as well. Highlights include the 3-mile Old Oak Nature Trail, North Dakota's first National Recreation Trail. Grab a brochure at the trailhead or the park office to learn about the wetlands, forest groves, and meadows along the route and throughout the park.

Look for delicate violets and the white blossoms of false Solomon's seal in spring and goldenrod and purple fireweed during the summer. Downy woodpeckers tap and squirrels and chipmunks scurry. Foragers can taste (but not harvest) wild strawberries, juneberries, chokecherries, beaked hazelnuts, and wild sarsaparilla. Lake Metigoshe Outdoor Learning Center offers workshops and hands-on learning opportunities in spring, summer and fall. Geocaching is a popular pastime all year long.

The park's three campgrounds stay busy through the fall, when the bur oak, quaking aspen, green ash and balsam poplars erupt into a riot of yellow, gold and honey brown foliage. Select a shady spot from 85 modern campsites, 39 primitive campsites, and three group sites. Parties of 20 or more can bunk in the dorms.

Four year-round, full-service cabins provide creature comforts like full kitchens and indoor bathrooms. Three are ADA-accessible and include gas fireplaces. Two rustic camping cabins (including a hike-in cabin in the backcountry without water or electricity) and a handicap-accessible yurt contain more basic amenities like charcoal grills or a wood burning stove.

Lake Metigoshe State Park glitters under newly fallen snow. The entire trail network is groomed for snowshoeing and skiing. Rent skis, snowshoes, kicksleds, or skishoes rentals at the warming house near the sledding hill. Ice fishing is popular and a 3.7-mile section of the Peace Garden Snowmobile Trail runs through the park. When you're done playing in the snow, relax by a crackling fire at a cabin or yurt just steps from the trail.

Icelandic State Park

The shady grounds of Icelandic State Park attract nature lovers, pioneer history fans, and camping enthusiasts from both sides of the U.S./Canadian border. Find this 912-acre park perched on the shore of Lake Renwick, five miles west of Cavalier in the northeastern corner of the state.

The four-mile trail system (most of which is groomed for cross-country skiing and snowshoeing) weaves through the evergreens, along the banks of the Tongue River, and deep into the 200-acre Gunlogson Nature Preserve. A series of pretty footbridges crosses streams and springs, whisking you past rushes, ferns, and cheery marsh marigolds. Hikers might spot rare birds like the pileated woodpecker or see river otters and beavers splashing in the water. A dozen kicksleds are available for rent when the snow falls.

Some trails pass by the historic buildings which highlight homesteading history. The Pioneer Heritage Center includes exhibits and a genealogy library. Annual events like a pancake breakfast at Hallson Church and square dancing at Akra Hall allow visitors to step back in time.

Placid Lake Renwick is a perfect place to take up water sports. Rent kayaks, a canoe, or stand-up paddle boards by the hour or for the day. Families build sandcastles on the swimming beach, fish from the dock, and picnic under the towering oak trees.

The large campground is one of the largest in the State Park system. It offers 140 modern campsites, 10 primitive campsites, seven group sites, and three camping cabins with air conditioning, electricity, refrigerators, fire rings, and picnic tables.

Grahams Island State Park

Located on the ever-changing shores of Devils Lake, 18 miles west of the city with the same name, Grahams Island State Park is an angler's dream. People come from all over the world to fish for walleye, perch, white bass, and northern pike in these storied waters and to compete in regional and national fishing tournaments. So Grahams Island State Park (no, there's no apostrophe) caters to anglers all year long.

The four-lane boat ramp with five courtesy docks keeps lake traffic moving and the bait shop stocks anything you might have forgotten. You can fuel up and use the fish cleaning station right in the park. There's a swimming beach on the property and it's common to see people shore fishing too.

Play a game of horseshoes or volleyball after a day on the water. Or take a short, 2.1-mile hike. (Three miles of cross-country skiing trails open each winter.) You can rent two picnic shelters under the oaks or let your pups run in the leash-free dog park.

The sheltered campground is shady and cool in the summer. Six camping cabins each sleep five and offer air conditioning, heat, electricity, refrigerators and fire rings.

And since the fish still bite when Devils Lake freezes over, Graham's Island State Park offers the only non-seasonal campground in the North Dakota State Park system. It offers 38 modern plus campsites (it's one of the rare parks that includes sewer hook-ups), 70 modern campsites, nine primitive sites, and several group sites.

Region: East

Fort Ransom State Park

Eastern North Dakota isn't all prairies and farm fields. Head to Fort Ransom State Park when you're craving a little chlorophyll. This heavily wooded spot sits along the Sheyenne River, near the city of Fort Ransom. It's also a stop along the Sheyenne River Valley National Scenic Byway, a

63-mile route that links historical sites, mom and pop shops, and picturesque vistas between Valley City and Lisbon.

See the park from the river in a canoe or kayak. Bring your own or rent a kayak. (Life jackets and paddles are included here and at all North Dakota state parks.) Staff can pick you up 5.2 miles downstream for an additional fee.

The roughly 1-mile Little Twig Nature Trail offers an interpretive overview of the park's habitats, which include woodlands thick with green ash and American elm, clusters of mighty oak trees, and mixed-prairie meadows where wildflowers and big bluestem grasses sway. Birders come to spot black and white bobolinks, several types of swallows, red-tailed hawks, and black-capped chickadees.

Most of the nearly 16-mile trail system is relatively flat grass or dirt, so it's suitable for beginners and open to hikers, snowshoers, mountain bikers, cross-country skiers, and horseback riders. (Skis are available for rent by the day if you need them.). A few steeper sections climb through the trees and up the prairie slopes for a bit of a challenge. Footbridges cross Bjorn Creek, offering shady spots with a soothing soundtrack of running water.

A wide and easy 2.2-mile segment along the Sheyenne River is the most famous stretch of trail in Fort Ransom State Park. It's part of the North Country National Scenic Trail (NCT), a 4,800-mile interstate trail with one end in Vermont and the other in Lake Sakakawea State Park in central North Dakota.

The riverside campground is a peaceful place to relax and unwind. Most of the 39 modern campsites (with electric and water) and nine of the 20 primitive campsites (that offer electricity) are equestrian sites that include corrals. There's also an off-leash dog park and 11 group campsites.

Two spacious, handicap-accessible yurts sleep up to six and include all the comforts of home, including heat, air conditioning and electric outlets, a gas fireplace, a deck for soaking up the summer sun, and a full kitchen and bathroom. A small cabin sleeps two.

Fort Ransom State Park also boasts two unique forms of lodging that you won't find anywhere else in the North Dakota State Park system. Six people can sleep inside Bjone House, a cozy farmhouse with a deck, kitchen, and bathroom. If you prefer an earlier phase of pioneer history, book a stay in the Percheron Wagon. This covered wagon is equipped with air conditioning, a refrigerator and microwave, so you can try glamping, 1880s style. It sleeps four.

This park's homesteading history comes alive during the annual Sodbuster Days celebrations in July and September. Guests can watch haying, carpentry, and threshing demos and hear old-fashioned music. Rangers also lead regular Sunne Farm homestead tours during summer weekends.

Turtle River State Park

Wooded valleys keep Turtle River State Park shady in the summer and sheltered in the winter, so this forested valley is used for outdoor recreation all year long. Find it outside Arvilla, 20 miles west of Grand Forks.

The Turtle River is the heart of the park. It's full of northern pike and stocked with trout, so bring your fly-fishing gear. Water and trees are scarce among the farm fields of eastern North Dakota, so nearly 100 bird species breed here. Dozens more use Turtle River State Park as a rest stop during spring and fall migration, attracting birders from all over the region.

A 12-mile trail network crisscrosses the river, runs across the prairie, through wetlands, and along the riverbanks. It's open for hiking, cycling, snowshoeing, and skiing. The sledding hill and warming house are busy when the snow falls and geocaching attracts treasure hunters all year long.

Woodland Lodge's kitchen and dining hall holds 100 for meetings and reunions. Visitors can also rent a conference room in the Chalet. One picnic shelter is large enough for 40-50 guests. The second can hold up to 300.

The large campground includes 65 modern campsites, 26 primitive sites with electric hook-ups, and 3 modern group campsites. But the 12 Woodland Cabins are the stars of the show. Sleep in heated and air-conditioned comfort with electricity and a full bathroom. Ten of the duplex-style units sleep six people. Four handicap-accessible units accommodate four or five campers. Two units are available year-round.

Region: South

Fort Abraham Lincoln State Park

Indigenous roots and U.S. military history intersect at Fort Abraham Lincoln State Park, where the mighty Missouri River and the Heart River meet. Established in 1907, this is North Dakota's oldest state park. Find it just outside of the capital, Bismarck, seven miles south of Mandan.

The region's earliest residents inspired the city's name. "The People of the first Man" (the Mandan) have lived here for centuries. A thriving settlement of up to 1,000 people once stood within the park's boundaries, but it was already abandoned when Lewis and Clark sailed by on the Missouri in 1804. Now the reconstructed On-A-Slant Village (Miti O-pa-e-resh in Mandan) is a stop on the Lewis and Clark National Historic Trail. You can take a self-guided tour of the earthlodges, which kept extended families warm in the winter and cool in the summer, and learn more about the farmers, anglers, hunters, artisans, and traders who lived here.

The Visitor Center displays Mandan artifacts, as well as items that reference Lewis and Clark, and the site's heyday as a frontier military post. Lt. Col. George Armstrong Custer served here from 1873 until his death at the Battle of the Little Bighorn in 1876. The original 78 buildings were dismantled, but the Custer home, the stables, the commanding officer's quarters, a central barracks, granary, and commissary have been reconstructed.

Historic sites are open May through mid-September. Learn from costumed guides at the Custer house and take a guided tour of the officer's quarters. (Purchase tour passes at the Visitor Center or Commissary) Then stroll through the infantry post and climb the blockhouse for soaring views of the glinting rivers just beyond the earthlodge village.

Savor the same striking views from almost 19 miles of dirt, grass, or hard-packed single-track trails that climb up the buttes, cut through thickets, buffaloberry and snowberry shrubs, and descend among the cottonwoods along the river. Open to hikers, cyclists, equestrians, and snowshoers (not skiers), these are some of the only trails in mostly flat state where you'll encounter an incline. Keep an eye out for silvery sage, prolific prairie roses (North Dakota's State Flower), and the occasional deer in the underbrush. Listen to bobolinks and the western meadowlark (the State Bird) singing on the hilltop prairie.

Trail running sessions and group hikes that coincide with holidays are well-attended. The Haunted Fort serves up scares during October weekends.

Ride to and from the park in historic style aboard the Fort Lincoln Trolley. The nine-mile journey crosses three bridges from the 1880s in streetcars like the ones running in Bismarck a century ago. It departs from 2000 3rd St. SE in Mandan during summer afternoons. Don't forget to shop for souvenirs, history books, a snack, or fair-trade coffee at the Commissary Store before you leave.

The riverside campground includes 82 modern campsites with water and electric and 19 water-only sites. (Four are equestrian sites and include corral access.) There are also two seasonal camping cabins that each accommodate five. One is ADA-accessible.

Beaver Lake State Park

Soak up every second of summer sunshine at Beaver Lake State Park, where you can boat, camp, paddle, and swim under an endless prairie sky. This peaceful park is located in Wishek, deep in the heart of German-

Russian country in southern North Dakota. The park is a Depression-era Works Progress Administration (WPA) project built on top of an old horse racetrack, once one of the fastest in the state.

Pick up locally made sausage from Stan's Supermarket or Ashley Supervalu for your picnic. Beaver Lake State Park offers plenty of shady spots and two picnic shelters to choose from.

There are over 5 miles of hiking and cycling trails, but the lake is the main draw. Use the boat ramp to get out on the water and fish for perch or northern pike. Or splash and sun yourself on the swimming beach. (There are showers and bathrooms available if you just come for the day.) Renting a single or double kayak is a fun way to see the lake. Daylight stretches deep into the evening here, so you might as well spring for the day rental.

Choose from 25 modern campsites with water and electric or five primitive campsites with just electric hook-ups. (There are three group campsites too.)

Each of the three, ADA-accessible camping cabins sleep up to five people. Amenities include electricity, heat and air-conditioning, a fridge and microwave, and a picnic table and fire ring so you can enjoy the outdoors well after the spectacular prairie sunsets fade.

Region: West

Sully Creek State Park

Location matters. And Sully Creek State Park's location is better than most, tucked in between North Dakota's busiest tourist attractions and some of the state's most stunning scenery. But most visitors (and even many residents) don't even know it's there.

This rustic park is nestled at the foot of a badlands butte, just over two miles south of the shops, eateries, and entertainment in the tiny western town of Medora and the entrance to Theodore Roosevelt National Park. It's roughly the same distance from Bully Pulpit, one of America's Top

100 Public Golf Courses, which offers scenic vistas and serene river views. But this modest park, with its soaring bluffs, rusty red gravel roads, and silent stillness, feels like it's a world away from civilization.

An unassuming campground keeps the focus on the scenery. The littlest campers wade and splash in Sully Creek, which runs along its eastern edge. Older and more adventurous visitors paddle the Little Missouri River, which makes up the campground's western boundary. This free-flowing, 274-mile waterway is North Dakota's only State Scenic River and the park's canoe and kayak launch is a popular departure point in the spring, when water levels are higher.

Anglers can try fishing for catfish, carp, and bullheads from the shore. Anyone over 16 needs to purchase a fishing license (available online) from the North Dakota Game and Fish Department. Kids under 16 can fish without a license as long as they're accompanied by a license holder.

The park also provides easy access to the Maah Daah Hey Trail, one of the most stunning single-track trails in the United States. Hikers, mountain bikers, and equestrians follow the trail as it weaves 144 miles south through the badlands, crosses the Little Missouri River just northwest of Sully Creek State Park, and moves onto the rolling plains of the nearby Little Missouri National Grassland.

The views along this section of the trail are breathtaking--sometimes literally, if you've rented a mountain bike from Dakota Cyclery or brought your own. But the effort of climbing a particularly steep stretch is well worth it. The trail hugs the ridgeline, offering sweeping views of the colorful cliffs and the Little Missouri snaking through the valley.

Many people tackle the trail on horseback, so almost half of Sully Creek's 40-spot campground is dedicated to equestrian campsites, which include corrals. Choose from 16 modern campsites (6 are equestrian sites), 14 primitive campsites (2 are for groups), and 10 modern group equestrian campsites. Water is available at spigots near the park entrance—for everyone, both horses and humans. Vault toilets, a dump station, and shower facilities are available.

Take more water than you think you'll need, fill up often, and tell someone where you're going. Sully Creek State Park is dry enough to support cacti, yucca, and rattlesnakes. Cell phone coverage can be spotty, and water stations along the Maah Daah Hey are limited. Buy supplies before you arrive; there's no grocery store in Medora.

Little Missouri State Park

For a truly rugged badlands experience, visit Little Missouri State Park. It's located along a curve in the Little Missouri River, 17 miles north of Killdeer. The bluffs are still being sculpted by wind and water, so their colorful contours slowly shift with time.

Perch on the platform above the river basin to take photos and spot jackrabbits, mule deer, red foxes—and maybe even an elusive bobcat or coyote. Bring binoculars to watch bald eagles, Cooper's hawks, golden eagles, and prairie falcons or rent one of the three shelters for a picturesque picnic.

For badlands views few visitors ever see, explore over 45 miles of trails, which are only open to hikers and horseback riders. These trails climb the chalky buttes and descend deeper into the badlands for a glimpse of wild turkeys, tiny horned toads, prickly pear cacti, wild crocuses and pasque flowers in the spring and—if you're lucky—the rare wood lily. Some trails are challenging, so bring lots of water and pace yourself.

This seasonal oasis is only open May through October, so reserve your spot early. There are 28 modern campsites that only include electricity, three primitive sites, and a handful of group shelters for overnight camping. Amenities include a hay shed, round pen, and corrals for the horses and vault toilets, a dump station, and shower house for campers.

People come to Little Missouri State Park to reconnect with nature, to unplug and unwind. The silence and serenity linger long after you leave.

Lewis and Clark State Park

Get four landscapes in one at Lewis and Clark State Park, 19 miles southeast of Willison near Epping, in the northwestern corner of the state. Climb a badlands butte, trek through woody draws, and watch birds and butterflies flit between the blazing stars and coneflowers in the largest stretch of native mixed grass prairie of any North Dakota State Park. The self-guided Nature Trail (a route so old you can see ruts from covered wagon wheels) also contains an accessible boardwalk.

The water draws visitors like a magnet. The park sits on an upper bay of Lake Sakakawea, the third largest man-made reservoir in the nation. This massive lake is 180 miles long, with more shoreline than California.

Catch northern pike, walleye and sauger from its seemingly endless waters. The marina offers slip rentals, a four-lane boat ramp, fish cleaning station, and fuel. Trader's Bay Visitors Center stocks snacks, tackle, and supplies.

Rangers showcase aquatic species and share what life was like when the Lewis and Clark expedition passed through. Relax on the swimming beach, rent a kayak or canoe, or test your balance on a stand-up paddle board.

Campers can choose 43 modern plus campsites (including two group sites) with water, sewer and electric. There are also 50 modern sites (three for groups), eight primitive campsites, and two climate-controlled camping cabins. One is ADA-accessible.

Most of the 5.6-mile trail system is groomed for winter recreation and kids love the sledding hill. Rent snowshoes or fat tire bikes right in the park.

Region: Central

Fort Stevenson State Park

Kites bob in the breeze, buoyed by the same wind that propels elegant sail boats and darting windsurfers across a broad expanse of water that seems to stretch all the way to the horizon line. This charming scene unfolds every day at Fort Stevenson State Park, which juts out on a peninsula between two bays of Lake Sakakawea near Garrison.

Garrison bills itself as the Walleye Capital of the World, but people come here to fish for sauger, northern pike, white bass, and yellow perch too. The park welcomes them with a premium gas dock, sewage pump out service, a fish cleaning station, boat storage, and not one but two marinas. Two multi-lane boat ramps with courtesy docks provide easy access to de Trobriand Bay and the deep waters of Garrison Bay.

No boat? No worries. Fort Stevenson State Park is the only park in the North Dakota system that rents motorized boats, so you can take a 16 or 17-foot fishing boat or a 22-foot pontoon out for the day.

You can also check out paddleboats, canoes, kayaks, and stand-up paddle boards to see the bluffs from the water or rent an aqua pad to jump, play, and sun yourself on your own floating island.

Spend the afternoon on the swimming beach, then treat yourself to burgers, pizza, and sandwiches at the Sunset Grill restaurant. The marina store stocks snacks and drinks, bait and tackle, camping gear and plenty of ice cream.

Hike or bike almost 10 miles of trails that connect shrublands, woody ravines, towering ponderosa pines, tree plantings in the arboretum, and stretches of native prairie. Some of the prettiest trails trace the lake's shoreline and look out over the bay.

This is the home of the only trak wheelchair in the North Dakota State Park system, which means everyone can get out and enjoy the trails. Call the park at 701-337-5576 to reserve the trak chair or an ADA-compliant ramp that'll help you board your boat.

All but 0.7-miles of the trail system are groomed for cross-country skiing and snowshoeing, so they're open in every season. Rent snowshoes, cross-country skis, kicksleds, or fat tire bikes to go play in the snow. Bike rentals include helmets.

Fort Stevenson State Park's calendar is packed with special events. Come for Maple Sugaring Days in the spring or bring your kite to Sky Fest, an annual festival where expert kite flyers pilot massive kites over Memorial Day weekend. Cannons fire during Frontier Military Days, as living history demonstrations bring the park's past to life. The

Guardhouse Interpretive Center displays additional military history exhibits.

Campers can choose from 55 modern plus campsites (which include sewer, water, and electric), 74 modern campsites (including 18 for groups), and 17 primitive sites. Three camping cabins each sleep five and include air conditioning, heat, electricity and a refrigerator and charcoal grill. Whether you stay overnight or make it a day trip, make sure you stay to watch the sunset paint Lake Sakakawea's waters with bold strokes of orange, violet, and rose.

Lake Sakakawea State Park

It's wild to think that you can step onto the North Country National Scenic Trail in Lake Sakakawea State Park and walk 4,800 miles across the country. The nation's longest continuous hiking trail begins (or ends!) by the lakeside Visitor Center in this unassuming park outside Pick City. While this storied 1.78-mile stretch of trail draws through-hikers and the park is located on the Lewis and Clark National Historic Trail, most North Dakotans come here to go fishing, boating, and camping.

Lake Sakakawea is teeming with walleye, northern pike, sauger, trout, small-mouth bass, and even chinook salmon, which are raised at The National Fish Hatchery right next door. Come for the Great Planers Trout and Salmon Derby in the summer or try ice fishing in the winter.

Two boat ramps (one single and one multi-lane) provide easy access to the 368,000-acre lake. Courtesy docks, a fish cleaning station, gas dock, pump-out service, boat and camper storage, and a full-service marina make life easier for anglers. The Marina Store (open Memorial Day-Labor Day) rents life jackets and stocks bait, tackle, camping gear, souvenirs, and hand-dipped ice cream.

Beat the heat on the swimming beach, play a game of volleyball or horseshoes, or hike or bike 5.06 miles of trails. Then watch the sailboats and windsurfers glide across the water.

The campground is the largest of any North Dakota State Park. It contains 149 modern campsites, 42 primitive campsites, 10 group campsites, and two camping cabins that sleep five. One is ADA-accessible.

Cross Ranch State Park

The last free-flowing stretch of the Missouri River in North Dakota runs right by Cross Ranch State Park. Aside from the constantly shifting sandbars, the river view from this quiet park in Center hasn't changed much since Indigenous villages thrived along its banks and the Lewis and Clark expedition sailed its waters. This is a place where bison still roam.

Fish for catfish, salmon, pike, trout, bass, and walleye. Or rent a canoe or kayak and paddle two miles from the main campground to the boat ramp or try a nine-mile run from the city of Washburn. Contact the park staff to arrange transportation for an additional fee.

Nearly 17 miles of trails traverse the park and the Cross Ranch Preserve. Most are open for mountain biking, and all but two miles are groomed for winter recreation. Rent cross-country skis and snowshoes from the park office or bring your own. Geocaches are hidden throughout the park.

Look for bison along the 2-mile TNC Self-Guided Nature Trail and pass riverside Lewis and Clark campsites along the Ma-ak-oti "Old Village" trail. Some trails move through wooded channels and climb bluffs for peaceful river views. Others cross the nature preserve, where rare butterflies like the Ottoe skipper and regal fritillary thrive, and end at the backcountry campground.

If you're not ready to rough it, there are a total of 42 modern campsites and 28 primitive campsites (including group sites), six backcountry campsites, and four riverside yurts on the grounds. One yurt is handicap accessible. There are also three ADA-compliant cabins with a heat source, electricity, and mini-fridges.

Alicia Underlee Nelson has written for Thomson Reuters, Food Network, Delta Sky Magazine, AAA Living, Midwest Living, Rent.com, trivago Magazine, Matador Network, and craftbeer.com. Her photos have appeared in these outlets, as well as in USA Today, North Dakota Tourism, *and* Explore Minnesota *materials. Alicia is the author of* 100 Things To Do in Fargo Before You Die *and* North Dakota Beer: A Heady History, *the creator of prairestylefile.com, a KFGO AM contributor, and co-author of* Midwest Road Trip Adventures.

North Dakota State Parks Amenities

Please confirm availability of amenities with the state park system. For more information on North Dakota State Parks, visit their website at www.parkrec.nd.gov

A few notes about the amenities:
- RV – Full Hookups include access to electricity, water, and sewer at the campsite.
- RV – Partial Hookups include access to electricity and water, but not sewer.
- Tent: Tent only sites available.
- Primitive campsites generally only include a camping pad, although some offer water or electric. Check with the park for details.
- Backcountry: Camping in remote areas without amenities like bathrooms, picnic tables, trash cans, or any other man-made structures.
- Restrooms: Indicates the highest functional type of restroom available*.
- Paddling: Boat access; this could be kayaking, canoeing, and/or powered boats.
- Swimming: Selected if swimming is available, either at a beach or a pool.

*Little Missouri State Park and Sully Creek State Park both have a shower house, both only vault toilets. (No flush toilets, no comfort station)

Cross Ranch and Sully Creek State Parks offer backcountry camping. This is camping in remote areas without amenities like bathrooms, picnic tables, trash cans, or any other man-made structures.

Lake Metigoshe State Park also has a lodge, and Fort Ransom State Park has a covered wagon and a farmhouse available for rental.

Midwest State Park Adventures

State Park Name	Hiking # of miles	Camping RV - Full Hookups	Camping RV - Partial Hookups	Tent	Primitive	Lodging Cabin	Yurt
Beaver Lake State Park	5.14	☐	✓	✓	✓	✓	☐
Cross Ranch State Park	16.7	☐	✓	✓	✓	✓	✓
Fort Abraham Lincoln State Park	18.93	☐	✓	✓	✓	✓	☐
Fort Ransom State Park	15.46	☐	✓	✓	✓	✓	☐
Fort Stevenson State Park	9.54	✓	✓	✓	✓	✓	☐
Grahams Island State Park	5.1	✓	✓	✓	✓	✓	☐
Icelandic State Park	4.09	☐	✓	✓	✓	✓	☐
Lake Metigoshe State Park	13.8	☐	✓	✓	✓	✓	✓
Lake Sakakawea State Park	5.06	☐	✓	✓	✓	✓	☐
Lewis & Clark State Park	5.6	✓	✓	✓	✓	✓	☐
Little Missouri State Park	45+	☐	☐	✓	✓	☐	☐
Sully Creek State Park	0	☐	✓	✓	✓	☐	☐
Turtle River State Park	12.36	☐	✓	✓	✓	✓	☐

State Park Name	Restrooms	Visitor/ Nature Center	Swimming	Paddling	Store	Picnic	Fishing	Marina
Beaver Lake State Park	Showers	☐	✓	✓	☐	✓	✓	☐
Cross Ranch State Park	Showers	✓	☐	✓	☐	✓	✓	☐
Fort Abraham Lincoln State Park	Showers	✓	☐	☐	✓	✓	☐	☐
Fort Ransom State Park	Showers	✓	☐	✓	✓	✓	☐	☐
Fort Stevenson State Park	Showers	✓	✓	✓	✓	✓	✓	✓
Grahams Island State Park	Showers	☐	✓	☐	✓	✓	✓	☐
Icelandic State Park	Showers	✓	✓	✓	✓	✓	✓	☐
Lake Metigoshe State Park	Showers	✓	✓	✓	☐	✓	✓	☐
Lake Sakakawea State Park	Showers	✓	✓	☐	✓	✓	✓	✓
Lewis & Clark State Park	Showers	✓	✓	✓	✓	✓	✓	✓
Little Missouri State Park	Showers	☐	☐	☐	☐	✓	☐	☐
Sully Creek State Park	Showers	☐	☐	☐	☐	☐	☐	☐
Turtle River State Park	Showers	✓	☐	☐	✓	✓	✓	☐

OHIO

By Brandy Gleason

O hio has state parks from the shores and islands around Lake Erie all the way down to the mighty Ohio River. Truth be told, I took the Ohio state parks for granted until I began traveling to other places throughout America. I assumed all state parks were the same, and boy was I wrong. Ohio takes pride in its park system, taking time to improve and maintain them.

There are over 1,000 miles of hiking trails for visitors to explore in Ohio's state parks, with some crossing the Buckeye Trail system. Outdoor adventure seekers can plan backcountry camping trips to modern stays at one of the many state park lodges. Water lovers will find their happy place on Lake Erie, inland lakes, rivers, or streams where they can fish, kayak, swim, or watch a sunset. Winter adventures can be found in the months of January and February, giving cold-weather lovers a space to play.

What makes Ohio a unique place to experience a state park is the diversity throughout the state. Ohio is home to the "Little Smokies," raging waterfalls, glacial grooves, fossils, hanging bridges, geological wonders, snowshoeing, beach glass, stunning sunrises and sunsets, and hidden gems peppered throughout the regions.

The Midwest is full of differing features, topography, and various plant life, and Ohio encapsulates many of these outdoor marvels.

Education and conservation are two solid pillars that hold up everything that Ohio State Park is built on. They encourage sustainability and responsible travel within any state park; these are key to keeping natural spaces pristine for future generations.

I am an avid outdoors woman who loves nature, camping, and exploration; I hope you will find adventure, solace, and happiness within Ohio's state parks.

Ohio State Park Facts & Important Information

- ALL of Ohio state parks are FREE, yes you read that right, FREE
- There are 75 state parks in Ohio.
- The smallest state park is Oak Point State Park at 1.5 acres near Put-in-Bay
- The largest state park is Salt Fork, State Park
- Buckey Lake is the oldest state park
- Fish in Ohio include sunfish, bass, trout, perch, walleye, catfish, carp, pike, sauger, and saugeye
- Common animals native to Ohio you might see are white-tailed deer, turkey, squirrels, raccoons, turtles, and rat snakes; we are welcoming back the black bear.
- Plentiful geology and natural arches and bridges

A note about accessibility

Ohio offers ADA accessibility at some parks, please see the website for up to date information.

Ohio State Parks Map

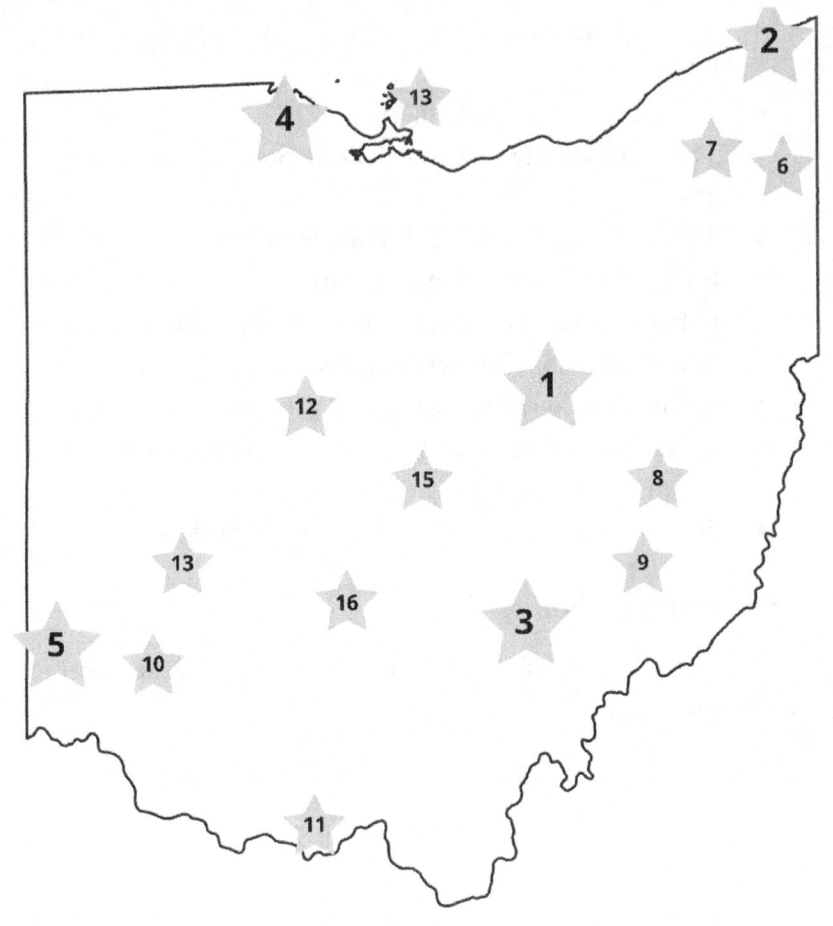

1. Mohican 2. Geneva 3. Hocking Hills 4. Maumee Bay 5. Hueston Woods 6. Mosquito Lake 7. Punderson 8. Salt Fork 9. Burr Oak 10. Caesar Creel 11. Shawnee 12. Indian Lake 13. South Bass 14. Alum Creek 15. Deer Creek

Region: Northeast

Geneva State Park

The Midwest is known for a lot of things, but a beachside resort might not be the first thing that comes to mind. Geneva State Park is home to fabulous Lake Erie sunsets, walleye fishing, and outdoor water activities.

One of the highlights of Geneva State Park is its campground. Featuring over 90 campsites, this campground offers visitors a chance to experience the great outdoors in comfort. The campsites are spacious and well-maintained, and many offer stunning views of the lake.

For those looking for a bit more luxury, Geneva State Park also features a beautiful lodge. Where guests can enjoy spacious rooms with stunning views of the lake, as well as a restaurant and lounge, guests can also take advantage of the lodge's indoor and outdoor pools, fitness center, and sauna.

Boaters and kayakers use the Geneva Mariana as a waypoint for boat and dock rentals, and it is a perfect place to book a charter rental for fishing on Lake Erie. If you are feeling adventurous, rent a jet ski for the afternoon.

One of the best things about Geneva State Park is its variety of activities. Whether you're looking to hike, swim, fish, or simply relax on the beach, this park has something for everyone. There are trails throughout the park that offer stunning views of the lake and the surrounding countryside. There are also plenty of opportunities for fishing, with Lake Erie being one of the best places in the country for walleye fishing.

Geneva State Park offers a 600-foot sand beach on Lake Erie with a marked swimming area where swimmers can enjoy a day of water play and sandcastle building. If you have brought man's best friend, there is a dog swimming area at the west end of the beach.

While the park is known for its summer activities, such as swimming and hiking, it also has plenty to offer during the winter months. The frozen lake provides the perfect setting for ice fishing, with plenty of fish to catch, including walleye, perch, and trout.

Despite its many attractions, Geneva State Park is still a relatively undiscovered gem. While it can get crowded during the summer months, especially on weekends, it is still possible to find quiet spots to relax and enjoy the natural beauty of the park. Whether you're looking for a peaceful retreat or an active outdoor adventure, Geneva State Park is an excellent choice.

Tip: Geneva on the Lake is known for its wine country; the lodge offers van tours from the state park to the local wineries. Just a short walk or golf cart ride from the lodge is the historic strip, where you can enjoy iconic places to eat and delve into the history of the resort town.

Mosquito Lake State Park

Nestled in the heart of Trumbull County, Ohio, Mosquito Lake State Park is a serene haven for nature lovers, adventure seekers, and anyone looking to unwind and reconnect with the great outdoors. Boasting 2,483 acres of lush forests, sparkling waters, and abundant wildlife, makes it the perfect destination for a weekend getaway or a day trip.

One of the main attractions of Mosquito Lake State Park is, of course, the lake itself. Covering over 7,000 acres, this expansive body of water offers endless opportunities for boating, fishing, and swimming. Anglers will be delighted to know that Mosquito Lake is home to a wide variety of fish, including walleye, muskie, bass, and catfish. If you're not into fishing, you can still enjoy the lake's scenic beauty by taking a leisurely boat ride or renting a kayak or paddleboard.

But Mosquito Lake State Park has much more to offer than just water activities. Hiking enthusiasts will love exploring the park's miles of trails, which wind through dense forests and along the lake's shoreline. Be sure to keep an eye out for the park's resident wildlife, which includes deer, foxes, and a variety of birds. For those who prefer a more relaxed pace, there are plenty of picnic areas and scenic overlooks where you can relax and take in the stunning views.

If you're looking for a little more adventure, Mosquito Lake State Park has got you covered. For a truly unique experience, check out the park's disc golf course, which is located on a scenic peninsula jutting out into the lake.

With so much to see and do, it's no wonder that Mosquito Lake State Park is a must-visit destination. Whether you're looking to escape the hustle and bustle of city life or just enjoy some quality time with family and friends, it is the perfect place to unwind and reconnect with nature.

Tip: Mosquito Lake State Park is named after Mosquito Creek and has nothing to do with the pesky summer pest.

Punderson State Park

Northeast Ohio is part of the snowbelt, so it isn't surprising that Punderson State Park is considered Ohio's winter playground. When the weather is just right, snow seekers flock to Punderson to sled on the lighted sledding hill that is outfitted with a tow rope or take a spin on the snowmobile trails. In late winter, the local maple trees are tapped to produce maple syrup, and visitors can experience a pancake breakfast in the lodge.

Adventurous guests will want to say in the English Tudor manor, which has been renovated into an updated lodge with lakeside dining. Some say the manor is haunted; others laugh it off, stay during one of the mystery dinners and find out for yourself.

Punderson Lake is a natural kettle lake, one of the largest and deepest of its kind in Ohio. Kayaks and canoes can be rented at the lodge to paddle out on this glacial-made body of water.

Punderson has one of the best disc golf courses in the state; thanks to the Friends of Punderson State Park, it's open year-round. One basket is uniquely placed on an island, making getting a hole-in-one challenging.

Region: Southeast
Hocking Hills State Park

Known as the crown jewel of the Ohio State Park system, Hocking Hills State Park is the most visited park in the Buckeye State. What makes this park the shining star? As I researched and asked Ohioans, the answers were varied, but the fantastic hiking trails made the top of everyone's bucket list. Lush green hemlocks surround visitors, and this park has year-round color, making it seem like you're in another world.

Adventure seekers' first stop in this park should be the Visitor Center located at The Old Man's Cave trailhead. Opened in 2019, the center welcomes guests to learn through interactive displays, exhibits, and wildlife showcases. Explore the gift shop filled with hiking necessities and gear for your journey to the caves.

Since hiking is the draw for thousands every year, planning your trip in advance is vital. Weekends here can be jam-packed. Visitors can arrive 30 minutes before sunrise and must be off the trails 30 minutes after sunset. Hocking Hills State Park's trail system is varied, and hikes range from difficult to easy. Waterfalls and stunning views are the biggest attractions for hikers, and every trail has something spectacular to see or experience.

Tip: Ash Cave Gorge ¼ mile is an easy trail that is handicap accessible; if you only have time for one trail while here, pick this one.

Take your fishing poles and spend the day casting a line into the 17-acre Rose Lake, where anglers can catch rainbow trout, channel catfish, bass, and bluegill. Kayaking and canoeing are welcome on Rose Lake, but you must carry your equipment in about a half mile to hand-launch them onto the lake.

The park has two mountain bike trails, which are not for the faint of heart; the purple 2-mile loop trail is considered moderate, while the Orange 2-mile Trail Loop is challenging. Each one is worth bringing your bike out to give them a shot.

Grab some picnic foods at Grandma Faye's near the Old Man's Cave and have an outdoor meal at one of the trailheads before heading out. Most picnic areas have pit toilets or restrooms with trash receptacles.

In 2022, the Hocking Hills State Park Lodge opened to welcome guests to this stunning part of Ohio, a home away from home to explore the Hocking Hills region. This lodge stands out because of the amenities, sustainability, and thoughtfulness they have incorporated into the property. Big timbered beams, wall-to-ceiling windows overlooking the beauty of nature will tantalize all your senses when you walk in. When you are not hiking or out exploring, live it up in the indoor pool with a year-round outdoor hot tub, then grab a delicious meal in the top-notch restaurant serving farm-to-table fare whenever possible. Book your stay well in advance.

Tip: Fall is a fantastic time to come to Hocking Hills State Park because of the striking autumn color and ideal temperatures for hiking; the waterfalls are not roaring this time of year unless it rains.

Salt Fork State Park

Rolling hills, colorful meadows, and a sprawling lake greet visitors as they head into Ohio's largest state park with a lodge. Plan on taking at least 30 minutes to drive into the heart of Salt Fork State Park, where you can park the car to begin exploring the 17,000-plus acres of public recreational land.

Since this park is so vast, plan on staying inside the park because there are plenty of ways to stay; large spacious cabins with hot tubs await on the banks of the water that boast beautiful sunsets and space to launch kayaks right from your cabin. Evenings are perfect for sitting at a campfire or on the screened-in porch that faces the water. Book a room in the lodge where the amenities will keep you busy in the evening after a day of outdoor exploration, with an indoor pool, game room, and rentable outdoor firepits. Campers are welcome; sites can accommodate RVs, tents, or car camping. Each pad in the campground has a picnic table, fire pit, and large space to enjoy the outdoor adventure.

Salt Fork State Park is known for its 2,954-acre body of water. Visitors come from all over the US to take advantage of the unlimited horsepower opportunities. Kids love to go tubing or fish for some of the wide variety found in the lake. Boaters can camp from their boats in the no-wake zones 50 feet from the shoreline.

Bring your fur baby to this park to enjoy the one-acre dog park located just off the main beach. Dogs have direct access to the water to play and swim on their own dog-friendly beach. Pets can go off-leash here.

History buffs will love the fully restored Kennedy Stone House. Built around 1837 Benjamin Kennedy had a large two-story home built with native sandstone blocks. These massive blocks range from 14" to 9' long. In the interior, volunteers have restored and decorated the house to the time period. Access to this home can be by trail, car, or boat; the docks are just east of the museum.

Burr Oak State Park

Burr Oak State Park is a beautiful park located in the rolling hills of southeastern Ohio. It is a perfect destination for anyone who loves the great outdoors. The park offers a wide range of activities, including camping, hiking, fishing, boating, and swimming.

One of the main attractions of Burr Oak State Park is its stunning lake, which spans over 600 acres and is surrounded by lush forest. The lake is perfect for fishing, with a variety of fish species including bass, crappie, and catfish. There are also several boat launch areas, allowing visitors to explore the lake by boat or kayak. If you don't own a boat rent one from the seasonal marina for a day out on the water,

For those who prefer to stay on land, Burr Oak State Park has miles of hiking trails that wind through the forest and along the lake. The trails vary in difficulty, from easy walks to challenging hikes, and offer stunning views of the park's natural beauty. There are also several picnic areas along the trails, making it easy to stop for a snack or lunch.

If you're looking for a place to stay, Burr Oak State Park offers several options for camping and lodging. The park has campsites for tents and

RVs, as well as several cabins, and for a more luxurious stay book a room in the rustic lodge with access to the indoor and outdoor pools and full-service restaurant. All the accommodations are located within the park, making it easy to access all of the activities.

Burr Oak State Park is a must-see destination for anyone looking to experience the beauty and tranquility of Ohio's natural landscape. Whether you're looking to hike, fish, camp, or simply relax in the great outdoors, this park has something for everyone making it a place to create unforgettable memories.

Region: Southwest

Hueston Woods State Park

Hueston Woods State Park catches one by surprise; located north of Cincinnati and outside the college town of Oxford, this state park enraptures first-time visitors and brings back lifelong lovers of the park. What makes this state park seem magical? Maybe it is the majestic lodge with floor-to-ceiling windows, the large lake, or the plentiful hiking trails; whatever it is, it enchants you.

This region is home to limestone and shale bedrock which has encased fossils of ancient marine mammals and attracts collectors year-round. While hiking, you can find many along the creekside trails and in certain collecting areas.

When you are not out collecting fossils, the nature center offers a wide variety of interactive displays, and a park ranger is on staff to answer guests' questions. On-site, you can also find live animals that can be found in this part of Ohio, like native fish, birds of prey, mammals, and reptiles.

One day is never enough at Hueston Woods; plan on booking a room in the lodge in one of the rooms facing Acton Lake; rooms offer balconies with comfortable chairs and a table where you can sip some local wine or a cup of coffee and watch the night sky. If you want a little more seclusion, try one of the cabins they offer, ranging from family-sized to couple-sized and even pet-friendly options. Are you more rugged? Stay at the large campground in tents or an RV, with many amenities for every visitor to enjoy, most sites offer partial hookups, but if you're lucky, you can snag one of the 20 full hook-up sites.

Birding is one of America's favorite past times, and Hueston Woods is a birder's paradise. The park is designated as an IBA (Important Birding Area) by the National Audubon Society due to its unique habitat of 200-acre old-growth beech-maple forests within the park's borders. This habitat is truly a special part of Ohio and should be cherished and preserved. The launch ramp and the 14-acre Hedgerow Project area have bird blinds where birds can be viewed without disturbing them.

Twelve miles of hiking trails course their way through the park creating a place where hikers can take paths by the shores of Acton Lake, through the dense forests, or along quiet streams bordered by wildflowers in the spring. Experience the American Discovery Trail™, a non-motorized multi-use trail that winds through the park.

Acton Lake, the beautiful backdrop to this park, is one of the major draws for boaters, anglers, and swimmers. Visit the marina to rent a boat or kayak for a lovely afternoon on the water.

Take a quick trip to the newest Preble County covered bridge that makes its home here, known as the Hueston Woods Covered Bridge. Spanning Four Mile Creek, this single-span bridge easily accommodates the paved two-lane road. One unique feature of the covered bridge is the pedestrian lane that is on each side, allowing safe passage for bikers and walkers to enjoy the scenic views.

Caesar Creek State Park

Beautiful lake views, miles and miles of hiking trails, and fossil fields draw nature seekers to Caesar Creek State Park. It is well known for camping, and campers love this southwestern state park. The Caesar Creek State Park campground offers 278 sites with a picnic table and fire ring, with large and spacious grassy areas. Outdoor lovers book months in advance to come and experience time within this well-loved park. The area's rich history and fossils go hand in hand here; plan on visiting when the Pioneer Village is open.

Fossils! This park is known for the fossils found here; obtain a fossil permit and head to the spillway to look for some. Familiarize yourself with the rules, what you can take home, and what must stay before you start the hunt.

Hikers will find multiple trails within the park, from moderate to strenuous, and the scenery is some of the best in this part of Ohio. Highlights on the trails include a swinging bridge, waterfalls, and views of the lake that are absolutely breathtaking. Grab a map before heading out on any of the trails because the trailheads are located in different places and are not all interconnected.

Shawnee State Park

Situated in the part of Ohio known as "The Little Smokies," seekers of serenity and beauty flock to this hidden gem in the southeast part of Ohio. Rugged rolling hills, rich and lush forests, and two lakes encapsulate the region. Don't overlook a visit to one of the places where the blue smoke starts to rise.

Shawnee State Park deserves more than a day, so book a room at the lodge, one of the modern cabins, or plan a camping trip. This state park has it all! Park visitors can fish in the lakes for bass, crappie, bluegill, and trout, play rounds of disk golf on the Black Bear Course, or check in at the seasonal Nature Center and Historic Log Cabin.

Backcountry hikers flock to this state park to experience the wilderness area that includes part of the 1,400-mile Buckeye trail. Seven backcountry campsites are located throughout the route; wayfarers must register at the trailhead. Latrines and drinking water are available at the campsites.

Each season in this park invites you to come to unwind at a crackling fire in the lodge during winter or around the summer campsite.

Region: Northwest

Maumee Bay State Park

Explore the 1,336 acres of outdoor adventure in the Northwest corner of Ohio. Situated on the shoreline of Lake Erie, Maumee Bay State Park provides breathtaking views of Lake Erie and stunning sunsets in the evenings. This state park is just a short 5 miles from Toledo; this park is an oasis away from the hustle and bustle of the city.

If you ask people one of the main reasons they come to Maumee Bay State Park, they will say enjoying Lake Erie is at the top of the list, but birders will tell you that birding should be right up there too. Marshland, wet woods, and lush marshes make this part of Ohio ripe to see all kinds of birds. In the springtime, Warblers come through as they migrate northward to their summer homes, and with those warblers come thousands of birders from all over the world to photograph and see them. Each year The Biggest Birding Week in American birding happens in May, and the conference is held at the lodge; if you have ever wanted to start birding, this is the place to be.

Sitting in the sun on the beach or looking for beach glass are ways to enjoy a day at Maumee Bay State Park. There are two ways to enjoy the water here: one beach is on Lake Erie, and another one is on the shore of an inland body of water. Both are great ways to enjoy swimming, kayaking, or just grabbing some rays. Restrooms and changing areas are provided, but leave Fido at home because pets are not allowed on the beaches.

Lake Erie is known as the walleye capital of the world, meaning fishing here is top-notch. Anglers will also find channel catfish, freshwater drum, smallmouth bass, and yellow perch within the lake's boundaries. However, if a more petite body of water is a better fit, there are several inland lakes that are wheelchair-accessible fishing piers, and a small pond near parking lot #7 is designated as a kid-friendly family fishing area.

Arthur Hills designed Maumee Bay State Park Golf Course, and this 18-hole course spans 1,850 acres with low rolling hills and beautiful views of the surrounding park. Deer and other wildlife might join you at the 14th hole. A PGA- certified professional is on staff in the golf pro shop.

Book a stay in the Maumee Bay State Park Lodge in a room with a balcony, where guests can take in the sweeping views of Lake Erie and enjoy the indoor amenities of the racket ball courts, hot tub, splash pad, and indoor pool. If you want seclusion, rent one of the stunning cottages where songbirds and nature are just steps outside your front door. Want a more rustic stay? The campground offers large sites with electric hookups.

This park offers cross-country skiing, ice skating, and a huge sledding hill just steps from the lodge in winter.

Indian Lake State Park

Locals love Indian Lake, and in recent years central Ohioans have been flocking to this hidden gem in Logan County. At one time, this was a passed-over park; however, it is now a day trip destination and overnight camping mecca.

Anglers experience the fight of the catch with large-mouth bass, walleye, and crappie from the shores or by boat in the 5,100-acre lake. If spending the day out on the water is calling your name, the Indian Lake Marina provides boat rentals where fun in the sun awaits.

Indian Lake State Park campground is one of the hidden gems in the park system, with premium waterfront sites and many full hook-up sites. One unique feature is the boat campsites located near the boat ramp in the campground. These are paved sites with electricity, and campers receive a reserved boat dock slip for their stay. Tents are not permitted for these sites, and campfire rings are not provided.

One of the best dog parks in the system is located here on Old Field Island, providing off-the-leash entertainment. Double-gated entry separates areas for large and small dogs. Bring your own drinking water for yourself and your pet; please don't forget clean-up bags; this is a pack-in and pack-out dog area.

South Bass Island State Park

If you are looking for a small state park that packs a big punch, South Bass Island State Park should make your list. While this is a small park that is only accessible by boat or by plane, it is worth the effort to get here.

Book campsites or the yurts here well in advance because they book up six months in advance. Campsites are tight, and you will want to ensure you read all the site information before booking. Recently Wi-Fi has been added to the campground since cell service is spotty. Tent campers have premium views from their cliff-side non-electric sites, but who needs amenities when Mother Nature paints the sky?

Fishing on Lake Erie is accessible from the shores, or rent a boat to spend the day out trying to catch walleye in the walleye capital of the world. Search for beach glass, swim at the small rocky beach, or enjoy a picnic as you watch one of the spectacular sunsets that can be seen from this state park.

Tip: Book a reservation with the Miller Ferry Line for yourself and to get your RV or overnight gear to the island.

Region: Central

Mohican State Park

With the beautiful Mohican River winding through it, Mohican State Park is one of Ohio's premier state parks for kayak, canoeing, and tubing. Lush forests of hardwood trees, evergreens, flora, and fauna cover the 1,100 acres comprising Mohican State Park; people come from far and wide to enjoy this outdoor playground. It is no surprise that visitors plan to stay in the area for more than one day with all the things there are to do in the state park and surrounding area.

Enjoy the scenic Clear Fork of the Mohican River as it winds its way through the campground and park by renting or buying a tube from the camp store. While the state park has many access points just outside the park's borders, there are several rental places for kayaks and canoes where you can spend the whole day on the river.

Mountain biking is another big draw for outdoor enthusiasts, with 25 miles of bike trails that pass through the state park and forest. Many consider the trails rigorous and challenging. Mountain Bike Action Magazine voted the mountain bike trail in Mohican State Park #1 in Ohio.

Plan to stay a night or two with so many things to enjoy considering there are a few unique ways to stay. Mohican State Park Lodge and Conference Center are tucked way back into the park, where the lodge sits overlooking Pleasant Hill Lake. While visitors are there to stay the night, the lodge will keep guests busy with plenty of onsite activities and amenities, like the indoor pool and sauna, fitness room, two game room areas, and campfire rings that can be rented for a night of storytelling and smores over the fading embers.

Bromfield Dining Room is a full-service restaurant on the property named after the Pulitzer-prize-winning author and naturalist Louis Bromfield, who once owned a nearby farm now known as Malabar Farm State Park, just a short drive from Mohican.

Cozy up in one of the modern deluxe two-bedroom cabins located on the Clear Fork River. Preferred cabins have heat and air conditioning, a full kitchen, and a private bathroom. Enjoy an evening on the screened-in back porch or hotdogs roasted on the fire ring.

Take a scenic drive through the park and visit the Pleasant Hill Dam, where you can park your car at the nearby trailhead. Hikers flock to Mohican throughout the year to experience every season in these dense woods. Walk the easy Pleasant Hill trail or make a day of it hiking to the Big and Little Lyons falls or to the Clear Fork Gorge.

Excellent opportunities for fishing are found in Wolf Creek or Clear Fork River, one of the few streams in Ohio that are stocked with Brown Trout. Visitors will need a valid fishing license to cast a line in Ohio waterways; those can be purchased on ohiodnr.gov.

Deer Creek State Park

Set in Ohio's rural farming country, Deer Creek State Park is central Ohio's premier state park destination for outdoor fun and recreation. Visitors to the park will find themselves surrounded by the 1,277-acre lake to enjoy boating, fishing, and water sports, a true gem amid the corn fields.

Book a stay at Deer Creek State Park Lodge, where you will find modern amenities with a bit of rustic charm. The lodge offers a restaurant with water views and a full-service menu for breakfast, lunch, and dinner menu. Looking for more of a rustic stay? Book one of the well-appointed cabins where you can sit by a campfire and roast marshmallows in the evening. Camping is another way to stay at Deer Creek State Park, with 200 electric sites to choose from. Campers can access full-service restrooms, a laundry facility, and a dump station. Kids will find fun at the volleyball, basketball, pickleball, and gaga ball courts.

Deer Creek State Park has a presidential past, and the 1.5-story fully resorted Harding Cabin sits on the banks of Deer Creek. Harding and his close friends, known as the "Ohio Gang," came and retreated here. Vacationers can book a stay in this cabin, updated with modern conveniences.

Water sports bring outdoor lovers to this hidden oasis every summer, where its body of water boasts unlimited horsepower for boating. Bring your boat or rent something from the marina for a day out on the lake. On sunny days you can see families tubing, fishing, and swim in the designated swimming area located in a cove near the lodge. Fishing at Deer Creek State Park entices anglers looking to hook a catfish, largemouth bass, or crappie.

All the trails within Deer Creek State Park are considered easy to moderate, making a day out in nature accessible for any fitness level. Wind your way on a path through the woods or along the banks of the water. If you are traveling with kids, take time to visit the storybook trail. At the beginning of the trail is a little library where you can take a book to read or leave on for the next little hiker.

Picnicking in the park is available, and visitors can enjoy one of the many pavilions or picnic tables scattered throughout the park. Shelter houses are on a first-come, first-served basis, and a few can be reserved in advance.

Traveling with man's best friend? Deer Creek State Park has a fenced-in dog park near the campground where your best friend can run and play unleashed within the designated area. If you are staying overnight, select cabins are pet friendly and can be booked in advance.

Love golf? Check out the 18-hole course designed by Jack Kidwell, and it has been a destination for golfers since 1982. Deer Creek Golf course is diverse and rated for all skill levels.

During winter, weather permitting, enjoy sledding, ice fishing, and ice skating. Snowmobiling is allowed on the 17-mile bridle trail when the snowpack is suitable.

Alum Creek State Park

Alum Creek State Park is the closest state park to Columbus and welcomes parkgoers every season of the year. This central Ohio park boasts the largest inland beach in the state, with over 3,000 feet of course sand to play in, with a large swimming area, volleyball courts, changing area, and beach vendors during the summer. Visitors will also enjoy 14 miles of mountain bike trails that zigzag their way through the landscape; the trails are known as some of the best in central Ohio. Alum Creek State Park is a park that is full of surprises and should make your must-visit list.

Camping and boating are two of the most significant amenities at Alum Creek. Visitors can book a night in one of the 286 campsites that offer eclectic or in one of the small rustic cabins; all the sites are large and offer fire rings and picnic tables.

Experience a day on the lake by renting a boat at the marina or bring your own to launch from one of the public launch areas. Rent a space in one of the overnight docks providing water and electricity for an overnight stay on the water. Seasonal rentals are made at the Park and

Watercraft office, and overnight rentals can be booked at the Marina Office.

Brandy Gleason is the CEO of Gleason Media, LLC. , chief writer at Gleason Family Adventure, and creator of the Ohio Road Trips Facebook group. She has written two books, 100 Things to Do in Ohio's Amish Country Before You Die, *and the Ohio section of* Midwest Road Trip Adventures; *currently, she is writing* 100 Things to Do in Ohio Before You Die. *She has spoken at National Conventions on education and virtual conferences on travel and was a brand ambassador for THOR industries in 2021, and is currently a Heartland RV's brand ambassador. Brandy loves to travel and explore and has a passion for the environment, sustainability, and the outdoors. She buckles up for a road trip any time she can, and her driving force behind her social media is to encourage others to find their own adventures. One of her favorite quotes is "In order to write about life first you must live it," by Ernest Hemingway, and she fully embraces each day.*

You can find Brandy at www.gleasonfamilyadventure.com

Ohio State Parks Amenities

Please confirm availability of amenities with the state park system For more information on Ohio State Parks, visit their website at ohiodnr.gov/home

A few notes about the amenities:
- RV – Full Hookups include access to electricity, water, and sewer at the campsite.
- RV – Partial Hookups include access to electricity and water, but not sewer.
- Tent: Tent only sites available.
- Primitive: Camping in remote areas without amenities like bathrooms, picnic tables, trash cans, or any other man-made structures.
- Restrooms: Indicates the highest functional type of restroom available.
- Paddling: Boat access; this could be kayaking, canoeing, and/or powered boats.
- Swimming: Selected if swimming is available, either at a beach or a pool.

Great Council State Park is opening in 2023.

Midwest State Park Adventures

State Park Name	Hiking # of miles	RV - Full Hookups	RV - Partial Hookups	Tent	Primitive	Cabin	Yurt	Lodge
A.W. Marion State Park	11.8	☐	☑	☑	☐	☐	☐	☐
Adams Lake State Park	1	☐	☐	☐	☐	☐	☐	☐
Alum Creek State Park	12.6	☑	☑	☑	☐	☑	☐	☐
Barkcamp State Park	11.4	☑	☑	☑	☐	☑	☐	☐
Beaver Creek State Park	5.75	☐	☑	☑	☐	☑	☐	☐
Blue Rock State Park	3	☐	☐	☐	☑	☑	☐	☐
Buck Creek State Park	5.79	☐	☑	☑	☐	☑	☐	☐
Buckeye Lake State Park	4.1	☐	☐	☐	☐	☐	☐	☐
Burr Oak State Park	45	☐	☑	☑	☐	☑	☐	☑
Caeser Creek State Park	24.3	☑	☑	☑	☐	☐	☐	☐
Catawba Island State Park	no	☐	☐	☐	☐	☐	☐	☐
Cowan Lake State Park	7.5	☐	☑	☑	☐	☑	☐	☐
Deer Creek State Park	5.8	☐	☑	☐	☐	☑	☐	☑
Delaware State Park	6.85	☐	☑	☑	☐	☐	☐	☐
Dillon State Park	9.4	☑	☑	☑	☐	☑	☐	☐
East Fork State Park	0.5	☑	☑	☐	☐	☐	☐	☐
East Harbor State Park	10.5	☑	☑	☑	☑	☐	☐	☐
Findley State Park	11.75	☑	☑	☑	☐	☑	☐	☐
Forked Run State Park	3.55	☐	☑	☑	☐	☑	☐	☐
Geneva State Park	6	☑	☑	☑	☐	☑	☐	☑
Grand Lake Saint Marys State Park	3.25	☑	☑	☑	☑	☑	☐	☐
Great Seal State Park	23	☐	☐	☑	☑	☐	☐	☐
Guilford Lake State Park	0.5	☐	☑	☑	☐	☐	☐	☐
Harrison Lake State Park	3.5	☐	☑	☑	☑	☑	☐	☐
Headland Beach State Park	1	☐	☐	☑	☐	☐	☐	☐
Hocking Hills State Park	9	☑	☑	☑	☐	☑	☐	☑
Hueston Woods State Park	12.7	☑	☑	☑	☐	☑	☑	☑
Independance Dam State Park	3	☐	☐	☑	☑	☐	☐	☐
Indian Lake State Park	5.72	☑	☑	☑	☐	☐	☐	☐
Jackson Lake State Park		☐	☑	☑	☐	☐	☐	☐
Jefferson Lake State Park	15.25	☐	☑	☑	☐	☐	☐	☐
Jesse Ownes State Park		☐	☐	☑	☑	☐	☐	☐
John Bryan State Park	10.4	☐	☑	☑	☐	☐	☐	☐
Kellys Island State Park	9	☑	☑	☑	☐	☐	☑	☐
Kiser Lake State Park	3.41	☐	☑	☑	☐	☑	☐	☐
Lake Alma State Park	4.19	☑	☑	☑	☐	☑	☐	☐
Lake Hope State Park	11.45	☐	☑	☑	☐	☑	☐	☐
Lake Logan State Park	1.25	☐	☐	☐	☐	☐	☐	☐
Lake Loramie State Park	9	☑	☑	☑	☐	☑	☐	☐
Lake Milton State Park	2.25	☐	☐	☐	☐	☐	☐	☐
Lake White State Park		☐	☐	☐	☐	☐	☐	☐
Little Miami State Park	50	☐	☐	☐	☐	☐	☐	☐
Madison Lake State Park	1	☐	☐	☐	☐	☐	☐	☐
Malabar Farm State Park	9.5	☐	☐	☑	☑	☑	☐	☐
Marblehead Lighthouse State Park	0	☐	☐	☐	☐	☐	☐	☐
Mary Jane Thurston State Park	2.95	☐	☑	☑	☐	☐	☐	☐
Maumee Bay State Park	12.3	☑	☑	☑	☐	☑	☐	☑
Middle Bass Island State Park		☐	☐	☑	☑	☐	☐	☐
Mohican State Park	13.07	☑	☑	☑	☐	☑	☐	☑
Mosquito Lake State Park	23.7	☑	☑	☑	☐	☐	☑	☐
Mt Gilead State Park	5.5	☑	☑	☑	☐	☐	☐	☐
Muskingum River State Park		☐	☐	☑	☑	☐	☐	☐

Ohio

State Park Name	Restrooms	Visitor/Nature Center	Swimming	Paddling	Store	Picnic	Fishing
A.W. Marion State Park		☐	☑	☑	☐	☑	☑
Adams Lake State Park		☑	☐	☑	☐	☑	☑
Alum Creek State Park	Flush	☑	☑	☑	☑	☑	☑
Barkcamp State Park	Flush	☑	☑	☑	☐	☑	☑
Beaver Creek State Park	Flush	☑	☐	☐	☐	☑	☑
Blue Rock State Park	Vault	☑	☑	☑	☐	☑	☑
Buck Creek State Park	Flush	☐	☑	☑	☑	☑	☑
Buckeye Lake State Park			☑	☑	☐	☑	☑
Burr Oak State Park	Flush	☑	☑	☑	☑	☑	☑
Caeser Creek State Park	Flush	☑	☑	☑	☐	☑	☑
Catawba Island State Park		☐	☐	☐	☐	☐	
Cowan Lake State Park	Flush	☑	☑	☑	☐	☑	☑
Deer Creek State Park	Flush	☑	☑	☑	☑	☑	☑
Delaware State Park	Flush	☐	☑	☑	☐	☑	☑
Dillon State Park	Flush	☑	☑	☑	☐	☑	☑
East Fork State Park	Flush	☑	☑	☑	☐	☑	☑
East Harbor State Park	Flush	☑	☑	☑	☑	☑	☑
Findley State Park	Flush	☑	☑	☑	☐	☑	☑
Forked Run State Park	Flush	☐	☑	☑	☐	☑	☑
Geneva State Park	Flush	☑	☑	☑	☑	☑	☑
Grand Lake Saint Marys State Park	Flush	☑	☑	☑	☑	☑	☑
Great Seal State Park	Vault	☐	☐	☐	☐	☑	☐
Guilford Lake State Park	Flush	☐	☑	☑	☐	☑	☑
Harrison Lake State Park	Flush	☐	☑	☑	☐	☑	☑
Headland Beach State Park	Flush	☐	☑	☐	☐	☑	☑
Hocking Hills State Park	Flush	☑	☑	☑	☑	☑	☑
Hueston Woods State Park	Flush	☑	☑	☑	☑	☑	☑
Independance Dam State Park		☐	☐	☐	☐	☑	☑
Indian Lake State Park	Flush	☐	☑	☑	☑	☑	☑
Jackson Lake State Park		☐	☑	☑	☐	☑	☑
Jefferson Lake State Park	Flush	☐	☑	☐	☐	☑	☑
Jesse Owens State Park	Vault	☐	☐	☑	☐	☑	☑
John Bryan State Park	Flush	☐	☐	☐	☐	☑	☑
Kellys Island State Park	Flush	☐	☑	☑	☐	☑	☑
Kiser Lake State Park	Flush	☑	☑	☑	☐	☑	☑
Lake Alma State Park	Flush	☐	☑	☑	☐	☑	☑
Lake Hope State Park	Flush	☑	☑	☑	☑	☑	☑
Lake Logan State Park	Flush	☐	☑	☑	☐	☑	☑
Lake Loramie State Park	Flush	☑	☑	☑	☐	☑	☑
Lake Milton State Park	Flush	☐	☑	☑	☐	☑	☑
Lake White State Park	Vault	☐	☐	☑	☐	☑	☑
Little Miami State Park	Vault	☐	☐	☑	☐	☑	☑
Madison Lake State Park	Flush	☐	☑	☑	☐	☑	☑
Malabar Farm State Park	Flush	☑	☐	☐	☑	☑	☑
Marblehead Lighthouse State Park	Flush	☑	☐	☐	☐	☑	☐
Mary Jane Thurston State Park	Flush	☐	☐	☐	☑	☑	☑
Maumee Bay State Park	Flush	☑	☑	☑	☑	☑	☑
Middle Bass Island State Park	Vault	☐	☐	☐	☐	☑	☑
Mohican State Park	Flush	☑	☑	☑	☑	☑	☑
Mosquito Lake State Park	Flush	☑	☑	☑	☑	☑	☑
Mt Gilead State Park	Flush	☑	☑	☑	☑	☑	☑
Muskingum River State Park	Vault	☐	☐	☑	☐	☑	☑

Midwest State Park Adventures

State Park Name	Hiking # of miles	RV - Full Hookups	RV - Partial Hookups	Tent	Primitive	Cabin	Yurt	Lodge
Nelson-Kennedy Ledges State Park	3	☐	☐	☐	☐	☐	☐	☐
North Bass Island State Park		☐	☐	✓	✓	✓	☐	☐
Oak Point State Park		☐	☐	☐	☐	☐	☐	☐
Paint Creek State Park	6	✓	✓	✓	☐	✓	☐	☐
Pike Lake State Park	3.8	☐	✓	✓	☐	✓	☐	☐
Portage Lakes State Park	1.1	☐	☐	☐	☐	☐	☐	☐
Punderson State Park	9.6	✓	✓	✓	☐	✓	☐	✓
Pymatuning State Park	3.2	✓	✓	✓	☐	✓	☐	☐
Rocky Fork State Park	1.8	✓	✓	✓	☐	☐	☐	☐
Salt Fork State Park	20.09	✓	✓	✓	☐	✓	☐	✓
Scioto Trail State Park	3.4	☐	✓	✓	☐	✓	☐	☐
Shawnee State Park	25	☐	✓	✓	☐	✓	☐	✓
South Bass State Park		✓	✓	✓	✓	☐	✓	☐
Stonelick State Park	3.88	☐	✓	✓	☐	✓	☐	☐
Strouds Run State Park	12	☐	☐	✓	✓	✓	☐	☐
Sycamore State Park	4.8	☐	☐	✓	✓	☐	☐	☐
Tar Hollow State Park	27	☐	✓	✓	☐	☐	☐	☐
Van Buren State Park	7	☐	✓	✓	☐	✓	☐	☐
West Branch State Park	14	✓	✓	✓	☐	☐	☐	☐
Wingfoot Lake State Park		☐	☐	☐	☐	☐	☐	☐
Wolf Run State Park	5.5	☐	✓	✓	☐	✓	☐	☐

State Park Name	Restrooms	Visitor/ Nature Center	Swimming	Paddling	Store	Picnic	Fishing
Nelson-Kennedy Ledges State Park	Vault	☐	☐	☐	☐	☐	☐
North Bass Island State Park	Flush	☐	☐	☐	☐	☐	✓
Oak Point State Park	Flush	☐	☐	✓	☐	✓	✓
Paint Creek State Park	Flush	✓	✓	✓	✓	✓	✓
Pike Lake State Park	Flush	✓	✓	✓	☐	✓	✓
Portage Lakes State Park		☐	✓	✓	☐	✓	✓
Punderson State Park	Flush	✓	✓	✓	✓	✓	✓
Pymatuning State Park	Flush	✓	✓	✓	✓	✓	✓
Rocky Fork State Park	Flush	☐	✓	✓	☐	✓	✓
Salt Fork State Park	Flush	✓	✓	✓	✓	✓	✓
Scioto Trail State Park	Flush	☐	✓	✓	☐	✓	✓
Shawnee State Park	Flush	✓	✓	✓	✓	✓	✓
South Bass State Park	Flush	☐	✓	✓	☐	✓	✓
Stonelick State Park	Flush	☐	✓	✓	☐	✓	✓
Strouds Run State Park	Flush	☐	✓	✓	☐	✓	✓
Sycamore State Park	Vault	☐	☐	☐	☐	✓	✓
Tar Hollow State Park	Vault	☐	✓	✓	☐	✓	✓
Van Buren State Park	Flush	☐	☐	☐	☐	☐	☐
West Branch State Park	Flush	☐	✓	✓	☐	✓	✓
Wingfoot Lake State Park		✓	☐	✓	☐	✓	✓
Wolf Run State Park	Flush	☐	✓	✓	☐	✓	✓

SOUTH DAKOTA

By Lindsay Hindman

South Dakota is home to lush green fields and barren desert lands; rolling hills and breathtaking rock formations from the Black Hills and Badlands in the west to Palisades and Big Stone Island in the east. It's also home to more than 60 state parks and state recreation areas. While these beautiful parks and recreation areas are scattered all around the state, there are a few major clusters: the Black Hills and Badlands in the western part of the state, Lake Oahe in the north central region, the recreational Missouri River basin in the central third, glacial lakes and the

Couteau des Prairies in the northeast, and the Missouri and Big Sioux River basins racing towards each other in the southeast until their eventual confluence.

The landscape of South Dakota comes with majestic views and contrasts. In the badlands, the land is stark, dry, and harsh, while the Black Hills themselves are so named because the tree cover is so dense that the hills appear black from below. In the northeast corner of the state, the landscape is dotted with glacial lakes and was nicknamed the slope of the prairie or Couteau des Prairies by explorer Joseph Nicollet. The state has been inhabited since prehistoric times, and South Dakota state parks share the history and continuing influence of these cultures including the Oneota, Woodland Culture, Lakota, and Cheyenne. South Dakota's state parks also share the history of nineteenth century pioneers, the Dakota Wars, and the twentieth century. At all of South Dakota's state parks, you can relax and enjoy the spectacular natural beauty of this great state—and I can't wait to tell you about some of the best.

The South Dakota Department of Game, Fish, and Parks is responsible for all South Dakota State Parks and State Recreation Areas, and gfp.SD.gov/parks is the official website for the state park system. Each park or recreation area has its own page accessible on that site.

South Dakota State Park Facts & Important Information

- The highest point in South Dakota is Black Elk Peak, accessible from the Sylvan Lake trailhead in Custer State Park.
- Black Elk Peak is also the highest point of elevation in the entire Midwest–or anywhere else east of the Rockies–at 7,242 feet above sea level!
- The lowest point of elevation in South Dakota is in Big Stone Lake, accessible from Hartford Beach State Park.
- The Black Hills is also known as one of the best dark sky sites for stargazing in the Midwest with a 1 rating on the Bortles scale.
- South Dakota's state parks are in two different time zones, both central and mountain.
- SD residents refer to regions of the state by which side of the Missouri River they're on: "east river" or "west river."
- Daily and annual park entrance licenses are available and are required at almost all SD state parks and state recreation areas.
- Many fossils, gems, and precious metals have been found in South Dakota state parks and other lands in the state.
- The prairie rattlesnake is South Dakota's only venomous snake–and it is found in some SD state parks.

A note about accessibility

The South Dakota Game, Fish, and Parks Department strives to provide accessible facilities and has ADA-compliant facilities for hunting, fishing, camping, and other activities at many state parks and recreation areas.

More info is available on the GFP website including gfp.sd.gov/ada-camping and gfp.sd.gov/fish-accessible-areas

South Dakota State Parks Map

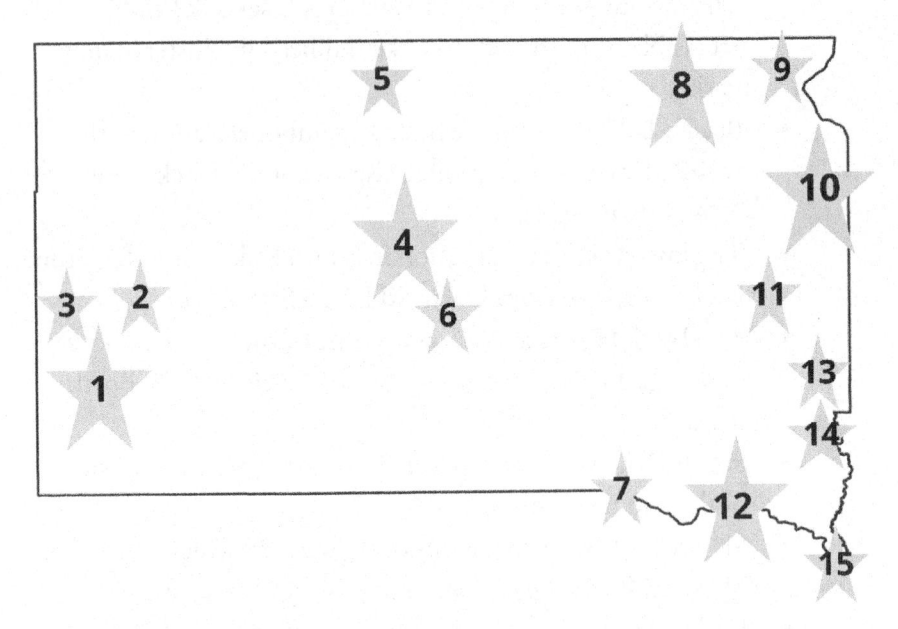

1. Custer 2. Bear Butte 3. Spearfish Canyon 4. Oahe Downstream 5. North Lake Oahe 6. Farm Island 7. Lake Francis Case 8. Fort Sisseton 9. Sica Hollow 10. Big Stone Lake 11. Sandy Shore 12. Lewis and Clark 13. Palisades 14. Good Earth 15. Adams Homestead

Region: West

Custer State Park

In western South Dakota, the Black Hills provide some of the most scenic and unique views in America, and plenty of places to enjoy them. And the crowning jewel is Custer State Park, South Dakota's oldest state park. It's also the largest state park in South Dakota, the largest state park in the Midwest, and one of the 10 biggest state parks in the nation! Custer State Park was established in 1919 and is flourishing into the twenty-first century with 71,000 acres of trails, waterways, campgrounds, amenities, and adventure. From the peaceful beauty of Sylvan Lake to the intense action at the annual Buffalo Roundup, Custer State Park offers visitors the best of the wild west.

South Dakota

There are more than a dozen campgrounds at Custer including ones for RVs, for tent camping, and for youth groups like scouts or church or school groups. Or you can stay at one of the five park lodges: Blue Bell, Sylvan Lake, Legion Lake, Creekside, and the State Game Lodge, which offer a variety of camping cabins and hotel rooms. The State Game Lodge is the most upscale, and presidents Calvin Coolidge and Dwight Eisenhower each stayed there with their staff while in office.

Custer State Park is home to notable restaurants at four of the lodges, serving up delicious food that ranges from haute cuisine to cozy Midwest comfort food. At the State Game Lodge visitors can enjoy menu items like buffalo ravioli with black truffle parmesan cream sauce, or spicy rabbit and rattlesnake sausage, and elk osso bucco paired with an extensive wine list. For more fine dining in the park, try the almond crusted walleye with a citrus beurre blanc at the Sylvan Lake Lodge. Across the park, the Blue Bell Lodge offers a more casual experience with buffalo chislic, onion rings, and Buffalo Burgers with Cowboy Beans. And visitors who want to keep enjoying the great outdoors even while dining will adore the Broasted Chicken Picnic Pickup Packs at the Legion Lake Lodge Dockside Grill, or the iconic Custer State Park Chuck Wagon Cookout.

Outside, look for the park's herd of over 1,000 bison, plus begging burros, prairie dogs, deer, pronghorn antelope, bighorn sheep, wild turkeys, mountain goats, and many more species of plants, animals, and insects. Then, head inside the Peter Norbeck Outdoor Education Center to learn more about the history, geology, flora, and fauna of the Custer State Park area, or to the Bison Center to learn more about the park's bison herd and annual Round Up.

For more outdoor entertainment, try fishing at Grace Coolidge Creek or one of Custer's other waterways, boating on Sylvan Lake, or hiking around the park. Or explore the park on open air jeep tours, buffalo safaris, or guided horseback tours. For indoor fun, watch a show at the Black Hills Playhouse or go shopping at the State Game Lodge, where the artist-in-residence might be busy creating an amazing new work.

Bear Butte State Park

Bear Butte is a geologically unique and culturally significant peak, towering around 1,200 feet above the surrounding plains. Butte is a misnomer; the eponymous mountain is actually a laccolith, a mass of igneous rock that jutted up and through layers of sedimentary rock, now long eroded.

Archaeological finds from the area show that humans have lived near or on Bear Butte for at least 10,000 years. In Cheyenne beliefs, Bear Butte is Noaha-vose or Nahkohe-vose, (giving hill or bear hill) and is revered as the place where Ma'heo'o (great spirit) gave knowledge to prophet Sweet Medicine.

To this day, Native American people make pilgrimages, conduct religious ceremonies on the mountain, and leave prayer cloths and tobacco bundle offerings on the trees, which other visitors are asked not to disrupt. Bear Butte is also sacred to the Lakota as a place to receive sacred visions.

The park is noted for its well-maintained hiking and equestrian use trails but they are quite narrow and steep in places, so hikers and riders should be cautious. Bear Butte State Park also includes 11-acre Bear Butte Lake, and connects to the end of the Centennial Trail, which hikers can follow all the way to Wind Cave National Park.

Spearfish Canyon Nature Area

For the best waterfalls in the Black Hills, it's hard to beat Spearfish Canyon Nature Area. This spectacular state park in Spearfish, South Dakota is home to thousand-foot limestone canyon walls as well as Bridal Veil's 70-foot falls and the multi-tiered Roughlock Falls. Spearfish Canyon is also home to the rare American Dipper bird, and to bobcats, deer, mountain goats, porcupines, and other remarkable wildlife.

Visitors can explore the area by hiking, snowmobiling, snowshoeing, rock climbing, and biking. Or take a break and do some fishing! Nearby Spearfish Canyon Rentals offers fishing gear, ATV rental, fat bikes, e-bikes, snowshoes, and snowmobiles, so no need to lug gear from home.

The canyon ends in the mining ghost town of Savoy and the beautiful Savoy Pond.

When you're tired and hungry, head to the Spearfish Canyon Lodge for food and lodgings. Originally built 1909 as the Glendoris Inn, using what remained of the McLaughlin Tie & Timber Sawmill, the Latchstring Inn and Restaurant at the lodge serves exceptionally cooked American fare, from biscuits & gravy to bison burgers, trout, and locally sourced steaks.

The lodge itself offers several options for accommodations including hotel rooms, suites, and a cabin. Film fans will also want to visit the nearby *Dances with Wolves* film site.

Region: Central

Oahe Downstream Recreation Area

Okobojo Point Recreation Area, Cow Creek Recreation Area, and Spring Creek Recreation Area provide a trio of options for riverside fun just north of 245-foot Oahe Dam, which creates 370,000 Lake Oahe and its 2,250 feet of shoreline. Okobojo Point and Cow Creek sit on opposite sides of an inlet of Lake Oahe and both are excellent spots for paddling sports and windsurfing as a result. as well as camping at Okobojo's 18 sites and Cow Creek's 46 campsites and 4 camping cabins. Visitors also enjoy walking the 2 miles of park roads at Okobojo and 3.5 miles at Cow Creek. The Outpost Lodge near Cow Creek offers additional cabins, plus guided tours for walleye fishing, pheasant hunting, and along with their own cozy fare like chicken strips and chislic, the Outpost Lodge also offers to cook your catch!

Just a bit further downstream, Spring Creek has the most extensive amenities, including a marina with up to 60-foot boat slips, convenience store, and The Boat House Bar & Grill. The Boat House executive chef serves surprisingly upscale fare for a state park, like a steak burger with smoked gouda, balsamic onion, and horseradish sour cream on a ciabatta bun and grilled ahi tuna with a sambal aioli. Spring Creek also has 12 modern cabins and 4 suites and is a great launch point for boating and paddling fun and fishing.

The closest state park to the dam itself is Oahe Downstream Recreation Area. This park near the Oahe Dam is one of the best places in the US for bald eagle viewing. The eagles love the reliable food source the churning water provides year-round, and roost in the mature cottonwood trees nearby, and even more eagles spend winter in the area!

Oahe Downstream Recreation Area is also a favorite for shore fun including hiking trails, an 18-hole disc golf course, and a beautiful prairie butterfly garden. Binoculars are available for checkout to help guests spot these eagles, butterflies, and other wildlife. Oahe Downstream is also a paradise for shooting sports, with an archery range and shooting complex. The park also manages a 400-acre off-highway vehicle area. And if that wears you out, stay for the night at an RV or tent camping site, or in one of the Oahe Downstream's camping cabins, modern cabins, or group lodge.

And while in the area, visitors can also explore the Oahe Dam itself and the surrounding area including the Oahe Chapel. The chapel was built in 1877 as part of the Oahe Mission, after which the dam and reservoir are both named. Then, head into the Oahe Dam Visitors Center to learn more about the dam itself. The earthen dam produces 2.7 billion kilowatt hours of electricity each year built and was completed in 1962, when it was dedicated by JFK. The Visitors Center has fascinating historical photos and information on the dam's operation and construction, President Kennedy's visit, the area and the Oahe Mission. The Oahe Dam Visitors Center is also home to the SD Missouri River Tourism Office, which offers tons of travel resources.

Indian Creek Recreation Area

Indian Creek State Recreation Area sits towards the northern part of South Dakota's sections of Lake Oahe. This area of Lake Oahe is home to a wide variety of fish species and is a favorite of anglers and boaters, and the park has a variety of accommodation options including campsites and cabins.

It's also home to the privately owned Bridge City Marina and Resort, which has everything boaters need from bait to beer, plus cabins, groceries, and delicious burgers and fries at its onsite eatery, Beef's. You can also check out things like fishing poles, kayaks, snowshoes, or floating water mats to make the most of your time here.

Nearby Revheim Bay State Recreation Area provides day use fun in the area with an archery range, lake access, and hiking and biking trails that connect to those at Indian Creek Recreation Area. Swan Creek State Recreation Area also in the area makes camping easy with two RV campsite areas, a tent camping area, and amenities including a dump station, fish cleaning station, flush toilets, a pair of boat ramps for lake access, and tons of scenic views of Lake Oahe.

Farm Island State Recreation Area

Farm Island State Recreation Area sits on an 1800-acre island in the Missouri River, with access to Lake Sharpe and Hipple Lake. As the Missouri River has risen and fallen, naturally and due to dam construction, varying amounts of the island have been underwater throughout the years.

In the early twentieth century, extensive recreational facilities were built on the island including an Izaak Walton League clubhouse, Boy Scout and Girl Scout camps, and a CCC camp, only to be later submerged, and now re-exposed. The island, causeway, and campground areas today offer 8+ miles of walking and hiking trails going past the ruins of these structures, through scenic areas and recreational facilities, and connecting to trails leading to LaFramboise Island and other Pierre-area attractions.

The shore includes playgrounds, picnic areas, an archery range, polo field, and amphitheater for fun, plus a swim beach and boat ramps for those who'd like to enjoy the water, and at the visitors center, guests can rent things like kayaks, bikes, canoes, life jackets, and GPS units for geocaching. The lake access makes the park popular with boaters and fishermen, and for wildlife viewing, with the varied habitats attracting everything from beavers to waterfowl. And visitors who aren't ready to leave the scenic beauty can stay at the park's cabins or campsites.

Randall Creek State Recreation Area

Randall Creek State Recreation Area is the closest state park to the Fort Randall Dam on the Missouri River, which creates the 11th largest reservoir in the United States: Lake Francis Case and is home to Fort Randall Eagle Roost, a National Natural Landmark.

The area was noted by the Corps of Discovery--and other visitors beginning in the early nineteenth century--for its "burning bluffs" where naturally emitted sulfuric acid and steam on the shale hills gave the illusion they were burning. And it's known as the area where the youngest member of that expedition, George Shannon, got lost when sent for water for the horses.

Today, visitors can also enjoy the beauty of the bluffs, the lake, the river, and the surrounding shore beauty at Snake Creek, Burke Lake, Platte Creek, North Wheeler, Pease Creek, North Point and Buryanek State Recreation Areas. Northpoint and South Shore in particular have beautiful sandy swimming beaches and boating beaches, and 102,000 acre Lake Francis Case is a great spot for paddling sports, boating, fishing, and other aquatic fun. The dam itself and the ruins of Fort Randall and its chapel are also well worth the visit.

Region: Northeast

Fort Sisseton Historical State Park

Built on the historic Couteau Des Prairies, Lake City's Fort Sisseton was an active military post known as Fort Wadsworth from 1864 to 1889, before eventually falling into disuse. It was eventually renamed after the nearby Sisseton tribe, and during the Great Depression, the Works Progress Administration restored 14 of the original 45 structures at Fort

Sisseton State Park. Those buildings are now open to the public to visit, and they're on the National Register of Historic Places, including officers' quarters, barracks, a school/library, a hospital and doctors' quarters, barn, blacksmith, guard house, and powder magazine.

Today, visitors can enjoy these historic buildings, along with a visitors center and gift shop, and outdoor artifacts like nineteenth century cannons. The park is popular for historical interest all year round, but is especially notable for its Fort Sisseton Festival each June which features shooting contests, a parade, a historical encampment, hoop dancing, and more, and for their Frontier Christmas celebration in December, complete with horse-drawn sleigh rides.

One notable hero of Fort Wadsworth is Scout Sam Brown. After hearing that a "war party" was approaching, he sent a warning to the next fort to the north, but he also prudently investigated further. He discovered a peaceful group of Lakota on a mission of peace. To prevent bloodshed, he rode through ice and snow and successfully intercepted his earlier message but developed severe frostbite and never walked again.

Fort Sisseton State Park is also known as an excellent place to go camping, with electric and non-electric sites as well as rustic cabins. Visitors ready to get active can check out life jackets and canoes to enjoy on the 3000-acre Kettle Lake, or hike the trails near the fort historic complex, including the Andrew Jackson Fisk quarter mile long boardwalk trail passing by the historic buildings, or the longer Fort Sisseton trail that passes through wetland, forest, and prairie habitats. Kettle Lake (sometimes also known as Cattail Lake, after high water levels in the 90s caused the two natural lakes to combine into one) is excellent for fishing, home to walleye, perch, bass, bluegill, pike, and bass.

And Fort Sisseton is a popular venue for weddings and special events, and is home to the Northern Fort Playhouse, which is a summer repertory theater company in partnership with Northern State University which stages live theater productions in the Fort Sisseton State Park south barracks.

Sica Hollow State Park

Sica Hollow offers one of the Midwest's most eerie camping and hiking experiences: iron deposits have tinted the water flowing through parts of Sica Hollow State Park, making the water appear bloody, leading to many legends about the park and to its name—Sica comes from the Lakota word for bad or evil.

Sica Hollow was known to and subject of legends by the Sioux for many years before a settler named Robert Roi in the 1840s became the first person to actually try to live there, and while a few others followed, the area eventually became uninhabited again, and was designated as a National Natural Landmark in 1967.

Inside the park, the Trail of the Spirits walking path was designated as a National Historic Trail in 1971. One of the park's amenities is 8 miles of horseback trails and 8 horse campsites. The extensive trails in this 900-acre park are also popular for hiking and bird watching year-round, leaf peeping in the fall, and snowshoeing in winter. But inexperienced visitors should stick closely to the trails–amidst the park's boggy grounds lurks quicksand-like surfaces, swamp gasses that sometimes glow or make strange noises, deep ravines, and other hazards!

Hartford Beach State Park

Big Stone Island Nature Area sits in Big Stone Lake or Íŋyaŋ Tháŋka Bdé, the 12,000-acre source of the Minnesota River. Big Stone Lake is the lowest point in the state of South Dakota, and there are state parks on both the South Dakota and Minnesota shores of the lake.

Big Stone Lake is the remnant of the Glacial River Warren that drained Glacial Lake Agassiz and created the Minnesota River Valley, and some say in the exposed granite and gneiss, visitors can sometimes spot fossilized shark teeth! The earliest known written records of Big Stone Island itself came from the expedition of Major Stephan Long and geologist William Keating and noted a Native American village on the island. By the late 1800s, the shores of the lake were covered in vacation resorts, and Big Stone Island at some point became home to a brothel. As local legend tells it, the wives of the men who frequented the island eventually got so fed up that they burned down the ferry to the island, and that was the end of that.

During WWII, the island was used by US Army pilots practicing their small-island landings before deploying to the Pacific, as described by Olympian-turned-bombardier Louis Zamperini in his biography *Unbroken*. Today, the island is a 100-acre state nature area accessible only by water. In addition to its historical interest, the island is also noted for its excellent fishing and scenic views. Big Stone Lake contains walleye, northern pike, yellow perch, largemouth bass, and bluegills.

Visitors wishing to launch from the South Dakota side usually start at Hartford Beach State Park. Near the park's campsites, visitors can walk along prairie grasses and wildflowers to find several historic sites. Along the Robar Trail, you'll find the historic Robar Trading Post and Mireau's Cabin. The trading post was open from 1863 to 1873 by Solomon Robar and his business partner Moses Mireau and was a hub of commerce for fur traders, pioneers, and Native Americans.

And on the Village View trail, you can check out Native American mounds dating from 300 to 1600 AD. Hartford Beach also offers lots of modern-day fun. At the park entrance booth, guests can check out gear like life jackets, then hit the water or the shore to make use of it. On shore, guests can use any of this gear or their own to play disc golf, toss horseshoes, and enjoy hiking trails along the shore of Big Stone Lake. In winter, visitors enjoy snowshoeing and xc skiing on the park's trails and ice fishing on the lake itself. When the ice is thawed, there are tons of opportunities to go fishing, kayak, canoeing, or boating, and Big Stone Lake is a popular place for fishing tournaments.

On the Minnesota side, visitors head to Big Stone Lake State Park, where they find several miles of hiking trails, boat access, and plenty of camping sites. Another must-see on the Minnesota side is the Bonanza Education Center, near the northeastern corner of the lake, which hosts nature education classes and events.

Sandy Shore State Recreation Area

South Dakota's smallest state park is Watertown's Sandy Shore State Recreation Area at just 19 acres! But don't be fooled by the park's small size, as it provides access to 5,520-acre glacial Lake Kampeska in the Couteau des Prairies region, known for its clear waters. On the lake, visitors enjoy boating, swimming, and fishing for walleye, bass, and more than a dozen other species of fish. Life jackets, kayaks, and lawn games are available for checkout.

Biking and walking the park roads are also popular, and the shore is sandy as promised, making a great place for sandcastles, swimming, and other fun. Camping cabins and RV and tent sites make Sandy Shore a great place to stay.

Lake Kampeska was settled as Kampeska City before Watertown itself was formed, and visitors who enjoy their time at Sandy Shore will want to stop at nearby Terry Redlin Museum, where many works of noted painter Terry Redlin feature Lake Kampeska.

In the nineteenth century, legend arose of a scaly Lake Kampeska Monster. Some people believe the beast to have been entirely fiction, while others propose it was an oversized sturgeon whose size was exaggerated to even more mythical proportions. At any size, the Lake Kampeska Monster hasn't been sighted in a century.

Region: Southeast

Lewis & Clark, Pierson Ranch, & Chief White Crane State Recreation Areas

In Yankton, the recreational Missouri River's southern end shines at a complementary trio of state parks: Lewis & Clark State Recreation Area, Pierson Ranch State Recreation Area, and Chief White Crane State Recreation Area. Upstream Lewis & Clark State Recreation Area is the largest and has more than a dozen miles of trail, including asphalt biking and pedestrian trails which connect to the crushed rock or wood chip multi-use trails in the park and to the trails in the city of Yankton, and nearby Pierson Ranch.

The park also has an impressive 28-target archery range and trail for visitors interested in shooting sports. Guests can stay in one of the park's 19 cabins, bring their own tent or RV to stay at one of 400+ campsites, or stay at the Lewis & Clark Resort. This area has been inhabited since about 3000-5000 BC by Archaic Period people, Woodland Culture, Yankton, Ponca, Omaha, and Santee, and nearby Calumet Bluff was the site of Lewis and Clark's first meeting with the Sioux. Today, visitors enjoy exploring, boating, swimming at sandy beaches, and naturalist-led nature education programs. The park also features an extensive marina with a boat store and an on-site restaurant, the Marina Grill.

Pierson Ranch State Recreation Area is the central and oldest of the Yankton trio, opened in 1959. It's also the closest state park or recreation area to the Gavin's Point Dam and Gavin's Point National Fish Hatchery. Built in 1957, the 1.9-mile dam is the most downstream dam on the Missouri and creates 31,000-acre Lewis & Clark Lake. The fish hatchery is one of the premier locations in the US for pallid sturgeon conservation, and has a small visitors center and aquarium open seasonally. Pierson Ranch has campgrounds with RV and tent camping areas and cute cabins so visitors can spend the night (or the week!) There are also tons of daytime fun including a playground, soccer and baseball fields, basketball, sand volleyball, and tennis courts, and a 9-hole disc golf course. There are bike and walking trails that connect to the other Yankton parks, and there's lake access for boating and fishing. Pierson Ranch is also known for hosting Homestead Days, Dutch Oven demonstrations, and other community events.

Just below the dam, Chief White Crane is considered one of the best places in the lower 48 states to see bald eagles in winter, where the mighty beasts love to fish, and you might even spot a bald eagle nest in the nearby cottonwood trees. Chief White Crane is also a great location for humans who want to go fishing, but human visitors are encouraged to stay at the park's 146 campsites including electric sites, tent sites, and cabins rather than nesting in the park's trees. The trails at Chief White Crane connect to the other Yankton trails, and the park features multiple playgrounds, horseshoe pits, and an amphitheater. And both the Missouri River and 250-acre Lake Yankton are accessible from the park, providing access to aquatic fun galore.

Palisades State Park

Palisades State Park shines with natural beauty and wild west legends near Garretson. At this 157-acre park, Split Rock Creek flows through astounding Sioux Quartzite formations including cliffs up to 50 feet tall. Paddle sports are popular on the creek, and the unique beauty of the quartzite is also well enjoyed on the park's hiking trails, or by climbing the rock face itself. Visitors who want to extend their stay can camp in a tent or RV, or enjoy the modern group lodge cabin at Palisades.

The 157-acre park also once contained about 300 silver claims after silver deposits were found in 1886, and a flour mill. The silver claims were quickly abandoned when the poor quality of the deposits became evident, but the mill was more prosperous, and its ruins are still visible on the riverbank. History lovers can aso follow Split Rock Creek north from Palisades to Devil's Gulch Park, north of Garretson, where infamous bandit Jesse James allegedly made a 20-foot leap to his horse while evading a posse after a bank robbery!

Good Earth State Park

South Dakota's newest state park also packs a big historical punch. Good Earth State Park is a day-use state park and home to the Blood Run National Historic Landmark, which is the oldest Oneota cultural site found to date.

At the Good Earth State Park Visitors Center, exhibits share more about the history of the Omaha, Ponca, Ioway, and Otoe who have been here since approximately 900 AD, and for whom the park site specifically served as an important trading site from around 1300-1700 AD for furs, catlinite (also known as "pipestone"), and other goods. Visitors can also check out gear from snowshoes to hammocks at the visitors center.

And Good Earth State Park is known for its programs like nature trivia nights and guided hikes for all ages, and for nature education events and summer day camps specifically for kids. Good Earth State Park offers a plethora of options for outdoor fun, with 7+ miles of hiking trails (including some with a view of the Big Sioux River), a small amphitheater, and an imaginative nature playscape for kids to climb on and explore.

Adams Homestead and Nature Preserve

Adams Homestead and Nature Preserve is a 1500-acre day-use park located on the Missouri River in North Sioux City, South Dakota. Once part of the homestead of Stephen Searls Adams, the park was gifted to the state of South Dakota in the 1980s by Adams' granddaughters, Mary and Maud.

The park features numerous historical buildings, including the Lamont Country School, Sha/Adams House, Stavenger Lutheran Church, and Brusseau Cabin. The Visitors Center provides educational exhibits, trail maps, and staff assistance. Outside, the park's 10 miles of crushed limestone trails offer excellent opportunities for walking, running, and biking in summer through marshy woodland and sandy riverside ecosystems.

In winter, the trails are groomed for xc skiing and snowshoeing. Year-round, visitors enjoy wildlife viewing as over 100 species of birds call Adams home, and scenic overlooks along the trails offer views of the two rivers and the animals that live in them. There's also an outdoor archery range, an updated playground, and a working farm. At Sonny's Acres, visitors learn about barnyard animals in a hands-on environment.

Adams Homestead and Nature Preserve hosts a wide variety of events, including nature education, archery practice sessions, community 5ks, and historical festivals including Homestead Holidays.

Lindsay Hindman is the author of 100 Things to do in Sioux City and Siouxland Before You Die, *a regular contributor to* Living Here Midwest *history magazine, and shares Siouxland and Midwest fun on SiouxlandFamilies.com. Her favorite state park to explore with her husband and their four kids is Stone State Park in Sioux City, Iowa.*

South Dakota State Parks Amenities

Please confirm availability of amenities with the state park system. For more information on South Dakota State Parks, visit their website at gfp.sd.gov

A few notes about the amenities:
- RV – Partial Hookups include access to electricity and water, but not sewer.
- Tent: Tent only sites available.
- Primitive: Camping in remote areas without amenities like bathrooms, picnic tables, trash cans, or any other man-made structures.
- Restrooms: Indicates the highest functional type of restroom available.
- Paddling: Boat access; this could be kayaking, canoeing, and/or powered boats.
- Swimming: Selected if swimming is available, either at a beach or a pool.

There are ten South Dakota parks with equestrian campgrounds. Please check the website for more information.

Midwest State Park Adventures

State Park Name	Hiking # of miles	RV - Partial Hookups	Tent	Primitive	Cabin	Lodge	Hotel/Resort
Adams Homestead and Nature Preserve	11.9	☐	☐	☐	☐	☐	☐
Angostura Recreation Area	5.4	☑	☑	☐	☑	☐	☑
Bear Butte State Park	5.8	☐	☑	☐	☐	☐	☐
Beaver Creek Nature Area	2	☐	☐	☐	☐	☐	☐
Big Sioux Recreation Area	7.4	☑	☐	☐	☐	☐	☐
Big Stone Island Nature Area	0	☐	☐	☐	☐	☐	☐
Burke Lake Recreation Area	0.7	☐	☐	☐	☐	☐	☐
Buryanek Recreation Area	0	☑	☐	☐	☐	☐	☐
Chief White Crane Recreation Area	1.1	☑	☐	☐	☐	☐	☐
Cow Creek Recreation Area	0	☑	☐	☐	☐	☐	☐
Custer State Park	117	☑	☑	☐	☑	☐	☑
Farm Island Recreation Area	7.5	☑	☐	☐	☐	☐	☐
Fisher Grove State Park	1	☑	☐	☐	☐	☐	☐
Fort Sisseton Historic State Park	1.8	☑	☑	☐	☑	☐	☐
Good Earth State Park	7	☐	☐	☐	☐	☐	☐
Hartford Beach State Park	5.6	☑	☑	☐	☑	☐	☐
Indian Creek Recreation Area	2.2	☑	☑	☐	☐	☐	☑
LaFramboise Island Nature Area	9.6	☐	☐	☐	☐	☐	☐
Lake Alvin Recreation Area	0.5	☐	☐	☐	☐	☐	☐
Lake Cochrane Recreation Area	1+	☑	☐	☐	☑	☐	☐
Lake Herman State Park	3.3	☑	☑	☐	☑	☐	☐
Lake Hiddenwood Recreation Area	1.9	☑	☐	☐	☐	☐	☐
Lake Louise Recreation Area	3.3	☑	☑	☐	☑	☐	☐
Lake Poinsett Recreation Area	3.3	☑	☑	☐	☑	☐	☐
Lake Thompson Recreation Area	2.9	☑	☑	☐	☑	☑	☐
Lake Vermillion Recreation Area	1.5	☑	☐	☐	☐	☐	☐
Lewis & Clark Recreation Area	12.6	☑	☐	☐	☐	☐	☐
Little Moreau Recreation Area	0.3	☐	☐	☐	☐	☐	☐
Llewellyn Johns Recreation Area	0	☑	☐	☐	☐	☐	☐
Mina Lake Recreation Area	0.7	☑	☐	☐	☑	☐	☐
Newton Hills State Park	9.6	☑	☐	☐	☐	☑	☑
North Point Recreation Area	4.3	☑	☐	☐	☐	☐	☐
North Wheeler Recreation Area	0	☐	☐	☐	☐	☐	☐
Oahe Downstream Recreation Area	4.2	☑	☐	☐	☐	☑	☐
Oakwood Lakes State Park	4.8	☑	☑	☐	☑	☐	☐
Okobojo Point Recreation Area	0	☐	☐	☐	☐	☐	☐
Palisades State Park	2.6	☑	☐	☐	☐	☑	☑
Pease Creek Recreation Area	3.4	☑	☐	☐	☐	☐	☐
Pelican Lake Recreation Area	6.3	☑	☐	☐	☑	☐	☐
Pickerel Lake Recreation Area	1.5	☑	☐	☐	☑	☐	☐
Pierson Ranch Recreation Area	0.8	☑	☐	☐	☐	☐	☐
Platte Creek Recreation Area	0	☑	☐	☐	☐	☐	☐
Randall Creek Recreation Area	0.7	☑	☐	☐	☐	☐	☐
Revheim Bay Recreation Area	1.5	☐	☐	☐	☐	☐	☐
Richmond Lake Recreation Area	7.1	☑	☐	☐	☑	☐	☐
Rocky Point Recreation Area	0.8	☑	☐	☐	☐	☐	☐
Roy Lake State Park	0.3	☑	☑	☐	☑	☐	☐
Sandy Shore Recreation Area	0	☑	☑	☐	☑	☐	☐
Shadehill Recreation Area	1.9	☑	☐	☐	☐	☑	☐
Sheps Canyon Recreation Area	1.3	☑	☐	☐	☐	☑	☐
Sica Hollow State Park	9.5	☑	☐	☐	☐	☐	☐
Snake Creek Recreation Area	1.4	☑	☐	☐	☐	☐	☑
Spearfish Canyon Nature Area	2.6	☐	☐	☐	☐	☐	☐

South Dakota

State Park Name	Restrooms	Visitor/Nature Center	Swimming	Paddling	Store	Picnic	Fishing
Adams Homestead and Nature Preserve	Flush	✓	☐	☐	✓	☐	☐
Angostura Recreation Area	Showers	✓	✓	✓	✓	✓	✓
Bear Butte State Park	Vault	✓	☐	☐	☐	✓	✓
Beaver Creek Nature Area	Vault	☐	☐	☐	☐	✓	☐
Big Sioux Recreation Area	Showers	☐	☐	✓	☐	✓	✓
Big Stone Island Nature Area	N/A	☐	☐	✓	☐	☐	✓
Burke Lake Recreation Area	Vault	☐	☐	☐	☐	✓	✓
Buryanek Recreation Area	Showers	☐	☐	☐	☐	✓	✓
Chief White Crane Recreation Area	Showers	☐	☐	✓	☐	✓	✓
Cow Creek Recreation Area	Showers	☐	☐	✓	☐	✓	✓
Custer State Park	Showers	✓	✓	✓	✓	✓	✓
Farm Island Recreation Area	Showers	✓	✓	✓	☐	✓	✓
Fisher Grove State Park	Showers	☐	☐	✓	✓	✓	✓
Fort Sisseton Historic State Park	Showers	✓	✓	✓	☐	✓	✓
Good Earth State Park	Flush	✓	☐	☐	☐	✓	✓
Hartford Beach State Park	Showers	☐	✓	✓	☐	✓	✓
Indian Creek Recreation Area	Showers	☐	☐	✓	✓	✓	✓
LaFramboise Island Nature Area	Vault	☐	☐	✓	☐	✓	✓
Lake Alvin Recreation Area	Vault	☐	✓	✓	☐	✓	✓
Lake Cochrane Recreation Area	Showers	☐	✓	☐	☐	✓	✓
Lake Herman State Park	Showers	☐	✓	✓	☐	✓	✓
Lake Hiddenwood Recreation Area	Vault	☐	☐	☐	☐	☐	☐
Lake Louise Recreation Area	Showers	☐	✓	✓	☐	✓	✓
Lake Poinsett Recreation Area	Showers	✓	✓	✓	☐	✓	✓
Lake Thompson Recreation Area	Showers	☐	✓	✓	☐	☐	✓
Lake Vermillion Recreation Area	Showers	☐	✓	✓	☐	✓	✓
Lewis & Clark Recreation Area	Showers	✓	✓	✓	✓	✓	✓
Little Moreau Recreation Area	Vault	☐	☐	✓	☐	✓	✓
Llewellyn Johns Recreation Area	Vault	☐	☐	☐	☐	✓	✓
Mina Lake Recreation Area	Showers	☐	☐	✓	☐	✓	✓
Newton Hills State Park	Showers	☐	✓	✓	☐	✓	✓
North Point Recreation Area	Showers	☐	✓	✓	✓	✓	✓
North Wheeler Recreation Area	Vault	☐	☐	☐	☐	☐	✓
Oahe Downstream Recreation Area	Showers	✓	✓	✓	☐	✓	✓
Oakwood Lakes State Park	Showers	☐	✓	✓	☐	✓	✓
Okobojo Point Recreation Area	Showers	☐	☐	✓	☐	✓	✓
Palisades State Park	Showers	☐	☐	✓	☐	✓	✓
Pease Creek Recreation Area	Showers	☐	☐	✓	☐	✓	✓
Pelican Lake Recreation Area	Showers	☐	✓	✓	☐	✓	✓
Pickerel Lake Recreation Area	Showers	☐	✓	✓	☐	✓	✓
Pierson Ranch Recreation Area	Showers	☐	☐	✓	☐	✓	✓
Platte Creek Recreation Area	Showers	☐	✓	☐	☐	☐	✓
Randall Creek Recreation Area	Showers	☐	☐	✓	☐	✓	✓
Revheim Bay Recreation Area	Vault	☐	✓	☐	☐	✓	✓
Richmond Lake Recreation Area	Showers	☐	✓	✓	☐	✓	✓
Rocky Point Recreation Area	Showers	☐	✓	☐	☐	✓	✓
Roy Lake State Park	Showers	☐	✓	✓	☐	✓	✓
Sandy Shore Recreation Area	Showers	☐	✓	✓	☐	✓	✓
Shadehill Recreation Area	Showers	✓	✓	✓	☐	✓	✓
Sheps Canyon Recreation Area	Showers	☐	☐	✓	☐	☐	✓
Sica Hollow State Park	Vault	☐	☐	☐	☐	☐	☐
Snake Creek Recreation Area	Showers	☐	✓	✓	✓	✓	✓
Spearfish Canyon Nature Area	Flush	☐	☐	☐	☐	☐	✓

Midwest State Park Adventures

State Park Name	Hiking # of miles	RV - Partial Hookups	Tent	Primitive	Lodging Cabin	Lodge	Hotel/Resort
Spirit Mound Historic Prairie	0.9	☐	☐	☐	☐	☐	☐
Spring Creek Recreation Area	0	☑	☐	☐	☐	☐	☐
Springfield Recreation Area	0.4	☑	☐	☐	☐	☐	☐
Swan Creek Recreation Area	0	☑	☐	☑	☐	☐	☐
Union Grove State Park	5.5	☑	☐	☐	☐	☐	☐
Walkers Point Recreation Area	0	☑	☑	☐	☑	☐	☐
West Bend Recreation Area	2.2	☑	☐	☐	☐	☐	☐
West Pollock Recreation Area	0	☑	☐	☐	☐	☐	☐
West Whitlock Recreation Area	1.9	☑	☐	☐	☐	☐	☐

State Park Name	Restrooms	Visitor/Nature Center	Swimming	Paddling	Store	Picnic	Fishing
Spirit Mound Historic Prairie	Vault	☐	☐	☐	☐	☐	☐
Spring Creek Recreation Area	Showers	☐	☐	☑	☑	☐	☑
Springfield Recreation Area	Showers	☐	☐	☑	☐	☑	☑
Swan Creek Recreation Area	Showers	☐	☐	☐	☐	☑	☑
Union Grove State Park	Showers	☐	☐	☐	☐	☐	☐
Walkers Point Recreation Area	Showers	☐	☐	☐	☐	☑	☑
West Bend Recreation Area	Showers	☐	☐	☐	☐	☑	☑
West Pollock Recreation Area	Showers	☐	☐	☐	☐	☐	☑
West Whitlock Recreation Area	Showers	☐	☑	☐	☐	☑	☑

WISCONSIN

By Dannelle Gay

Wisconsin is a state that truly embraces the beauty of nature. From its rolling hills to its deep forests, and from its pristine lakes and rivers to the impressive sandstone bluffs that rise high above the landscape, Wisconsin is a place that inspires awe in all who visit.

One of the best ways to experience Wisconsin's natural beauty is through its state park system. Managed by the Wisconsin Department of

Natural Resources (DNR), the system includes 49 state parks, 15 state forests, and 44 state trails. Each park is unique in its natural features, cultural history, and recreational opportunities, making Wisconsin a nature lover's paradise. They are truly dedicated to preserving and protecting the state's natural resources for future generations.

From Devil's Lake State Park in Baraboo, known for its stunning quartzite bluffs, clear blue waters, and panoramic views of the surrounding landscape, to Peninsula State Park on the Door County peninsula, offering scenic views of Green Bay and Lake Michigan, Wisconsin's state park system has something for everyone.

Even better, as the home to more than 15,000 lakes and 84,000 miles of streams and rivers, Wisconsin provides a wide variety of fishing experiences for both novice and experienced anglers. Many of Wisconsin's state parks have designated fishing areas or boat launches, making it easy for visitors to cast a line and reel in a catch. Some of the most popular fish species found in Wisconsin's lakes and streams include walleye, musky, northern pike, bass, and panfish.

So come and explore the breathtaking natural beauty of Wisconsin's state parks. Feel the rush of the wind in your hair as you hike through the forests, breathe in the fresh air as you relax by the lake, and marvel at the stunning sandstone formations that rise high above the landscape.

Whether you're seeking adventure, relaxation, or just a chance to connect with nature, Wisconsin's state parks offer endless possibilities for outdoor fun and exploration. Pack your bags, hit the road, and discover the wonders of Wisconsin's great outdoors for yourself!

Wisconsin State Park Facts & Important Information

- Wisconsin's state parks offer more than 2,700 miles of hiking trails, ranging from easy nature walks to challenging backcountry treks.
- Some of Wisconsin's state parks have unusual geological features, such as the sandstone bluffs at Devil's Lake State Park and the sea caves at Apostle Islands National Lakeshore.

- The Wisconsin state parks see more than 20 million visitors a year.
- Six state parks have amazing natures centers that make for fun educational opportunities for the kids.
- Wisconsin has two different kinds of Rattlesnakes so make sure to watch for them when hiking and keep a snake bite kit in your pack.
- The Wisconsin Explorer Program offers free books with nature activities, scavenger hunts, games, hikes, and more that will help you get the kids excited to get outdoors.
- You can hunt in every Wisconsin state park except for: Copper Culture State Park, Cross Plains State Park, Governor Nelson State Park, Heritage Hill State Park, Lakeshore State Park, and Lost Dauphin State Park.

A note about accessibility

The Wisconsin Department of Natural Resources (DNR) aims to make the outdoors accessible for all individuals, and therefore, they use the term "universally accessible" rather than "ADA-accessible" which may not apply to all elements of outdoor spaces. While hunting blinds are not mentioned in the ADA and cannot be labeled as "ADA-accessible," the DNR strives to adhere to accessibility standards for all other elements to make them as accessible as possible for people of all abilities.

Regarding compliance with accessibility requirements, the DNR works to meet and exceed ADA requirements at all of their properties. However, achieving "Barrier Free" status in large outdoor settings may not always be feasible.

To further improve accessibility, the DNR has placed posters at their properties asking visitors to provide feedback on any accessibility concerns or questions they may have. The DNR is committed to using this feedback to enhance accessibility in their state parks for future visitors.

Midwest State Park Adventures

Wisconsin State Parks Map

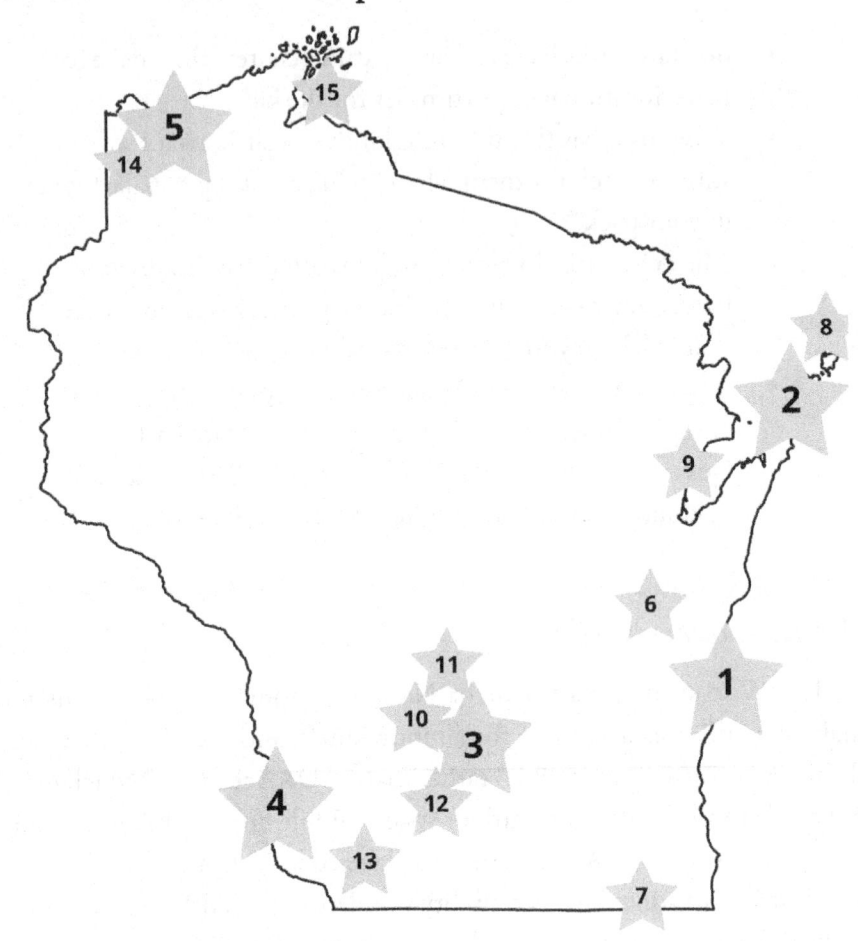

1. Kohler-Andre 2. Peninsula 3. Devil's Lake 4. Wyalusing 5. Amnicon Falls 6. High Cliff 7. Big Foot Beach 8. Copper Culture 9. Rock Island 10. Mirror Lake 11. Rocky Arbor 12.Blue Mound 13. Belmont Mound 14.Pattison 15.Big Bay

Region: Southeast

Kohler-Andrae State Park

Kohler-Andrae State Park is located in eastern Wisconsin, about six and a half miles from Sheboygan. The park comprises John Michael Kohler State Park on the north end, Terry Andrae State Park on the south end, and the area in between. The park is a unique natural preserve that offers visitors the opportunity to explore the shore of Lake Michigan. The park has two miles of sandy beach, fishing ponds, hiking trails through dunes and woods, and other recreational activities.

The park has a rich history that dates back 9500 years when Native Americans inhabited the area. The park was later inhabited by settlers, pioneers, and fishermen, and in 1928, Mrs. Elsbeth Andre donated her lakefront property to the state of Wisconsin. The park was named after her late husband, Terry Andrae.

In 1966, the Kohler Company donated 280 acres to the state of Wisconsin in memory of its founder, John Michael Kohler. Over the years, the state of Wisconsin purchased another 600 acres, and the state began overseeing the entire region, including both the parks and the land between them.

The park has several recreational activities for visitors to enjoy. On a warm day, the park's sandy beach is ideal for picnics, swimming, and paddle boating. The park has hiking trails, biking trails, horseback riding trails, and fishing ponds. The park's habitats host a wide range of wildlife, including deer, shorebirds, dune foxes, and marsh muskrats.

Camping is also available year-round in the park with 135 family campsites with fire rings and picnic tables. The park also has an accessible cabin equipped with modern conveniences that can accommodate six people and can be rented for up to four nights each year by the same person.

The park is also home to the Sanderling Nature Center, named after the sanderling shorebird. It offers interactive exhibits, nature films, books, educational programs, and souvenirs. The center's rooftop observation deck provides a great view of Lake Michigan's watercraft and waterfowl. Visitors can also explore the nearby keel of an 1853 shipwrecked schooner and the Creeping Juniper Nature Trail.

The park offers a range of water recreation activities to enjoy, including swimming, paddle boating, and fishing. Visitors should use caution when swimming because the water can be chilly and there is usually a brisk wind on Lake Michigan.

The park's Friends Fishing Pond is two acres in area and fourteen feet deep, and it is an urban fishing pond that has special regulations with the intent of promoting recreational fishing.

Kohler-Andrae State Park is an excellent destination for those looking to explore Lake Michigan's natural preserve. This park offers various recreational activities, including camping, hiking, fishing, bird watching, and swimming. Visitors can walk sandy beaches along Lake Michigan, enjoy towering sand dunes, and peaceful woodlands.

It is easy to see why Kohler-Andrae State Park is a popular destination for nature lovers, outdoor enthusiasts, and anyone seeking a peaceful escape from the hustle and bustle of daily life.

High Cliff State Park

High Cliff State Park is a popular Wisconsin state park located in the scenic Kettle Moraine, on the northeast corner of Lake Winnebago in the town of Sherwood. It is the only state-owned recreational area on Lake Winnebago, Wisconsin's largest lake.

The park is famous for offering year-round activities for visitors such as camping, hiking, and biking, and it is known for its historical and cultural significance. The rocks at High Cliff are primarily sandstone, and they were formed by streams that once ran through the area millions of years ago.

Nomadic Siouan Native Americans once inhabited the area, and they left 30 effigy mounds behind, nine of which remain today. The park was once a successful limestone mining operation from 1855 to 1956, which supported a small "company town" consisting of 16 houses for workers, a store, and a tavern.

High Cliff State Park is also home to a Red Bird statue that honors a leader of the Winnebago Native American tribe who fought in the Winnebago War against the United States.

The park's effigy mounds are believed to be haunted, and there have been reports of a "warm wind" or "cold wind" in the area, as well as a special kind of green moss that ONLY grows on the effigy mounds. The park is a great destination for families who want to learn more about Wisconsin's history and culture, while enjoying the great outdoors.

Big Foot Beach State Park

Big Foot Beach State Park is a 271-acre park located on the shores of Lake Geneva in the Southern Unit of Kettle Moraine State Forest. It is a popular summer vacation destination with campers, hikers, and outdoor enthusiasts who enjoy the fantastic attractions found in the park and Lake Geneva nearby.

The park is named after Chief Big Foot, a Potawatomi tribal chief who led his people to settle in the region because of the rich resources that were present there.

Lake Geneva is a large, natural freshwater lake that is accessible to the public for swimming and water sports, including boating, kayaking, and scuba diving. The lake has four beaches, including Big Foot Beach, Fontana Beach, Riviera Beach, and Williams Bay Beach.

The region is also popular for fishing, with Ceylon Lagoon being a favorite spot for campers and hikers. The park has over 100 wooded campsites, accommodating both RV and tent campers, and numerous open spaces for families to camp. The park also has beautiful trails and scenic picnic spots that are wheelchair-accessible, making it ideal for peaceful and tranquil walks.

Region: East

Peninsula State Park

Nestled in the heart of Door County, Peninsula State Park is a 3,776-acre state park that welcomes around one million visitors annually. The park has eight miles of shoreline on Green Bay and offers a range of activities for visitors, including camping, hiking, biking, and skiing. The park is also known for its stunning views, particularly during the fall, when the trees offer a display of various colors.

Peninsula State Park was established in 1910, and it became Wisconsin's second state park. During the Great Depression, the Civilian Conservation Corps completed several projects, including the rebuilding of Eagle Tower and the construction of stone fences. During World War II, a German prison camp was established in Fish Creek, and inmates were used for park construction projects.

The park has four campgrounds that cater to visitors with different preferences. The Nicolet Bay camping area has 188 campsites, 33 of which have electricity, and shower and flush toilet facilities are available throughout the campground.

Tennison Bay is the largest campground with 188 campsites, 56 of which are electric, and it has playgrounds and kayak launches. The Weborg campground has twelve electric sites and is popular with RV and trailer campers, while Welcker's Point is an 81-site non-electric campground located in a heavily wooded area that's ideal for tent and small trailer campers.

The park offers numerous activities for visitors who prefer not to camp, including hiking, biking, hunting, and fishing. The park has many hiking trails, with some looping through forests or over bluffs that offer views of Lake Michigan and Green Bay.

Being in the middle of Door County, you are a short drive from many incredible gift shops, restaurants, light houses, and even a drive-in movie theater! You can be sure to enjoy some quality unplugged time here.

Overall, Peninsula State Park is an excellent place to visit for nature lovers, as it offers breathtaking views, outdoor activities, and the chance to connect with nature.

Copper Culture State Park

Copper Culture State Park is an incredible historic site that is home to the oldest known Native burial site in Wisconsin. While you cannot camp overnight here, you can enjoy a variety of outdoor activities like hiking, bird watching, and snowshoeing in the winter. Outdoor lovers will find beautiful, isolated, and quiet hiking trails inside this park.

The park covers 42 acres and sits on the banks of the Oconto River. The site was once the burial ground for the Menominee, the first inhabitants of the region. The Menominee were known for their use of copper in tools and decorations, and their remains, some of which date back over 7,000 years, have been found at the site.

There are an estimated 200 burial grounds still present – please be respectful. The burial grounds showed that the deceased people were interred close to their place of death, and some were buried with copper tools, ornaments, and bone tools, indicating a strong belief in the afterlife.

The Werrebroeck home inside the park serves as the Copper Culture State Park museum and is an incredible way to learn more about the people who had settled here. You will learn things like why they were referred to as "The Copper Culture People" and how the Menomonee were hunters, fishermen, and gatherers, and traded their copper goods for other items they needed.

Rock Island State Park

Rock Island State Park is a small, remote park located on Rock Island, which is about six miles from Washington Island on the Door Peninsula in Wisconsin. The park covers most of the island, which is less than two miles long and a little over a mile wide. It is only open during the summer season from Memorial Day Weekend to Columbus Day due to the harsh winter environment. Visitors must take two ferries to get to the island, which makes it unique and remarkable.

Rock Island has a rich history, with Native American tribes as the original inhabitants, followed by European explorers, settlers, lighthouse keepers, and even Scandinavian inventor Chester Thordarson, who bought most of the island's acreage in 1910 and had several stone buildings constructed. The park has several historical sites, including the oldest lighthouse in Wisconsin, Pottawotami Light, and the historic boathouse, also known as "Viking Hall."

To visit Rock Island State Park, visitors must take a large ferry to Washington Island and then take the passenger-only Rock Island Ferry. Passengers with canoes and kayaks may be able to bring them on the ferry for an extra fee. There are no bicycles or vehicles allowed on the island, so visitors may want to rent a wagon at the ferry dock to transport their gear.

Region: South Central

Devil's Lake State Park

Devil's Lake State Park is home to several unique animal sightings, including a "monster in the lake," a large alligator, and even Bigfoot. There are also ghost stories, including the 10-ton ghosts of Baraboo, which were said to be deceased ghost circus elephants that roamed the area.

The park is also home to several effigy mounds, including a Bird, Panther, Bear, and Lynx. These mounds are sacred spaces and are not meant to be walked on and they are protected People can learn more about them at the Devil's Lake State Park Nature Center.

The park has three campgrounds with a total of 423 sites that each accommodate a family of up to six people, but there are no campgrounds near or on the shoreline of Devil's Lake itself. The park offers something for every adventurer, with over 29 miles of hiking trails, two sandy beaches, and opportunities for scuba diving, fishing, swimming, kayaking, boating, and canoeing. However, gas motors are not allowed on the lake.

Devil's Lake is also the home to exceptional rock climbing in the Midwest, with highly qualified instructors, climbing guides, and outfitters available at the park. Whether you're a novice or a pro, you can take advantage of private or group anchor courses, climbing trips, bouldering, and traditional lessons.

Mirror Lake State Park

Mirror Lake State Park, located three miles south of Wisconsin Dells, is a beautiful 137-acre lake with a glassy-smooth surface, surrounded by a 2,000-acre park that includes natural features such as dense pine forests, sandstone bluffs, and marshlands, creating a great habitat for wildlife and a perfect outdoor destination for nature lovers.

The park was officially opened in 1966 and includes Mirror Lake, from which it derives its name. The lake was created by damming Dell Creek, and its deep, clean waters make it a great location for scuba diving. It also offers excellent fishing grounds, and visitors can find a variety of fish, including northern pikes, panfish, walleyes, bluegill, trout, and largemouth bass.

Mirror Lake State Park offers 151 campsites divided into three separate campgrounds that are open from April to October. There are many fun activities available to visitors, including white-water rafting, swimming, kayaking, and canoeing, and there are also hiking trails, mountain biking trails, and snowshoeing.

The park is home to the Seth Peterson Cottage, the only structure designed by renowned architect Frank Lloyd Wright that is available for rent.

Rocky Arbor State Park

Rocky Arbor State Park, located in south-central Wisconsin, is a popular destination for outdoor enthusiasts. Visitors can enjoy hiking, camping, picnicking, and snowshoeing. The park features a gorge with cliffs, mixed woodlands, wetlands, and unique rock outcroppings. The park's geologic formations of sandstone ledges and rock outcroppings were protected when the park was established in 1932.

Camping at Rocky Arbor State Park is a popular choice for those who want to explore the park and the surrounding area. The campground has 89 wooded sites, and there are several vault toilets and water stations available throughout the campground. The campground is open from Memorial Day to Labor Day, and sites with power and water are available in the second loop.

The park's hiking trail is almost one and a half miles long and includes the former bed of the Wisconsin River, wetlands, sandstone structures, and the ridge of the gorge. Visitors can appreciate spring blossoms, fall foliage, and a variety of species, including frogs, smaller mammals, and deer. The trail has an elevation gain of 95 feet and includes overgrowth, fallen trees, rock steps, and wooden stairs.

Rocky Arbor State Park is only a mile and a half from The Dells and is frequently visited in combination with other state parks in the area. The park is open to foot traffic all year, but vehicles are only permitted in the park between Memorial Day and Labor Day weekends.

Region: Southwest

Wyalusing State Park

Wyalusing is a beautiful state park located in southwestern Wisconsin, where the Wisconsin and Mississippi Rivers meet, just off the Great River Road. The park covers an area of almost 2,700 acres and is one of Wisconsin's oldest state parks, established in 1917.

The name Wyalusing comes from a Native American word meaning "home of the warrior." The park's location has historical significance as the site was once inhabited by the Hopewell and the Effigy Mound Builders. Europeans, fur traders, miners, and farmers all left their mark here to create a rich history that is fun to explore.

Stargazers flock here to take advantage of the Huser Astronomy Center. With several high powered telescopes, the local StarSplitters

Wisconsin

Astronomy Club offers regular free public programs from May to October.

The park is also a dream for those who love to cast for panfish, bass, northern pike and walleye. There's an accessible fishing pier at the boat landing, and boat rentals are available for those who prefer to fish from the water. There is even a six mile canoe trail through the backwaters of the Mississippi River that has blue and white canoe trail signs to guide you.

Visitors to Wyalusing State Park can enjoy a range of outdoor activities. The park offers 14 miles of hiking between nine trails that wind through forests, bluffs, and along the riverbanks. The trails range in difficulty from easy to challenging and offer scenic views of the river valley. Some of the park's most popular trails include the Sentinel Ridge Trail and the Bluff Trail, which includes a flight of stairs that leads to Treasure Cave, which is a small limestone cavern.

Bird lovers will take delight in the over 90 species that they can observe, and there is an amazing sunset view if you climb to Lookout Point. One of the park's unique features is the 64 Native American burial mounds that are scattered throughout the park. You can learn more if you hike the Sentinel Ridge Tail.

What makes this park different for campers is that besides the two family campgrounds that have 109 sites, they have the Hugh Harper Indoor Group Camp. With four dorms that can hold up to 108 people, this is perfect for larger families or that business retreat. It has a full commercial kitchen, nice dining area, and even a recreation room.

Wyalusing State Park is a beautiful and diverse park that offers something for everyone. From hiking and camping to fishing and boating, the park provides endless opportunities for outdoor recreation. It is close to local historic Villa Louis and Wisconsin's only War of 1812 Battlefield.

Blue Mound State Park

Blue Mound State Park is located in Southern Wisconsin and covers an area of 1,153 acres. It is known for its observation towers, which offer spectacular views of the Wisconsin River valley, the Driftless Area forests, the plains, and the city of Madison.

The park was founded in 1959 by the Wisconsin Department of Natural Resources and has many amenities, including 77 wooded sites for camping, RV sites, tent sites, an accessible cabin for people with disabilities, and is the only state park with a swimming pool.

Visitors can also take advantage of the park's trails, which offer varying levels of difficulty, from easy walks to more challenging hikes. Bicycle enthusiasts can cycle through the 15.5 miles of off-road trails, which are moderate to hard in terms of challenge.

The park also hosts a variety of nature programs and guided hikes, with a nature center providing educational programs. Blue Mound State Park is a unique ecosystem with bountiful wildlife due to the region being largely untouched by glaciers. However, visitors should be wary of the raccoons at the park and store your food accordingly.

Belmont Mound State Park

Belmont Mound State Park, located off Highway 151 in Wisconsin's southwest corner, is a non-profit day-use-only park run by the Belmont Lions Club, established in 1961. It offers a range of recreational activities, including hiking, biking, snowshoeing, hunting, and trapping.

The park is in the Wisconsin Driftless Area, an area never covered by ice during the ice age. Belmont Mound, which rises four hundred feet above the surrounding landscape, is one of two mounds in the area used as navigational aids, making Wisconsin's first capitol easy to find in Wisconsin's territorial wilderness.

Belmont Mound was once a mountain, and natural erosion has turned it into the present-day Belmont Mound, with limestone cliffs, small caves, and unique rock formations that visitors can enjoy. The park has two and a half miles of hiking trails, with three main trails, and a lightly trafficked

1.9-mile loop trail, the Belmont Mound Extended Loop Trail. The trail goes through a dense forest with lush outcroppings, cliffs, and interesting rock formations.

Although camping is not allowed within the park, there are two campgrounds nearby, Lake Joy Campground and Yellowstone Lake State Park, which offer numerous water sports activities and entertainment options for families.

Region: Northwest
Amnicon Falls State Park

Amnicon Falls State Park, located in Wisconsin's far northwest region, is a popular tourist destination with activities suitable for all ages. The park covers 850 acres and features four named waterfalls that are very close to visitors, allowing them to feel the spray of the falls. Visitors can take a leisurely stroll along the hiking routes and photograph the waterfalls set against a stunning backdrop. This park is a family-friendly destination with something for everyone, and it can be explored in an hour or when you camp overnight.

Native Americans have settled in the Amnicon Falls State Park area since the last glacier melted, using copper found in the rocks along the Amnicon riverbanks to make tools and weapons. The area became part of Wisconsin State due to the Westward Expansion, and Native Americans continue to live here and play a vital role in the conservation of wildlife. The name Amnicon comes from the Ojibwe word "aminikan," meaning "where fish spawn."

Amnicon Falls State Park began as a privately owned park, with copper miners and lumberjacks operating in the area. The Wisconsin DNR took ownership of the park over the years, and the final acreage was purchased in 1977. The park is historically significant due to the Douglas Fault running through it, making it an attractive site for geologists and other visitors to study and monitor the fault.

Visitors to this park can immerse themselves in the park's unique outdoor environment by wading in the river and exploring the waterfalls. The park features four waterfalls: Upper Falls, Lower Falls, Now and Then Falls, and Snake Pit Falls. Now and Then Falls are intermittent, only flowing in the spring and after rainfall. Visitors can take a selfie at the selfie station located downstream from the bridge and Lower Falls. They can also view the waterfalls from the historic "Horton Bridge," a 55-foot covered footbridge, and the covered bridge, with its perspective of the falls, is a popular attraction for visitors to the park.

Amnicon Falls State Park is a place where visitors can relax and enjoy the natural surroundings. It's an excellent destination for families or anyone looking for a break from the city's hustle and bustle. Visitors can camp overnight or explore the park's attractions in an hour. The park is accessible via a short drive from Superior or Duluth, making it an ideal location for a day trip.

Pattison State Park

If you like the falls at Amnicon, you need to check out Pattison State Park. Located in northern Wisconsin, it is one of the state's oldest state parks, established in 1920. The park is home to two waterfalls, Big Manitou Falls, which is the state's highest waterfall, and Little Manitou Falls, which is located about a mile and a half from Big Manitou Falls.

The park covers 1,400 acres of land, including a lake with a sandy beach, trails, and camping sites. There is also a backpacking campground area with three primitive camping sites, only with vault toilets, tables, and fire rings.

In addition to camping, visitors can paddle on Interfalls Lake, go fishing, hunting, camping, cross-country skiing, and explore the park's wildlife. This park is home to about fifty mammal species and two hundred bird species. The park also has a Nature Center with interpretive displays, and visitors can borrow activities for children to enjoy.

The Civilian Conservation Corps continued to improve the park from the 1930s to WWII. Visitors can thank Martin Pattison's foresight and investment as well as the CCC's "Camp Pattison" for the park features of Big Manitou Falls, old growth forest, and the artificial beachfront enjoyed today.

Big Bay State Park

Big Bay State Park is located on Madeline Island, the largest island in the Apostle Islands chain in Lake Superior, Ashland County. The park covers 2,350 acres and is the largest protected area in the Apostle Islands. Visitors can drive, bike, hike, or take the ferry to the park. The ferry ride provides stunning views of the lake and the surrounding area.

This park has a rich history and connection to the Ojibwa/Chippewa community (Native Americans). The island was named after Michel Cadotte's wife, Madeline, who was the daughter of an Ojibwa chief. The Ojibwa community considered the island a spiritual center, and petitions by the chief led to the treaty of La Pointe (in 1854) that offered them permanent reservations on the island and around the Big Bay State Park, successfully ending years of conflicts with the Mississippi cohort. Visitors can drive, bike, hike, or take the ferry to the park. The ferry ride provides stunning views of the lake and the surrounding area.

The park's jagged, uneven coastline is a fascination for travelers, providing stunning photo opportunities and a great place to sit and enjoy the cool sea breeze. The park also offers 60 campsites, including 21 family campsites and two outdoor group camps. All campsites come equipped with amenities, and instructions on how to camp can be found at the campground center.

Lake Superior creates a stunning beach that stretches for about 1.5 miles along the shore, with soft, small-grained sands and a shallow shore that allows for a great swimming experience. The water of Lake Superior is so clean you can see the bottom of the lake, and water sports like scuba diving, swimming, kayaking, and boating are common activities. The park's east-facing beach warms up as the sun rises, making it ideal for a great morning kayaking adventure.

Dannelle Gay, AKA The Traveling Cheesehead, is a travel writer, TV host, and camping enthusiast. She's a published author of 100 Things to Do in Wisconsin Before You Die, the brains behind the website Crazy Camping Girl, and often works with GoRving.com to create recipes to enhance outdoor adventures. Despite her busy schedule, she finds time to camp and to disconnect from modern life.

Wisconsin

Wisconsin State Parks Amenities

Please confirm availability of amenities with the state park system For more information on Wisconsin State Parks, visit their website at dnr.wisconsin.gov/topic/Parks

A few notes about the amenities:
- RV – Partial Hookups include access to electricity and water, but not sewer.
- Tent: Tent only sites available.
- Primitive: Camping in remote areas without amenities like bathrooms, picnic tables, trash cans, or any other man-made structures.
- Restrooms: Indicates the highest functional type of restroom available.
- Paddling: Boat access; this could be kayaking, canoeing, and/or powered boats.
- Swimming: Selected if swimming is available, either at a beach or a pool.

Notes about specific state parks:
- Heritage Hill State Historical Park is a living history museum and Wisconsin state park that features over 25 historic buildings, interactive exhibits, and costumed interpreters, offering visitors a glimpse into Wisconsin's rich history from the fur trading era to the early 1900s. This place has its own admission fee, as the Wisconsin State Park Pass does not cover it.
- Lost Dauphin: While technically a state park, the Town of Lawrence Parks and Recreation Department runs Lost Dauphin State Park. It is a 19-acre day-use-only park and sports a porta-potty for convenience.

Midwest State Park Adventures

State Park Name	Hiking # of miles	RV - Partial Hookups	Tent	Primitive	Cabin
Amnicon Falls State Park	1.8	☑	☑	☑	☐
Aztalan State Park	2	☐	☐	☐	☐
Belmont Mound State Park	2.5	☐	☐	☐	☐
Big Bay State Park	7	☑	☑	☑	☐
Big Foot Beach State Park	5	☑	☑	☐	☐
Blue Mound State Park	20	☑	☑	☐	☑
Brunet Island State Park	8	☑	☑	☐	☐
Buckhorn State Park	4	☑	☑	☑	☑
Copper Culture State Park	10	☐	☐	☐	☐
Copper Falls State Park	17	☑	☑	☐	☑
Council Grounds State Park	3.5	☑	☑	☐	☐
Cross Plains State Park	0	☐	☐	☐	☐
Devil's Lake State Park	29	☑	☑	☐	☐
Governor Dodge State Park	40	☑	☑	☐	☐
Governor Nelson State Park	8	☐	☐	☐	☐
Governor Thompson State Park	16	☑	☑	☐	☐
Harrington Beach State Park	7	☑	☑	☐	☑
Hartman Creek State Park	10	☑	☑	☐	☐
High Cliff State Park	8	☑	☑	☐	☑
Interstate State Park	9	☑	☑	☐	☐
Kinnickinnic State Park	10	☐	☐	☐	☐
Kohler-Andrae State Park	7	☑	☑	☐	☑
Lake Kegonsa State Park	5	☑	☑	☐	☐
Lake Wissota State Park	7	☑	☑	☐	☐
Lakeshore State Park	1	☐	☐	☐	☐
Lizard Mound State Park	1	☐	☐	☐	☐
Merrick State Park	3	☑	☑	☐	☐
Mill Bluff State Park	2	☑	☑	☐	☐
Mirror Lake State Park	19	☑	☑	☐	☑
Natural Bridge State Park	1	☐	☐	☐	☐
Nelson Dewey State Park	2	☑	☑	☑	☐
New Glarus Woods State Park	5.5	☐	☑	☑	☐
Newport State Park	30	☐	☑	☑	☐
Pattison State Park	7	☑	☑	☐	☐
Peninsula State Park	20	☑	☑	☐	☐
Perrot State Park	12.5	☑	☑	☐	☐
Potawatomi State Park	9.5	☑	☑	☐	☑
Rib Mountain State Park	13	☐	☐	☐	☐
Roche-a-Cri State Park	6	☑	☑	☐	☐
Rock Island State Park	10	☐	☐	☑	☐
Rocky Arbor State Park	1	☑	☑	☐	☐
Straight Lake State Park	8.5	☐	☐	☑	☐
Tower Hill State Park	2	☐	☑	☐	☐
Whitefish Dunes State Park	14.5	☐	☐	☐	☐
Wildcat Mountain State Park	20	☑	☑	☑	☐
Willow River State Park	13	☑	☑	☐	☐
Wyalusing State Park	14	☑	☑	☐	☑
Yellowstone Lake State Park	13	☑	☑	☐	☐

Wisconsin

State Park Name	Restrooms	Visitor/Nature Center	Swimming	Paddling	Store	Picnic	Fishing
Amnicon Falls State Park	Vault	☐	✓	☐	☐	✓	✓
Aztalan State Park	Pit	☐	☐	✓	☐	✓	✓
Belmont Mound State Park	N/A	☐	☐	☐	☐	✓	☐
Big Bay State Park	Showers	☐	☐	✓	☐	✓	✓
Big Foot Beach State Park	Showers	☐	✓	✓	☐	✓	✓
Blue Mound State Park	Showers	☐	✓	☐	☐	✓	☐
Brunet Island State Park	Showers	☐	✓	✓	☐	☐	✓
Buckhorn State Park	Showers	☐	✓	✓	☐	✓	✓
Copper Culture State Park	N/A	☐	☐	☐	☐	✓	☐
Copper Falls State Park	Showers	☐	✓	✓	☐	✓	✓
Council Grounds State Park	Showers	☐	✓	✓	☐	✓	✓
Cross Plains State Park	N/A	☐	☐	☐	☐	☐	✓
Devil's Lake State Park	Showers	✓	✓	✓	✓	✓	✓
Governor Dodge State Park	Showers	☐	✓	✓	☐	✓	✓
Governor Nelson State Park	Flush	☐	✓	✓	☐	✓	✓
Governor Thompson State Park	Showers	☐	✓	✓	☐	✓	✓
Harrington Beach State Park	Showers	☐	✓	✓	☐	✓	✓
Hartman Creek State Park	Flush	☐	✓	✓	☐	✓	✓
High Cliff State Park	Showers	☐	✓	✓	☐	✓	✓
Interstate State Park	Showers	☐	✓	✓	☐	✓	✓
Kinnickinnic State Park	Vault	☐	✓	✓	☐	✓	✓
Kohler-Andrae State Park	Showers	✓	✓	✓	✓	✓	✓
Lake Kegonsa State Park	Showers	☐	✓	✓	☐	✓	✓
Lake Wissota State Park	Showers	☐	✓	✓	☐	✓	✓
Lakeshore State Park	N/A	☐	☐	✓	☐	✓	✓
Lizard Mound State Park	Vault	✓	☐	☐	☐	✓	☐
Merrick State Park	Showers	☐	✓	✓	☐	✓	✓
Mill Bluff State Park	Vault	☐	✓	☐	☐	✓	☐
Mirror Lake State Park	Showers	☐	✓	✓	☐	✓	✓
Natural Bridge State Park	N/A	☐	☐	☐	☐	☐	☐
Nelson Dewey State Park	Flush	☐	☐	✓	☐	✓	✓
New Glarus Woods State Park	Vault	☐	☐	☐	☐	✓	☐
Newport State Park	Pit	☐	☐	✓	☐	✓	✓
Pattison State Park	Showers	☐	✓	☐	☐	✓	✓
Peninsula State Park	Vault	✓	✓	✓	☐	✓	☐
Perrot State Park	Showers	☐	☐	✓	☐	✓	✓
Potawatomi State Park	Showers	☐	☐	✓	☐	✓	✓
Rib Mountain State Park	Vault	☐	☐	☐	☐	✓	☐
Roche-a-Cri State Park	Vault	☐	☐	☐	☐	✓	✓
Rock Island State Park	Pit	☐	✓	✓	☐	✓	✓
Rocky Arbor State Park	Showers	☐	☐	☐	☐	✓	☐
Straight Lake State Park	N/A	☐	☐	✓	☐	☐	✓
Tower Hill State Park	Vault	☐	☐	✓	☐	✓	✓
Whitefish Dunes State Park	Vault	✓	✓	✓	✓	✓	✓
Wildcat Mountain State Park	Flush	☐	☐	✓	☐	✓	✓
Willow River State Park	Flush	✓	✓	✓	☐	✓	✓
Wyalusing State Park	Flush	☐	☐	☐	☐	✓	✓
Yellowstone Lake State Park	Showers	☐	✓	✓	☐	✓	✓

STATE CONTACT INFORMATION

Contact information for each state's parks management organization.

Illinois Department of Natural Resources
One Natural Resources Way
Springfield, IL 62702
(217) 782-6302
dnr.illinois.gov

Indiana Department of Natural Resources
402 W. Washington St.
Indianapolis, IN 46204
(317) 232-4200
in.gov/dnr

Iowa Department of Natural Resources
Wallace State Office Building
502 E. 9th St.
Des Moines, IA 50319
(515) 725-8200
www.iowadnr.gov

State Contact Information

Kansas Department of Wildlife and Parks
1020 S. Kansas Ave.
Topeka, KS 66612
(785) 296-2281
ksoutdoors.com

Michigan Department of Natural Resources
525 W. Allegan St.
Lansing, MI 48933
(517) 284-7275
michigan.gov/dnr

Minnesota Department of Natural Resources
500 Lafayette Road
St. Paul, MN 55155
(651) 296-6157 or (888) 646-6367
dnr.state.mn.us

Missouri Department of Conservation
P.O. Box 180
Jefferson City, MO 65102
(573) 751-4115
mdc.mo.gov

Nebraska Game and Parks Commission
2200 N. 33rd St.
Lincoln, NE 68503
(402) 471-0641
outdoornebraska.gov

North Dakota Game and Fish Department
100 N. Bismarck Expressway
Bismarck, ND 58501
(701) 328-6300
gf.nd.gov

Ohio Department of Natural Resources
2045 Morse Road
Columbus, OH 43229
(614) 265-6565
ohiodnr.gov

South Dakota Game, Fish, and Parks
523 E. Capitol Ave.
Pierre, SD 57501
(605) 223-7660
gfp.sd.gov

Wisconsin Department of Natural Resources
101 S. Webster St.
Madison, WI 53707
(608) 266-2621 or (888) 936-7463
dnr.wisconsin.gov

INDEX

Abe Martin Lodge............................ 44
ADA-accessible......... 10, 13, 31, 35, 55, 57, 63, 99, 108, 176, 188, 190, 196, 197, 200, 203, 255
Aquatic Center........................ 45, 176
archery range....... 10, 78, 174, 238, 239, 245, 247
backcountry camping........ 83, 205, 207
badlands 87, 185, 197, 198, 199, 232
bald eagles........ 6, 18, 21, 40, 51, 76, 77, 80, 90, 97, 101, 149, 199, 238, 245
basketball...33, 39, 43, 45, 87, 224, 245
beach 10, 14, 34, 39, 40, 57, 64, 65, 66, 68, 80, 86, 88, 90, 92, 97, 99, 102, 107, 108, 113, 114, 131, 140, 149, 150, 151, 152, 163, 183, 190, 191, 192, 197, 200, 201, 202, 205, 208, 211, 216, 220, 222, 225, 227, 239, 240, 249, 257, 259, 268, 269, 271
Bigfoot 262
biking 9, 33, 38, 44, 45, 51, 66, 106, 112, 113, 126, 129, 130, 132, 146, 153, 156, 162, 169, 174, 223, 236, 239, 244, 247, 257, 258, 260, 263, 266

mountain63, 66, 78, 83, 89, 107, 179, 193, 198, 203

birding..... 18, 34, 58, 61, 85, 106, 132, 146, 171, 218, 220

bison ..6, 38, 39, 61, 90, 133, 134, 135, 169, 170, 171, 203, 235, 237
bow hunting.. 10
Buffalo Soldiers................................ 180
butterfly garden 57, 238
Cahokia Mounds State Historic Site19
canoe.... 14, 40, 42, 47, 57, 65, 83, 127, 130, 136, 138, 146, 152, 173, 174, 186, 189, 191, 193, 198, 200, 203, 214, 222, 243, 262, 263, 265
cave 16, 38, 46, 54, 55, 86, 131, 137, 155, 177
CCC..39, 54, 59, 60, 62, 83, 239, 269, *See* Civilian Conservation Corps
Civil War 12, 81, 84, 159
Civilian Conservation Corps 15, 24, 39, 42, 54, 58, 59, 62, 83, 260, 268
Clark, George Rogers 17
Clean Streams Register........................ 9
Colonel Richard Lieber..............29, 41
Coolidge, Calvin 235
Corps of Engineers .. 76, 79, 81, 83, 89
covered bridge 218, 268
covered wagon........ 186, 194, 200, 205
Crazy Horse 168, 180
dark sky........................... 100, 103, 233
Dark Sky Park........................ 100, 167
Daughters of the American Revolution 17
disc golf course....... ...78, 150, 213, 238, 245

Driftless Region 52, 130
dunes...10, 34, 104, 109, 110, 257, 258
earthlodge 195, 196
effigy mounds.................. 258, 259, 262
Eisenhower, Dwight 235
Eisenhower, Mamie Doud 60
equestrian 38, 66, 77, 127, 130, 131, 135, 174, 175, 196, 198
   camping...10, 14, 161, 170, 178, 198, 249
   trail................ 9, 10, 14, 77, 112, 161
   trails 257
Father Jacques Marquette .... *See* Marquette, Pere Jacques
fossils.......30, 37, 55, 88, 131, 169, 174, 208, 217, 219, 233
Fox River 11
Frank Lloyd Wright 52, 56, 263
Gateway Arch National Park 19
glamping.................................. 175, 194
Grand Portage National Park.........129
Great Lakes 58, 95, 101, 113
Great River Road National Scenic Byway 55
Hernando DeSoto............................17
horseback riding...........................9, 33
horseshoe 66, 78, 180, 202, 243, 246
hunting 7, 9, 10, 11, 17, 18, 19, 21, 24, 38, 81, 83, 88, 97, 102, 129, 233, 237, 260, 266, 268
ice fishing....33, 51, 202, 212, 225, 243
ice skating 221, 225
Illinois River 18, 19, 21, 22
Jensen, Jens 10
Joliet, Louis 18, 22
kayak 6, 33, 39, 40, 47, 51, 57, 63, 65, 83, 97, 99, 100, 113, 126, 127, 136, 138, 146, 155, 173, 186, 189, 191, 193, 197, 198, 200, 201, 203, 208, 212, 214, 215, 216, 218, 220, 222, 223, 239, 243, 244, 259, 260, 262, 263, 269
kicksleds 186, 190, 191, 201
Lake Erie......... 207, 208, 211, 220, 222
Lake Michigan.. ....6, 10, 19, 34, 102, 103, 104, 105, 108, 109, 254, 257, 258, 260
Lake Superior............99, 100, 128, 269
Lewis and Clark ...6, 17, 189, 195, 200, 202, 203, 234, 245
lighthouse.... 96, 97, 99, 102, 104, 106, 108, 113, 262
Lincoln, Abraham 13, 195
living history 17, 43, 131, 201, 271
marina. 11, 40, 150, 151, 176, 200, 201, 202, 216, 218, 221, 224, 225, 237, 239, 245
Marquette, Pere Jacques 17
Mississippi River.........6, 14, 17, 19, 20, 23, 55, 125, 126, 130, 132, 137, 153, 265
Missouri River.. ....66, 154, 168, 169, 171, 177, 195, 198, 199, 203, 231, 233, 238, 239, 240, 244, 246, 247
Mormons 20, 62
motocross..152
National Audubon Society............218
National Historic Landmark..153, 246
National Historic Trail ...17, 195, 202, 242
National Natural Landmark...23, 240, 242
National Register Historic District 125
National Register of Historic Places 22, 35, 52, 99, 110, 123, 135, 151, 241

Index

Native American 9, 17, 18, 20, 22, 23, 33, 43, 55, 61, 62, 81, 97, 110, 125, 132, 151, 168, 180, 186, 236, 242, 243, 257, 258, 259, 262, 264, 265, 267, 269
Nature Preserve 10, 15, 40, 41, 191, 247
Niobrara River 170, 172, 173
Norbeck, Peter 235
observation tower 127, 175
Ohio River 6, 16, 17, 35, 36, 37, 207
Ozarks 74, 84, 159
paddleboat 33, 201
petroglyphs 90, 97, 110, 111, 177
pickleball 224
railroad tunnel 36
rattlesnakes 132, 199
Revolutionary War 17, 105
rock climbing 134, 137, 176, 236, 263
sailing 56, 89, 106
Santa Fe Trail 74
scuba diving 259, 262, 263, 269
Shawnee National Forest 6, 15
shooting range 80
skiing 151, 177, 190, 194, 243, 247, 260
    cross-country 12, 20, 24, 33, 51, 55, 60, 61, 63, 66, 101, 107, 112, 170, 191, 192, 193, 201, 203, 221, 268
    water 57
skishoes 186, 190
sledding .... .12, 20, 33, 101, 180, 191, 194, 200, 213, 221, 225

snowmobiling 9, 66, 101, 236
snowshoeing 55, 101, 138, 186, 190, 191, 194, 200, 201, 203, 208, 236, 239, 242, 243, 247, 261, 263, 266
St. Louis 19, 22, 157
tallgrass prairie 78, 80, 81, 133
Tecumseh 43
Tenskwatawa 43
toboggan run 33
Trine State Recreation Area 33
tubing 57, 130, 177, 190, 216, 222, 224
Underground Railroad 6
UNESCO World Heritage Site 19
Upper Peninsula . 95, 96, 99, 100, 101, 105
volleyball 33, 39, 40, 45, 66, 78, 87, 180, 192, 202, 224, 225, 245
water tower 158
waterfall 9, 35, 45, 128, 129, 132, 133, 135, 136, 137, 152, 168, 171, 172, 173, 174, 214, 268
waterpark 43
Weldon, Judge Lawrence 12
Weldon, Lincoln 12
Wind Cave National Park 236
windsurfing 89, 237
Works Progress Administration 54, 197, 240
World War II 40, 109, 181, 243, 260
WWII .... *See* World War II
Yosemite National Park 29
zipline 167, 176

279